New Geometric Data Structures for Collision Detection and Haptics

Springer Series on Touch and Haptic Systems

For further volumes:
www.springer.com/series/8786

René Weller

New Geometric Data Structures for Collision Detection and Haptics

 Springer

René Weller
Department of Computer Science
University of Bremen
Bremen, Germany

ISSN 2192-2977   ISSN 2192-2985 (electronic)
Springer Series on Touch and Haptic Systems
ISBN 978-3-319-03318-1   ISBN 978-3-319-01020-5 (eBook)
DOI 10.1007/978-3-319-01020-5
Springer Cham Heidelberg New York Dordrecht London

Printed on acid-free paper

Springer is part of Springer Science+Business Media (www.springer.com)

Dedicated to my parents

Series Editors' Foreword

This is the eighth volume of the "Springer Series on Touch and Haptic Systems", which is published in collaboration between **Springer** and the **EuroHaptics Society**.

New Geometric Data Structures for Collision Detection and Haptics is focused on solving the collision detection problem effectively. This volume represents a strong contribution to improving algorithms and methods that evaluate simulated collisions in object interaction. This topic has a long tradition going back to the beginning of computer graphical simulations. Currently, there are new hardware and software tools that can solve computations much faster. From the haptics point of view, collision detection frequency update is a critical aspect to consider since realism and stability are strongly related to the capability of checking collisions in real time.

Dr. René Weller has received the EuroHaptics 2012 Ph.D. award. In recognition of this award, he was invited to publish his work in the Springer Series on Touch and Haptic Systems. Weller's thesis was selected from among many other excellent theses defended around the world in 2012. We believe that, with the publication of this volume, the "Springer Series on Touch and Haptic Systems" is continuing to set out cutting edge topics that demonstrate the vibrancy of the field of haptics.

April 2013

Manuel Ferre
Marc Ernst
Alan Wing

Preface

Collision detection is a fundamental problem in many fields of computer science, including physically-based simulation, path-planning and haptic rendering. Many algorithms have been proposed in the last decades to accelerate collision queries. However, there are still some open challenges: For instance, the extremely high frequencies that are required for haptic rendering. In this book we present a novel geometric data structure for collision detection at haptic rates between arbitrary rigid objects. The main idea is to bound objects from the *inside* with a set of *non-overlapping* spheres. Based on such sphere packings, an "inner bounding volume hierarchy" can be constructed. Our data structure that we call *Inner Sphere Trees* supports different kinds of queries; namely proximity queries as well as time of impact computations and a new method to measure the amount of interpenetration, the *penetration volume*. The penetration volume is related to the water displacement of the overlapping region and thus, corresponds to a physically motivated force. Moreover, these penalty forces and torques are continuous both in direction and magnitude.

In order to compute such dense sphere packings, we have developed a new algorithm that extends the idea of space filling Apollonian sphere packings to arbitrary objects. Our method relies on prototype-based approaches known from machine learning and leads to a parallel algorithm. As a by-product our algorithm yields an approximation of the object's medial axis that has applications ranging from path-planning to surface reconstruction.

Collision detection for deformable objects is another open challenge, because pre-computed data structures become invalid under deformations. In this book, we present novel algorithms for efficiently updating bounding volume hierarchies of objects undergoing arbitrary deformations. The event-based approach of the kinetic data structures framework enables us to prove that our algorithms are optimal in the number of updates. Additionally, we extend the idea of kinetic data structures even to the collision detection process itself. Our new acceleration approach, the *kinetic Separation-List*, supports fast continuous collision detection of deformable objects for both, pairwise and self-collision detection.

In order to guarantee a fair comparison of different collision detection algorithms we propose several new methods both in theory and in the real world. This includes a model for the theoretic running time of hierarchical collision detection algorithms and an open source benchmarking suite that evaluates both the performance as well as the quality of the collision response.

Finally, our new data structures enabled us to realize some new applications. For instance, we adopted our sphere packings to define a new volume preserving deformation scheme, the *sphere-spring system*, that extends the classical mass-spring systems. Furthermore, we present an application of our Inner Sphere Trees to real-time obstacle avoidance in dynamic environments for autonomous robots, and last but not least we show the results of a comprehensive user study that evaluates the influence of the degrees of freedom on the users performance in complex bi-manual haptic interaction tasks.

Bremen, Germany   René Weller
March 2013

Acknowledgements

First of all, I would like to thank my supervisor Prof. Dr. Gabriel Zachmann. He always helped with precious advices, comments and insightful discussions.

I also would like to express my gratitude to Prof. Dr. Andreas Weber for accepting the co-advisorship.

Obviously, thanks go to all scientific and industrial collaborators for the fruitful joint work, namely, Dr. Jan Klein from Fraunhofer MEVIS, Mikel Sagardia, Thomas Hulin and Carsten Preusche from DLR, and Marinus Danzer and Uwe Zimmermann from KUKA Robotics Corp. Special thanks to Dr. Jérôme Perret of Haption for lending us the 6 DOF devices for our user study and the demonstration at the JVRC 2010.

I would also like to thank all my students for their efforts (roughly in chronological order): Sven Trenkel, Jörn Hoppe, Stephan Mock, Stefan Thiele, Weiyu Yi, Yingbing Hua and Jörn Teuber.

Almost all members of the Department of Computer Science of the Clausthal University contributed to this work, whether they realized it or not. I always enjoyed the very friendly atmosphere and interesting discussions. In particular, I would like to thank the members of the computer graphics group David Mainzer and Daniel Mohr but also my colleagues from the other groups, especially (in no particular order) Jens Drieseberg, René Fritzsche, Sascha Lützel, Dr. Nils Bulling, Michael Köster, Prof. Dr. Barbara Hammer, Dr. Alexander Hasenfuss, Dr. Tim Winkler, Sven Birkenfeld and Steffen Harneit.

Last but not least, I would like to thank my sister Dr. Simone Pagels for designing the cute haptic goddess and Iris Beier and Jens Reifenröther for proofreading parts of my manuscript (Obviously, only those parts that are now error-free).

Contents

Part I   That Was Then, This Is Now

1   Introduction   3
    1.1   Contributions   4
    References   7

2   A Brief Overview of Collision Detection   9
    2.1   Broad Phase Collision Detection   12
    2.2   Narrow Phase Basics   13
    2.3   Narrow Phase Advanced: Distances, Penetration Depths
        and Penetration Volumes   18
        2.3.1   Distances   18
        2.3.2   Continuous Collision Detection   19
        2.3.3   Penetration Depth   21
        2.3.4   Penetration Volume   22
    2.4   Time Critical Collision Detection   22
        2.4.1   Collision Detection in Haptic Environments   24
    2.5   Collision Detection for Deformable Objects   26
        2.5.1   Excursus: GPU-Based Methods   29
    2.6   Related Fields   30
        2.6.1   Excursus: Ray Tracing   30
    References   31

Part II   Algorithms and Data Structures

3   Kinetic Data Structures for Collision Detection   49
    3.1   Recap: Kinetic Data Structures   51
    3.2   Kinetic Bounding Volume Hierarchies   52
        3.2.1   Kinetic AABB-Tree   53
        3.2.2   Kinetic BoxTree   59
        3.2.3   Dead Ends   63

3.3   Kinetic Separation-List   66
       3.3.1   Kinetization of the Separation-List   66
       3.3.2   Analysis of the Kinetic Separation-List   70
       3.3.3   Self-collision Detection   73
       3.3.4   Implementation Details   73
3.4   Event Calculation   75
3.5   Results   77
3.6   Conclusion and Future Work   83
       3.6.1   Future Work   85
References   88

4   **Sphere Packings for Arbitrary Objects**   91
4.1   Related Work   92
       4.1.1   Polydisperse Sphere Packings   93
       4.1.2   Apollonian Sphere Packings   94
       4.1.3   Sphere Packings for Arbitrary Objects   94
       4.1.4   Voronoi Diagrams of Spheres   95
4.2   Voxel-Based Sphere Packings   96
4.3   Protosphere: Prototype-Based Sphere Packings   98
       4.3.1   Apollonian Sphere Packings for Arbitrary Objects   99
       4.3.2   Parallelization   103
       4.3.3   Results   105
4.4   Conclusions and Future Work   105
       4.4.1   Future Work   107
References   109

5   **Inner Sphere Trees**   113
5.1   Sphere Packings   114
5.2   Hierarchy Creation   115
       5.2.1   Batch Neural Gas Hierarchy Clustering   115
5.3   Traversal Algorithms   120
       5.3.1   Distances   121
       5.3.2   Penetration Volume   122
       5.3.3   Unified Algorithm for Distance and Volume Queries   125
       5.3.4   Time-Critical Distance and Volume Queries   126
       5.3.5   Continuous Collision Detection   128
5.4   Continuous Volumetric Collision Response   130
       5.4.1   Contact Forces   133
       5.4.2   Torques   134
5.5   Excursus: Volumetric Collision Detection with Tetrahedral
       Packings   135
5.6   Results   136
5.7   Conclusions and Future Work   138
       5.7.1   Future Work   141
References   143

Part III   Evaluation and Application

6   Evaluation and Analysis of Collision Detection Algorithms 147
   6.1   Related Work   148
      6.1.1   Theoretical Analysis 148
      6.1.2   Performance Benchmarks 149
      6.1.3   Quality Benchmarks 150
   6.2   Theoretical Analysis 150
      6.2.1   Analyzing Simultaneous Hierarchy Traversals 152
      6.2.2   Probability of Box Overlap 154
      6.2.3   Experimental Support 156
      6.2.4   Application to Time-Critical Collision Detection 159
   6.3   Performance Benchmark 160
      6.3.1   Benchmarking Scenarios   162
      6.3.2   Benchmarking Procedure   166
      6.3.3   Implementation   166
      6.3.4   Results 169
   6.4   Quality Benchmark   176
      6.4.1   Force and Torque Quality Benchmark 178
      6.4.2   Benchmarking Scenarios   178
      6.4.3   Evaluation Method 180
      6.4.4   Equivalent Resolutions for Comparing Different
             Algorithms 181
      6.4.5   Results 182
   6.5   Conclusion and Future Work   186
      6.5.1   Future Work   189
   References 190

7   Applications 193
   7.1   Related Work   194
      7.1.1   General Deformation Models of Deformable Objects 194
      7.1.2   Hand Animation 195
      7.1.3   Obstacle Avoidance in Robotics 196
      7.1.4   Evaluation of Haptic Interactions 197
   7.2   Sphere–Spring Systems and Their Application to Hand
      Animation   199
      7.2.1   Sphere–Spring System 199
      7.2.2   Parallelization of the Sphere–Spring System   203
      7.2.3   Application to a Virtual Human Hand Model 204
      7.2.4   Results 205
   7.3   Real-Time Obstacle Avoidance in Dynamic Environments 207
      7.3.1   The Scenario 208
      7.3.2   Accelerating Distance Queries for Point Clouds   208
      7.3.3   Results 211

7.4   3 DOF vs. 6 DOF—Playful Evaluation of Complex Haptic
        Interactions 213
        7.4.1   Haptesha—A Multi-user Haptic Workspace 215
        7.4.2   The Design of the Study: A Haptic Game 216
        7.4.3   The User Study 219
7.5   Conclusions and Future Work 226
        7.5.1   Future Work 227
References 228

Part IV   Every End Is Just a New Beginning

8   Epilogue 235
8.1   Summary 235
8.2   Future Directions 237
        8.2.1   Parallelization 238
        8.2.2   Point Clouds 238
        8.2.3   Natural Interaction 238
        8.2.4   Haptics 239
        8.2.5   Global Illumination 239
        8.2.6   Sound Rendering 240

Part I
That Was Then, This Is Now

Chapter 1
Introduction

The degree of realism of interactive computer simulated environments has increased significantly during the past decades. Stunning improvements in visual and audible presentations have emerged. Real-time tracking systems that were hidden in a handful of VR laboratories just a few years ago can be found in every child's room today. These novel input technologies, like Nintendo's Wii, Sony's Move or Microsoft's Kinect have opened a completely new, more natural way of interaction in 3D environments to a wide audience.

However, an immersive experience in interactive virtual environments requires not only realistic sounds, graphics and interaction metaphors, but also plausible behavior of the objects that we interact with. For instance, if objects in the real world interact, i.e. if they collide, they may bounce off each other or break into pieces when they are rigid. In case of non-rigidity, they deform. Obviously, we expect a similar behavior in computer simulated environments.

In fact, psychophysical experiments on perception have shown that we quickly feel distracted by unusual physical behavior [16], predominantly by visual cues [17]. For instance, O'Sullivan and Dingliana [15] showed that a time delay between a collision and its response reduces the perception of causality significantly. Fortunately, further experiments suggest that we do not compute Newtons' laws of motion exactly when interacting with the world, but judgments about collision are usually made by heuristics based on the objects' kinematic data [8]. Consequently, it is sufficient to provide physically *plausible* instead of physically *correct* behavior [1].

However, in a computer generated world, objects are usually represented by an abstract geometric model. For instance, we approximate their surfaces with polygons or describe them by mathematical functions, like NURBS. Such abstract representations have no physical properties per se. In fact, they would simply float through each other. Therefore, we have to add an appropriate algorithmic handling of contacts.

In detail, we first have to *find* contacts between moving objects. This process is called *collision detection*. In a second step, we have to *resolve* these collisions in a physically plausible manner. We call this the *collision response*.

R. Weller, *New Geometric Data Structures for Collision Detection and Haptics*, Springer Series on Touch and Haptic Systems, DOI 10.1007/978-3-319-01020-5_1, © Springer International Publishing Switzerland 2013

Fig. 1.1 The intersection of
two Chazelle polyhedra is a
worst case for collision
detection algorithms

    This fundamental technique is not restricted to interactive physics-based real-
time simulations that are widely used in computer graphics [3], computer games [2],
virtual reality [6] or virtual assembly tasks [10]. Actually, it is needed for all those
tasks involving the simulated motion of objects that are not allowed to penetrate
one another. This includes real-time animations [5] as well as animations in CGI
movies [12], but also applications in robotics where collision detection helps to
avoid obstacles [4] and self-collisions between parts of a robot [11]. Moreover, it is
required for path planning [13], molecular docking tasks [18] and multi-axis NC-
machining [9] to name but a few.
    This wide spectrum of different applications to collision detection is evidence
that there has already been done some research on this topic. Actually, hundreds,
if not thousands, of different research papers have been written about solutions to
collision detection problems in the last decades. For instance, a Google-Scholar
query for the phrase "collision detection" lists more than 44 000 results.
    Obviously, this raises several questions:

- What makes the detection of collisions so difficult that there has had to be done
  so much work on it?
- Is there still room for improvements? Or has everything already been told about
  this topic?

    In the next section, we will answer these questions and outline our contributions
to the field of collision detection as presented in this book.

1.1 Contributions

Actually, it turns out that finding collisions between geometric objects is a very
complicated problem. In most of the applications mentioned above, collision detection is, due to its inherent complexity, the computational bottleneck. Just think of
two objects in a polygonal surface representation, each of them being modeled by
n polygons. A brute-force approach for a collision detection algorithm could be to
simply test each polygon of one object against each polygon of the other object.

This results in a complexity of $O(n^2)$. Actually, if the objects are of bad shape it is possible to construct configurations with $O(n^2)$ colliding polygons (see Fig. 1.1).[1] These cases seem to be artificial and may not occur very often in practically relevant situations. In fact, in Chap. 6 we present a new theoretic model to estimate the *average* running-time of collision detection algorithms by tracking only a few simple parameters. For many real-world scenarios we could prove the complexity to be $O(n \log n)$. However, collision detection algorithms have to handle also worst cases correctly. Thus, the theoretical complexity of most collision detection algorithms is in the worst case $O(n^2)$.

Most collision detection algorithms are based on some clever data structures that provide an output sensitive acceleration of collision detection queries. In Chap. 2, we give an overview of classical and recent developments in this field.

Usually, these data structures are built in a time consuming pre-processing step. Unfortunately, if the objects are not rigid, i.e. the objects deform over time, these pre-computed data structures become invalid and must be re-computed or updated. Almost all previous collision detection approaches did this on a per-frame basis, and this means that they update their underlying data structures before each collision query. Obviously, this is very time consuming, and this is one reason for the restriction of deformable objects to a relatively low object resolution.

In Chap. 3 we present several new methods that are able to update such acceleration data structure *independently* of the query frequency. Moreover, we prove a lower bound of $O(n \log n)$ on the number of necessary updates, and we show that our new data structures do not exceed this lower bound. Consequently, our data structures are optimal in the number of updates.

However, *finding* collisions is only one side of the coin. As mentioned above, collisions must also be resolved during the collision handling process. In order to compute physically plausible collision responses, some kind of contact data is required that must be delivered by the collision detection algorithm. Basically, there exist four different kinds of contact information that can be used by different collision response solvers: we can either track the *minimum distances* between pairs of objects, we can determine the exact *time of impact*, we can define a minimum translational vector to separate the objects, the so-called *penetration depth*, or we can compute the *penetration volume* (see Fig. 1.2). We will discuss the advantages and disadvantages of the different penetration measures in more detail in Chap. 2.

According to Fisher and Lin [7, Sect. 5.1], the *penetration volume* is "the most complicated yet accurate method" to define the extent of an intersection. However, to our knowledge, there are no algorithms to compute it in real time for a reasonable number of polygons, i.e. more than a dozen of polygons, as yet.

In Chap. 5 we contribute the first data structure, the so-called *Inner Sphere Trees*, which yields an approximation of the penetration volume for objects consisting of hundreds of thousands of polygons. Moreover, we could not only achieve visual

---

[1]By the way, Chazelle's polyhedron also has other interesting properties: for instance, it requires $O(n^2)$ additional Steiner points for its tetrahedrization.

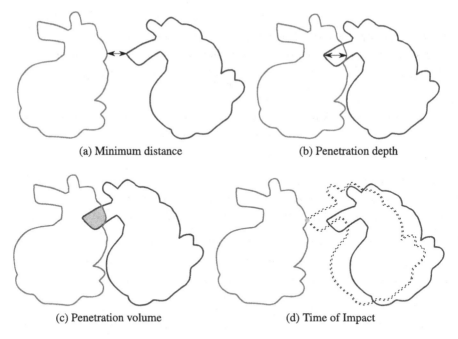

(a) Minimum distance   (b) Penetration depth

(c) Penetration volume   (d) Time of Impact

Fig. 1.2 Different penetration measures

real-time, but our data structure is also applicable to haptic rendering. Actually, in-tegrating force feedback into interactive real-time virtual environments causes addi-tional challenges: for a smooth visual sensation, update rates of 30 Hz are sufficient. But the temporal resolution of the human tactile sense is much higher. In fact, haptic rendering requires an update frequency of 1000 Hz for hard surfaces to be felt as realistic [14].

Our *Inner Sphere Trees* gain their efficiency from filling the objects' interior with sets of *non-overlapping* spheres. Surprisingly, there does not exist any algorithm that could compute such sphere packings yet. Consequently, we have developed a new method that we present in Chap. 4. Basically, it extends the idea of space-filling Apollonian sphere packings to arbitrary objects. Therefore, we used a prototype-based approach that can easily be parallelized. It turns out that our new algorithm has some amazing side-effects: for instance, it yields an approximation of an object's medial axis in nearly real time.

In Chap. 7 we present some applications of our new data structures that were hardly realizable without them. More precisely, we propose a new method to sim-ulate volume preserving deformable objects, the *Sphere–Spring systems*, based on our sphere packings. Moreover, we applied our Inner Sphere Trees to real-time col-lision avoidance for autonomous moving robots. Finally, we have implemented a haptic workspace that allows simultaneous bi-manual haptic interaction for multi-ple users in complex scenarios. We used this workspace to investigate the influence of the degrees of freedom of haptic devices in demanding bi-manual haptic tasks.

However, our data structures are still not an all-in-one solution that is suitable for every purpose. They also have their drawbacks; e.g. our Inner Sphere Trees are, until now, restricted to watertight objects. Hence, also other collision detection approaches have a right to exist. However, a programmer who wants to integrate collision detection into his application still has to choose from hundreds of different approaches. Obviously, this is almost impossible without studying the literature for years. But even for experts it is hard to judge the performance of collision detection algorithms correctly by reading research papers, because almost every researcher presents his results with only certain, well chosen, scenarios. As a remedy, we have developed a standardized benchmarking suite for collision detection algorithms, which we present in Chap. 6. It allows a fair and realistic comparison of different algorithms for a broad spectrum of interesting contact scenarios and many different objects. Moreover, we included a benchmark to compare also the quality of the forces and torques of collision response schemes.

References

1. Barzel, R., Hughes, J. F., & Wood, D. N. (1996). Plausible motion simulation for computer graphics animation. In *Proceedings of the eurographics workshop on computer animation and simulation '96* (pp. 183–197). New York: Springer. ISBN3-211-82885-0. URL http://dl.acm.org/citation.cfm?id=274976.274989.
2. Bishop, L., Eberly, D., Whitted, T., Finch, M., & Shantz, M. (1998). Designing a pc game engine. *IEEE Computer Graphics and Applications, 18*(1), 46–53.
3. Bouma, W. J., & Vanecek, G. Jr. (1991). Collision detection and analysis in a physically based simulation. In *Eurographics workshop on animation and simulation* (pp. 191–203).
4. Chakravarthy, A., & Ghose, D. (1998). Obstacle avoidance in a dynamic environment: a collision cone approach. *IEEE Transactions on Systems, Man and Cybernetics, Part A, 28*(5), 562–574.
5. Cordier, F., & Magnenat Thalmann, N. (2002). Real-time animation of dressed virtual humans. *Computer Graphics Forum, 21*(3), 327–335.
6. Eckstein, J., & Schömer, E. (1999). Dynamic collision detection in virtual reality applications. In V. Skala (Ed.), *WSCG'99 conference proceedings*. URL citeseer.ist.psu.edu/eckstein99dynamic.html.
7. Fisher, S., & Lin, M. (2001). Fast penetration depth estimation for elastic bodies using deformed distance fields. In *Proc. international conf. on intelligent robots and systems (IROS)* (pp. 330–336).
8. Gilden, D. L., & Proffitt, D. R. (1989). Understanding collision dynamics. *Journal of Experimental Psychology. Human Perception and Performance, 15*, 372–383.
9. Ilushin, O., Elber, G., Halperin, D., Wein, R., & Kim, M.-S. (2005). Precise global collision detection in multi-axis nc-machining. *Computer Aided Design, 37*(9), 909–920. doi:10.1016/j.cad.2004.09.018.
10. Kim, H. S., Ko, H., Lee, K., & Lee, C.-W. (1995). A collision detection method for real time assembly simulation. In *IEEE international symposium on assembly and task planning* (Vol. 0:0387). doi:10.1109/ISATP.1995.518799.
11. Kuffner, J., Nishiwaki, K., Kagami, S., Kuniyoshi, Y., Inaba, M., & Inoue, H. (2002). Self-collision detection and prevention for humanoid robots. In *Proceedings of the IEEE international conference on robotics and automation* (pp. 2265–2270).
12. Lafleur, B., Magnenat Thalmann, N., & Thalmann, D. (1991). Cloth animation with self-collision detection. In *Proc. of the conf. on modeling in comp. graphics* (pp. 179–187). Berlin: Springer.

13. LaValle, S. M. (2004). *Planning algorithms.*
14. Mark, W. R., Randolph, S. C., Finch, M., Van Verth, J. M., & Taylor, R. M. II (1996). Adding force feedback to graphics systems: issues and solutions. In *Proceedings of the 23rd annual conference on computer graphics and interactive techniques, SIGGRAPH '96* (pp. 447–452). New York: ACM. ISBN 0-89791-746-4. doi:10.1145/237170.237284. URL http://doi.acm.org/10.1145/237170.237284.
15. O'Sullivan, C., & Dingliana, J. (2001). Collisions and perception. *ACM Transactions on Graphics, 20*(3), 151–168. doi:10.1145/501786.501788. URL http://doi.acm.org/10.1145/501786.501788.
16. O'Sullivan, C., Dingliana, J., Giang, T., & Kaiser, M. K. (2003). Evaluating the visual fidelity of physically based animations. *ACM Transactions on Graphics, 22*(3), 527–536. doi:10.1145/882262.882303. URL http://doi.acm.org/10.1145/882262.882303.
17. Reitsma, P. S. A., & O'Sullivan, C. (2008). Effect of scenario on perceptual sensitivity to errors in animation. In *Proceedings of the 5th symposium on applied perception in graphics and visualization, APGV '08* (pp. 115–121). New York: ACM. ISBN 978-1-59593-981-4. doi:10.1145/1394281.1394302. URL http://doi.acm.org/10.1145/1394281.1394302.
18. Turk, G. (1989). *Interactive collision detection for molecular graphics* (Technical report). University of North Carolina at Chapel Hill. URL http://citeseerx.ist.psu.edu/viewdoc/summary?doi=10.1.1.93.4927.

Chapter 2
A Brief Overview of Collision Detection

In this chapter we will provide a short overview on classical and recent research in collision detection. In the introduction, we already mentioned the general complexity of the collision detection problem due to its theoretical quadratic running time for polygonal models like Chazelle's polyhedron (see Fig. 1.1).

However, this is an artificial example, and in most real world cases there are only very few colliding polygons. Hence, the goal of collision detection algorithms is to provide an output sensitive running time. This means that they try to eliminate as many of the $O(n^2)$ primitive tests as possible, for example by an early exclusion of large parts of the objects that cannot collide. Consequently, the collision detection problem can be regarded as a filtering process.

Recent physics simulation libraries like PhysX [163], Bullet [36] or ODE [203] implement several levels of filtering in a so-called *collision detection pipeline*.

Usually, a scene does not consist only of a single pair of objects, but of a larger set of 3D models that are typically organized in a scenegraph. In a first filtering step, the *broad phase* or *N-body culling*, a fast test enumerates all pairs of potentially colliding objects (the so-called *potentially collision set (PCS)*) to be checked for exact intersection in a second step, which is called the *narrow phase*. The narrow phase is typically divided into two parts: first a filter to achieve pairs of potentially colliding geometric primitives is applied and finally these pairs of primitives are checked for collision. Depending on the scene, more filtering levels between these two major steps can be used to further speed-up the collision detection process [247]. Figure 2.1 shows the design of CollDet [250], a typical collision detection pipeline. All data structures that are developed for this work have been integrated into the CollDet framework.

However, the chronological order of the collision detection pipeline is only one way to classify collision detection algorithms, and there exist many more distinctive factors. Other classifications are e.g. rigid bodies vs. deformable objects. Usually, the filtering steps rely on geometric acceleration data structures that are set up in a pre-processing step. If the objects are deformable, these pre-calculated data structures can become invalid. Consequently, deformable objects require other data structures or, at least, additional steps to update or re-compute the pre-processed struc-

R. Weller, *New Geometric Data Structures for Collision Detection and Haptics*,
Springer Series on Touch and Haptic Systems, DOI 10.1007/978-3-319-01020-5_2,
© Springer International Publishing Switzerland 2013

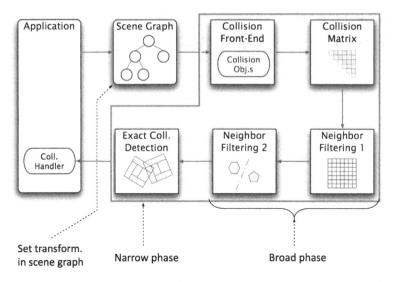

Fig. 2.1 The typical design of a collision detection pipeline

tures. Additionally, deformable objects require a check for self-collisions. Some of these methods are described in Sect. 2.5.

Another distinctive feature is the representation of the geometric objects. Especially in computer graphics, the boundary of objects is usually approximated by polygons. Hence, most collision detection algorithms are designed for polygonal objects. However, in CAD/CAM applications also curved surface representations like *non-uniform rational B-splines* (*NURBS*) play an important role. For instance, Page and Guibault [175] described a method based on oriented bounding boxes (OBBs) especially for NURBS surfaces. Lau et al. [131] developed an approach based on axis aligned bounding boxes (AABBs) for inter-objects as well as self-collision detection between deformable NURBS. Greß et al. [76] also used an AABB hierarchy for trimmed NURBS but transferred the computation to the GPU. Kim et al. [108] proposed an algorithm based on bounding coons patches with offset volumes for NURBS surfaces. Another object modeling technique often used in CAD/CAM is the *constructive solid geometry* (*CSG*). Objects are recursively defined by union, intersection or difference operations of basic shapes like spheres or cylinders. In order to detect collisions between CSG objects, Zeiller [251] used an octree-like data structure for the CSG tree. Su et al. [208] described an adaptive selection strategy of optimal bounding volumes for sub-trees of objects in order to realize a fast localization of possible collision regions.

Point clouds become more and more popular due to cheap depth-cameras that can be used for 3D scanning like Microsoft's Kinect [94]. One of the first approaches to detect collision between point clouds was developed by Klein and Zachmann [116]. They use a bounding volume hierarchy in combination with a sphere covering of parts of the surface. Klein and Zachmann [117] proposed an interpolation search approach of the two implicit functions in a proximity graph in combination with randomized sampling. El-Far et al. [47] support only collisions between a single point probe and a point cloud. For this, they fill the gaps surrounding the points with AABBs and use an octree for further acceleration. Figueiredo et al. [53] used R-trees, a hierarchical data structure that stores geometric objects with intervals in several dimensions [80], in combination with a grid for the broad phase. Pan et al. [177] described a stochastic traversal of a bounding volume hierarchy. By using machine learning techniques, their approach is also able to handle noisy point clouds. In addition to simple collision tests, they support the computation of minimum distances [178].

This directly leads to the next classification feature: The kind of information that is provided by the collision detection algorithm. Actually, almost all simulation methods work discretely; this means that they check only at discrete points in time whether the simulated objects collide. As a consequence, inter-penetration between simulated objects is often unavoidable. However, in order to simulate a physically plausible world, objects should not pass through each other and objects should move as expected when pushed or pulled. As a result, there exist a number of collision response algorithms to resolve inter-penetrations. For example, the penalty-based method computes non-penetration constraint forces based on the amount of inter-penetration [207]. Other approaches like the impulse-based method or constraint-based algorithms need information about the exact time of contact to apply impulsive forces [110].

Basic collision detection algorithms simply report whether or not two objects intersect. Additionally, some of these approaches provide access to a single pair of intersecting polygons or they yield the set of all intersecting polygons. Unfortunately, this is not sufficient to provide the information required for most collision response schemes. Hence, there also exist methods that are able to compute some kind of *penetration depth*, e.g. a minimum translational vector to separate the objects. More advanced algorithms provide the *penetration volume*. Especially in path-planning tasks, but also in constraint-based simulations, it is helpful to track the *minimum separation distance* between the objects in order to avoid collisions. Finally, the *continuous collision detection* computes the exact point in time when a collision occurs between two object configurations. Section 2.3 provides an overview over algorithms that compute these different penetration measurements. Usually, the more information the collision detection algorithm provide, the longer is its query time.

More classifications of collision detection algorithms are possible. For instance, real-time vs. offline, hierarchical vs. non-hierarchical, convex vs. non-convex, GPU-based methods vs. CPU, etc. This already shows the great variety of different approaches.

Actually, collision detection has been researched for almost three decades. A complete overview over all existing approaches would fill libraries and thus is far beyond the scope of this chapter. So, in the following, we will present classic methods that are still of interest, as well as recent directions that are directly related to our work. As a starting point for further information on the wide field of collision detection we refer the interested reader to the books by Ericson [49], Coutinho [37], Zachmann and Langetepe [249], Eberly [43], Den Bergen [228], Bicchi et al. [18]

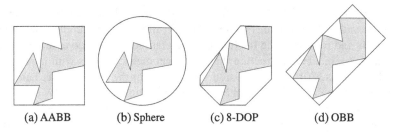

| (a) AABB | (b) Sphere | (c) 8-DOP | (d) OBB |

Fig. 2.2 Different bounding volumes

or Lin et al. [141] and the surveys by Jimenez et al. [97], Kobbelt and Botsch [120], Ganjugunte [60], Lin and Gottschalk [140], Avril et al. [8], Kockara et al. [121], Gottschalk [71], Fares and Hamam [51], Teschner et al. [218] and Kamat [103].

2.1 Broad Phase Collision Detection

The first part of the pipeline, called the *broad-phase*, should provide an efficient removal of those pairs of objects that are not in collision. Therefore, objects are usually enclosed into basic shapes that can be tested very quickly for overlap. Typical basic shapes are *axis aligned bounding boxes (AABB)*, spheres, *discrete oriented polytopes (k-DOP)* or *oriented bounding boxes (OBB)* (see Fig. 2.2).

The most simple method for the neighbor finding phase is a brute-force approach that compares each object's bounding volume with all others' bounding volumes. The complexity of this approach is $O(n^2)$, where n denotes the number of objects in the scene. Woulfe et al. [241] implemented this brute-force method on a Field-Programmable Gate Array (FPGA) using AABBs. However, even this hardware-based approach cannot override the quadratic complexity.

Moreover, Edelsbrunner and Maurer [45] have shown that the optimal algorithm to find intersections of n AABBs in 3D has a complexity of $O(n \log^2 n + k)$, where k denotes the number of objects that actually intersect. Two main approaches have been proposed to take this into account: spatial partitioning and topological methods.

Spatial partitioning algorithms divide the space into cells. Objects whose bounding volumes share the same cell are selected for the narrow phase. Examples for such spatial partitioning data structures are regular grids [247], hierarchical spatial hash tables [156], octrees [12], kd-trees [17] and binary space partitions (BSP-trees) [162]. The main disadvantage of spatial subdivision schemes for collision detection is their static nature: they have to be rebuilt or updated every time the objects change their configuration. For uniform grids such an update can be performed in constant time and grids are perfectly suited for parallelization. Mazhar [149] presented a GPU implementation for this kind of uniform subdivision. However, the effectiveness of uniform grids disappears if the objects are of widely varying sizes. Luque et al. [147] proposed a semi-adjusting BSP-tree that does not require a complete re-structuring, but adjusts itself while maintaining desirable balancing and height properties.

In contrast to space partitioning approaches, the topological methods are based on the position of an object in relation to the other objects. The most famous method is called *Sweep-and-Prune* [32]. The main idea is to project the objects' bounding volume on one or more axes (e.g. the three coordinate axis (x, y, z)). Only those pairs of objects whose projected bounding volumes overlap on all axes have to be considered for the narrow phase. Usually, this method does not construct any internal structure but starts from scratch at each collision check.

Several attempts have been proposed to parallelize the classical Sweep-And-Prune approach. For instance, Avril et al. [10] developed an adaptive method that runs on multi-core and multi-threaded architectures [9] and uses all three coordinate axes. Moreover, they presented an automatic workload distribution based on off-line simulations to determine fields of optimal performance [11]. Liu et al. [143] ported the Sweep-and-Prune approach to the GPU using the CUDA framework. They use a principal component analysis to determine a good sweep direction and combine it with an additional spatial subdivision.

Tavares and Comba [217] proposed a topological algorithm that is based on Delaunay triangulations instead of Sweep-and-Prune. The vertices of the triangulation represent the center of mass of the objects and the edges are the object pairs to be checked in the narrow phase.

However, even if all these algorithms are close to the optimal solution proved by Edelsbrunner and Maurer [45], in accordance to Zachmann [247], they are profitable over the brute-force method only in scenarios with more than 100 dynamically simulated objects. This is due to the high constant factor that is hidden in the asymptotic notation. Maybe this is also why much more research is done on the acceleration of the narrow phase.

2.2 Narrow Phase Basics

While the broad phase lists pairs of possible colliding objects, the objective of the narrow phase is to determine exact collision checks between these pairs.

A brute force solution for the narrow phase could simply check all geometric primitives of one object against all primitives of the other object. Surely this would again result in quadratic complexity. Due to the fast evolution of modern graphics hardware, objects can consist of millions of polygons today, and a quadratic running time is not an option. Consequently, more intelligent algorithms are required.

Actually, the narrow phase can be divided into two phases by itself. In a first phase, non-overlapping parts of the objects are culled; in a second step, an accurate collision detection is performed between pairs of geometric primitives that are not culled in the first phase.

Instead of data structures that partition the world-space in the broad phase, in the narrow phase, most often object partitioning techniques are used for the culling

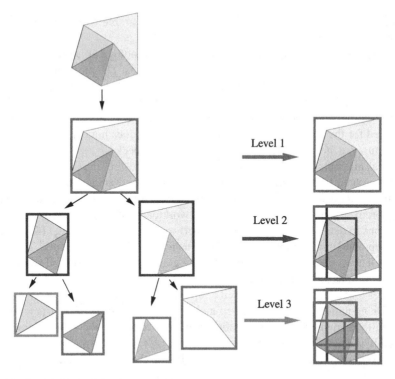

Fig. 2.3 The BVH principle: Geometric objects are divided recursively into subsets of their geometric primitives (*left*) and each node on the tree realizes a bounding volume for all primitives in its sub-tree (*right*)

stage. The common data structures for this task are *bounding volume hierarchies* (*BVHs*). The technique of bounding volumes, known from the previous section (Fig. 2.2), is recursively applied to a whole object. This results in a tree-like structure. Each node in such a tree is associated to a bounding volume that encloses all primitives in its sub-tree (see Fig. 2.3).

Usually, a BVH is constructed in a pre-processing step that can be computationally more or less expensive. During running time a simultaneous recursive traversal of the BVHs of two objects allows a conservative non-intersection pruning: if an intersection is detected in the root of the BVH, the traversal proceeds by checking the bounding volumes of the root node's children and so on until the leaf nodes are reached and an exact collision test between the geometric primitives can be performed. Non-overlapping BVs are discarded from further consideration. The whole traversal algorithm results in a *bounding volume test tree* (*BVTT*) (see Fig. 2.4).

Usually, BVs for the BVHs are spheres [92, 185], AABBs [182, 225] and their memory optimized derivative called BoxTree [248], which is closely related to kd-Trees, k-DOPs [118, 245], a generalization of AABBs, OBBs [2, 15, 70] or convex hull trees [46]. Additionally, a wide variety of special BVs for spe-

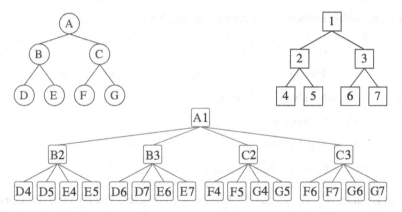

Fig. 2.4 The simultaneous recursive traversal of two BVHs during the collision check results in a bounding volume test tree

cial applications has been developed. For instance, we have spherical shells [125], swept spheres [126], spheres that are cut by two parallel planes called slab cut balls [130], quantized orientation slabs with primary orientations (QuOSPO) trees [85] that combine OBBs with k-DOPs, or combinations of spherical shells with OBBs as proposed by Krishnan et al. [124] for objects that are modeled by Bezier patches.

The optimal bounding volume should

- tightly fit the underlying geometry
- provide fast intersection tests
- be invariant undergoing rigid motion
- not use too much memory
- be able to be build automatically and fast

Unfortunately, these factors are contradictory. For example, spheres offer very fast overlap and distance tests and can be stored very memory efficiently, but they poorly fit flat geometries. AABBs also offer fast intersection tests, but they need to be realigned after rotations. Or, if no realignment is used, a more expensive OBB overlap test is required. But in this case, the tighter fitting OBBs could be used directly. However, they also require more memory. Convex hulls offer the tightest fit among convex BVs, but the overlap test is very complex and their memory consumption depends on the underlying geometry.

Consequently, choosing the right BVHs is always a compromise and depends on the scenario. Basically, the quality of BVH-based algorithms can be measured by the following cost function, which was introduced by Weghorst et al. [235] to analyze hierarchical methods for ray tracing and later was adapted to hierarchical collision detection methods by Gottschalk et al. [70]:

$$T = N_v C_v + N_p C_p \text{ with}$$

$$T = \text{Total cost of testing a pair of models for intersection}$$

$$N_v = \text{Number of BV Tests}$$

$$C_v = \text{Cost of a BV Test}$$ (2.1)

$$N_p = \text{Number of Primitive Tests}$$

$$C_p = \text{Cost of a Primitive Test}$$

In addition to the shape of the BV, there are more factors that affect the efficiency of a BVH, including the height of the hierarchy, which may but should not be influenced by its arity or the traversal order during collision queries. The first two factors have to be considered already during the construction of the BVH.

Basically, there exist two major strategies to build BVHs: bottom-up and top-down. The bottom-up approach starts with elementary BVs of leaf nodes and merges them recursively together until the root BV is reached. A very simple merging heuristic is to visit all nearest neighbors and minimize the size of the combined parent nodes in the same level [191]. Less greedy strategies combine BVs by using tilings [137].

However, the most popular method is the top-down approach. The general idea is to start with the complete set of elementary BVs, then split that into some parts and create a BVH for each part recursively. The main problem is to choose a good splitting criterion. A classical splitting criterion is to simply pick the longest axis and split it in the middle of this axis. Another simple heuristic is to split along the median of the elementary bounding boxes along the longest axis. However, it is easy to construct worst case scenarios for these simple heuristics. The *surface area heuristic (SAH)* tries to avoid these worst cases by optimizing the surface area and the number of geometric primitives over all possible split plane candidates [68]. Originally developed for ray tracing, it is today also used for collision detection. The computational costs can be reduced to $O(n \log n)$ [232, 233] and there exist parallel algorithms for the fast construction on the GPU [132]. Many other splitting criteria were compared by Zachmann [246].

In addition to the splitting criterion, also the choice of the BV affects the performance of the hierarchy creation process. Even if this is a pre-processing step, extremely high running times are undesirable in many applications. Computing an AABB for a set of polygons or a set of other AABBs is straightforward. Also k-DOPs can be computed relatively easy. But the only optimal solution for OBB computation is $O(n^3)$ and very hard to implement [166]. Chang et al. [24] presented a close to optimal solution based on a hybrid method combining genetic and Nelder-Mead algorithms. Other heuristics, like principal component analysis [100], are not able to guarantee the desired quality in all cases. On the other hand, very complicated BVs, like the convex hull, can be computed efficiently in $O(n \log n)$ [102].

With OBBs, also the computation of a minimum enclosing sphere turns out to be very complicated. Welzl [236] formulated it as a linear programming problem.

However, the choice of spheres as BVs also points to another challenge: the set of elementary BVs. For AABBs, OBBs or k-DOPs, usually a single primitive or a set of adjacent primitives are enclosed in an elementary BV. For spheres this is not an optimal solution, because proximate primitives, often represented by polygons, usually form some kind of flat geometry that poorly fits into a sphere. Therefore, Bradshaw and O'Sullivan [20] presented a method based on the medial axis to group also distant spheres in the same elementary BV.

The influence of the trees' branching factor is widely neglected in the literature. Usually, most authors simply use binary trees for collision detection. But according to Zachmann and Langetepe [249] the optimum can be larger. Mezger et al. [155] stated that, especially for deformable objects, 4-ary or 8-ary trees could improve the performance. This is mainly due to the smaller number of BV updates. However, we will return to this topic in Sect. 2.5.

During running time, the performance of the BVH depends on the traversal order. Usually, a simultaneous recursive traversal of both BVHs is applied. The easiest way to do this is via the *depth-first-search* (*DFS*). Gottschalk [72] additionally proposed a *breath-first-search* (*BFS*) traversal using a queue. For complex objects with many polygons and hence deep trees, the DFS can lead to a stack overflow. However, on modern CPUs with large stack sizes, the DFS is much faster. O'Sullivan and Dingliana [168] proposed a *best-first-search* method for sphere trees. It simply descends into sub-trees with largest BV-overlap first. However, in our experience, the time to keep a priority queue often exceeds its advantages.

The final step in the collision detection pipeline is the primitive test. Most often the surfaces of the objects are represented by polygons or, more specific, triangles. A general polygon–polygon intersection test is described by Chin and Wang [29]. For the special case of triangles, there exist a wide variety of fast intersection tests, e.g. by Möller [159] or Tropp et al. [222]. Even today new optimized approaches are proposed for special cases: for instance Chang and Kim [25] described a triangle test that takes into account that many intermediate computation results from an OBB test can be re-used for the triangle intersection. Many fast intersection tests are implemented by Held [87] and Schneider and Eberly [197].

Another important class of geometric primitives are convex polytopes. Not only because they are widely used in physics-based simulations, but also from an historical point of view: some of the first collision detection algorithms are based on them. Moreover, they can be used as both geometric primitives and bounding volumes. Actually, there exist two main approaches for convex polytopes: feature-based algorithms and simplex-based algorithms.

The first feature-based method was proposed by Lin and Canny [139]. Features of a convex polyhedron are vertices, edges and faces. The Lin–Canny algorithm performs a local search on these features using a pre-computed Voronoi diagram [231]. The convexity guarantees that local minima are avoided. Furthermore, the algorithm uses spatial and temporal coherence between two distinctive queries: usually, objects do not move too much between two frames of a physics-based simulation.

Hence, the closest feature in the current frame is close to the closest feature from the next frame. A major drawback of the algorithm is that it cannot handle intersections. In this case it runs in an endless loop. V-Clip [157], an extension of the classical Linn–Canny method, eliminates this serious defect.

The best known simplex-based algorithm was developed by Gilbert et al. [65]. Instead of using Voronoi diagrams, the GJK-algorithm is based on Minkowski differences. In addition to the boolean collision detection that simply reports whether two objects collide or not, the GJK-algorithm also returns a measure of the interpenetration [22]. Moreover, it achieves the same almost constant time complexity as Lin–Canny. A stable and fast implementation of the enhanced GJK algorithms was presented by Bergen [226].

Both kinds of algorithms are designed for convex polyhedra. However, by using a convex decomposition of well-behaved concave polyhedrons, they can also be extended to other objects [26]. But finding good convex decompositions is not straightforward and is still an active field of research [81, 138].

2.3 Narrow Phase Advanced: Distances, Penetration Depths and Penetration Volumes

For physics-based simulations a simple boolean answer at discrete points in time to whether a pair of objects intersect or not is often not sufficient. Usually, some kind of contact information is required to compute repelling forces or non-intersection constraints.

As long as a pair of objects rests in a collision-free configuration, a simple way to characterize the extent of repelling forces is to use the *minimum distance* between them. However, collisions are often unavoidable due to the discrete structure of the simulation process. Therefore, a penetration measure is required for configurations where the objects overlap. Some authors proposed a minimum translational vector to separate the objects. This is often called the *penetration depth*. The most complicated, but also the only physically plausible inter-penetration measure is the penetration volume [164], which corresponds directly to the amount of water being displaced by the overlapping parts of the objects. Last but not least, it is possible to compute the exact point in time between two discrete collision checks; this is called *continuous collision detection*. In fact, it is not a measure of the amount of inter-penetration, but the techniques that are used for its computation are very similar to other penetration depth computations.

2.3.1 Distances

The Lin–Canny algorithm, described in the previous section, is already an example of one using minimum distance computations. Tracking of the closest features directly delivers the required distances. Actually, computing minimum distances can be performed in a very similar way to conventional boolean collision detection using BVHs.

The traditional recursive BVH traversal algorithm, described above, tests whether two BVs—one from each BVH—overlap. If this is the case, the recursion continues to their children. If they do not, the recursion terminates. If two leaves are reached, a primitive intersection test is performed.

The simple recursive scheme can be modified easily for minimum distance computations: just the intersection test of the primitives has to be replaced by a distance computation between the primitives and the intersection test between the BVs by a distance test between the BVs. During the traversal, an upper bound for the distance between two primitives is maintained by a variable δ. This variable can be initialized with ∞ or the distance between any pair of primitives. δ has to be updated if a pair of primitives with a smaller distance is found.

Obviously, BVs with larger distances than δ can be culled, because if the BVs have a larger distance, this must also be true for all enclosed primitives. This is exactly the way most authors using BVHs implemented their algorithms; e.g. Larsen et al. [126] used the swept-sphere method as BVs together with several speed-up techniques, Quinlan [185] proposed sphere trees, Bergen [226] used AABBs in combination with the GJK-based Minkowski difference; Lauterbach et al. [133] implemented OBB trees running on the GPU. Johnson and Cohen [98] generalized the basic BVH-based distance computation in the framework of minimum distance computations.

Actually, all these approaches can be interrupted at any time and they deliver an upper bound for the minimum distance. Other approaches are able to additionally provide a lower bound, like the spherical sector representation presented by Bonner and Kelley [19], or the inner–outer ellipsoids by Ju et al. [101] and Liu et al. [144].

Another alternative for distance computations are distance fields [56], which can also be combined with BVHs [58].

However, all these approaches use the Euclidean distance between the objects. Other authors also proposed different metrics like the Hausdorff-distance, which defines the maximum deviation of one object from the other object [213, 243]. Zhang et al. [256] used a so-called *DISP distance*, which is defined as the maximum length of the displacement vector over every point on the model at two different configurations. This metric can be used for motion planning tasks [134].

A *local* minimum distance for a stable force feedback computation was proposed by Johnson et al. [99]. They used spatialized normal cone pruning for the collision detection. The normal cone approach differs from prior works using BVHs, because it searched for extrema of a minimum distance formulation in the space of normals rather than in Euclidean space.

2.3.2 Continuous Collision Detection

Computing repelling forces on the separating distance can lead to visual artifacts in physics-based simulations, e.g. when the objects bounce away before they really are in visual contact. Moreover, if the objects move too fast, or the time step between two collision queries is too large, the objects could pass through each other. To avoid errors like this tunneling effect, it would be better to really compute the exact time of impact between a pair of objects [35]. Several techniques have been proposed to solve this *continuous collision detection* problem, which is sometimes also called *dynamic collision detection*.

The easiest way is to simply reuse the well researched and stable algorithms known from static collision detection. Visual interactive applications usually require updating rates of 30 frames per second, i.e. there passes about 30 milliseconds of time between two static collision checks. Recent boolean collision detection algorithms require only a few milliseconds, depending on the objects' configuration. Hence, there is plenty of time to perform more than one query between two frames. A simple method, the so called method of *pseudo-continuous collision*, realizes exactly this strategy: it performs static collision detection with smaller time steps [88]. Even with a higher sampling frequency, it is, however, still possible to miss contacts between thin objects.

Conservative advancement is another simple technique that avoids these problems. The objects are repeatedly advanced by a certain time-step, which guarantees a non-penetration constraint [158]. Usually, the minimum distance is used to compute iteratively new upper bounds for the advancement [259]. Conservative advancement is also perceived as a discrete ancestor of the kinetic data structures that we will review in the next chapter.

Another method is to simply enclose the bounding volumes at the beginning and at the end of a motion step by a swept volume. This can be done very efficiently for AABBs [44]. Coming and Staadt [34] described a velocity-aligned DOP as swept volume for underlying spheres as BVs, and Redon et al. [189] proposed an algorithm for OBBs. Taeubig and Frese [210] used sphere swept convex hulls. Also ellipsoids are an option [30].

The swept volumes guarantee conservative bounds for their underlying primitives, and consequently the swept BVHs can be traversed similarly to the discrete BVHs. However, an additional continuous collision test for the primitives is required to achieve the exact time of impact. Actually, these tests (and in fact, also the tests between the BVs) depend on the trajectories of the primitives, which are usually not known between two simulation steps. Often, a simple linear interpolation is used to approximate the in-between motion [239]. For a pair of triangles this yields six face–vertex and nine edge–edge tests. Each of these elementary tests requires one to solve a cubic equation. This is computationally relatively costly. Therefore, some authors additionally proposed feature-based pre-tests, like the subspace filters by Tang et al. [211] or additional BVs like k-DOPs for the edges [93].

However, more accurate but also more complicated interpolation schemes have been described as well. Canny [23] proposed quaternions instead of Euler angles but still got a 6D complexity. Screw motions are often used [105] because they can also be computed by solving cubic polynomials. Redon et al. [187] combined them with interval arithmetic. Zhang et al. [260] defined Taylor models for articulated models with non-convex links. Von Herzen et al. [230] used Lipschitz bounds and binary subdivision for parametric surfaces.

There exist a few other acceleration techniques; e.g. Kim et al. [106] implement a dynamic task assignment for multi-threaded platforms, or Fahn and Wang [50] avoid BVHs by using a regular grid in combination with an azimuth elevation map. However, continuous collision detection is still computationally too expensive for real-time applications, especially, when many complex dynamic objects are simulated simultaneously.

2.3.3 Penetration Depth

The minimum distance is not a good measure to define repelling forces, and computing the exact time of impact using continuous collision detection is too time consuming for real-time applications. Consequently, in research one has developed another penetration measure: the *penetration depth*. In fact, it is not entirely correct to speak about *the* penetration depth, because there exist many different, partly contradictory, definitions. A widely used definition describes it as the distance that corresponds to the shortest translation required to separate two intersecting objects [41].

The same authors also delivered a method for their computation based on the Dobkin and Kirkpatrick hierarchy and Minkowski differences. They derived a complexity of $O(n^2)$ for convex and $O(n^4)$ for non-convex polyhedral objects consisting of n polygons. Cameron [22] presented a similar approach for convex objects, which can additionally track the minimum distance in non-intersection cases. Especially the computation of the Minkowski difference is very time consuming and difficult. Therefore, several approximation schemes have been developed: for instance Bergen [227] described an expanding polytope algorithm that yields a polyhedral approximation of the Minkowski difference. Agarwal et al. [1] proposed an approximation algorithm based on ray-shooting for convex polyhedra. Kim et al. [109] implicitly constructed the Minkowski difference by local dual mapping on the Gaussian map. Additionally, the authors enhanced their algorithm by using heuristics to reduce the number of features [111, 113]. Other approximations rely on discretized objects and distance fields [54].

Some authors computed *local* approximations of the penetration depth if the objects intersect in multiple disjoint zones. Therefore, penetrating zones were partitioned into coherent regions and a local penetration depth was computed for each of these regions separately. Redon and Lin [188] computed a local penetration direction for these regions and then used this information to estimate a local penetration depth on the GPU. Je et al. [96] presented a method based on their continuous collision detection algorithm using conservative advancement [212]: they constructed a linear convex cone around the collision free configuration found via CCD and then formulated a projection of the colliding configuration onto this cone as a linear complementarity problem iteratively.

Also other metrics have been proposed for the characterization of penetrating objects: for instance, Zhang et al. [255] presented an extended definition of the penetration depth that also takes the rotational component into account, called the *generalized penetration depth*. It differs from the translational penetration depth only in non-convex cases, and the computation of an upper bound can be reduced to the convex containment problem if at least one object is convex [257]. Gilbert and Ong [66] defined a *growth distance* that unifies the penetration measure for intersecting but also disjoint convex objects: basically, it measures how much the objects must be grown so that they were just in contact. Also an algorithm for the computation of the growth distance was presented [165]. Zhu et al. [261] used a gauge function [90] instead of the Euclidean norm to define pseudo-distances for overlapping objects and they presented a constrained optimization-based algorithm for its calculation.

The publication years presented in this subsection already show that penetration depth computation has recently become a very active field of research. This is mainly because computing the penetration depth is still computationally very expensive and becomes practically relevant only on very fast machines. However, using the classical penetration depth still has another serious drawback: the translational vector is not continuous at points lying on the medial axis. This results in flipping directions of the contact normals when used directly as penalty force vector. Moreover, it is not straightforward to model multiple simultaneous contacts. Tang et al. [214] tried to avoid these problems by accumulating penalty forces along the penetration time intervals between the overlapping feature pairs using a linear CCD approach.

2.3.4 Penetration Volume

Compared to other penetration measures, the literature on penetration volume computation is sparse. More precisely, there exist only two other algorithms apart from our approach: one method, proposed by Hasegawa and Sato [84], constructs the intersection volume of convex polyhedra explicitly. For this reason, it is applicable only to very simple geometries, like cubes, at interactive rates.

The other algorithm was developed by Faure et al. [52] simultaneously with our *Inner Sphere Trees*. They compute an approximation of the intersection volume from layered depth images on the GPU. This approach is applicable to deformable geometries but restricted to image space precision. And apart from that, it is relatively slow and it cannot provide continuous forces and torques for collision response.

2.4 Time Critical Collision Detection

Despite the computational power available, the performance of collision detection algorithms is still critical in many applications, especially if a required time budget must never be exceeded. This problem arises in almost all interactive real-time applications where frame rates of at least 30 fps are needed for a smooth visual

feedback. Consequently, only 30 msec remain for rendering and physics-based simulation. For the rendering step, there exists the technique of levels-of-details (LOD)
to reduce the workload of the graphics pipeline [146]. The main idea is to store
geometric data in several decreasing resolutions and choose the right LOD for rendering according to the distance from the viewpoint. Similar techniques can also be
applied to the physics-based simulation; more precisely, to the collision detection
step. Hence, this so-called *time-critical collision detection* reduces the computation
time at the cost of accuracy.

Typically, time-critical collision detection methods rely on simplifications of the
complex objects like the visual LOD representations. This can be done either explicitly or implicitly. Moreover, they often use frame-to-frame coherence because in
physics-based simulations there should usually be no discontinuities, and hence the
contact information between two collision checks does not differ too much.

For instance, the BVTT derived from a simultaneous BVH traversal (see Fig. 2.4
in the previous section) holds in each node the result of the query between two BVs.
Those BV pairs where the traversal stops build a list in the BVTT, the *separation
list* [27]. In case of high coherence, the traversal does not have to be restarted at the
roots of the BVHs for each query, but this list can be directly re-used. Ehmann and
Lin [46] called this the generalized front tracking. Lin and Li [142] enhanced this
method by defining an incremental algorithm that prioritizes the visiting order: dan-
gerous regions where collisions may occur with a high probability are prioritized.

These are, however, just examples for coherence. In fact, the classical simultaneous BVH traversal lends itself well to time-critical collision detection: the traversal
can simply be interrupted when the time budget is exhausted. This was first proposed by Hubbard [92], who additionally used a round-robin order for the collision
checks. This approach was later extended by O'Sullivan and Dingliana [168, 169]
and Dingliana and O'Sullivan [39]: like Hubbard [92] they also used an interruptible sphere tree traversal but added a more appropriate collision response solution
to Hubbard's elementary response model. A similar method can also be adopted
for deformable objects [154]. Another extension using sphere trees with a closest
feature map to avoid over-estimations of the contact information was presented by
Giang and O'Sullivan [62, 63].

Klein and Zachmann [115] described an average case approach for time-critical
traversals (ADB-trees): for each pair of BVs they computed the probability that
an intersection of the underlying primitives will occur. Coming and Staadt [33]
presented an event-based time-critical collision detection scheme relying on stride-
scheduling in combination with kinetic Sweep-and-Prune and an interruptible GJK
version.

Other authors created the LOD explicitly. For example, Otaduy and Lin [171]
presented a dual hierarchy for both the multi-resolution representation of the geometry and its BVH using convex hulls. A similar approach, called clustered hierarchy
of progressive meshes, was developed by Yoon et al. [243] for very large scenes
that require out-of-core techniques. James and Pai [95] used the reduced models not
only for fast collision detection, but also presented a deformation method based on
their bounded deformation trees.

2.4.1 Collision Detection in Haptic Environments

Almost all collision detection approaches described above are primarily designed to work in at least visual real-time. As mentioned in the introduction, for a smooth visual sensation update-rates of 30 Hz are sufficient, whereas haptic rendering requires an update frequency of 1000 Hz for a realistic haptic sensation. Moreover, detailed contact information has to be provided for a realistic perception.

None of the previously described methods, especially those computing penetration depths or times of impact, can be accelerated by a factor of 30 out of the box for reasonable scene complexities in haptic environments. Consequently, collision detection for haptics often leads to further simplifications in order to guarantee the high frequency, but also to compute plausible forces.

2.4.1.1 3 DOF

In the early times of haptic human–computer history, the beginning 1990s [195], a major simplification affected both the design of haptic hardware interfaces and the collision detection: instead of simulating the complex interaction of rigid bodies, only a single point probe was used for the interaction. This required only the computation of three force components at the probe's tip. As a result, many 3 DOF haptic devices, like the SensAble Phantom Omni Massie and Salisbury [148], entered the market and also a lot of research was done on 3 DOF haptic rendering algorithms.

One of the first algorithms for this problem was presented by Zilles and Salisbury [262]. They proposed the usage of a two different points: one represents the real position of the probe's tip, whereas the second, they call it *god object*, is constrained to the surface of the polygonal object. A spring–damper model between these points defines the force. Ruspini et al. [194] extended this approach by sweeping a sphere instead of using a single point in order to avoid the god object slipping into a virtual object through small gaps. Ho et al. [89] also took the movement of the god object into account by using a line between its previous and its recent position. BVHs can be used for accelerating the collision detection. For example, Gregory et al. [75] developed a hybrid hierarchical representation consisting of uniform grids and OBBs.

Also algorithms for other than polygonal object representations have been proposed: Thompson et al. [220] developed an algorithm that is applicable for 3 DOF rendering of NURBS surfaces without the use of any intermediate representation. Gibson [64] and Avila and Sobierajski [7] described approaches for volumetric representations. More recent works also included the GPU for faster collision detection using local occupancy maps [107].

Fig. 2.5 The Voxmap-Pointshell approach for 6 DOF haptic rendering uses two different data structures: A voxelization (*left*) and a point-sampling of the objects' surface (*right*)

2.4.1.2 6 DOF

Many applications, like training or virtual prototyping, require interaction with complex virtual tools instead of just a single point probe to ensure a sufficient degree of realism. As soon as the haptic probe includes 3D objects, the additional rendering of torques becomes important. Also, simultaneous multiple contacts with the environment may occur. This significantly increases the complexity of the collision detection but also of the collision response. Generally, a complete 6 DOF rigid-body simulation, including forces and torques, has to be performed in only 1 millisecond.

For very simple objects, consisting of only a few hundred polygons, the traditional collision approaches described above can be used. Ortega et al. [167] extended the god-object method to 6 DOF haptic rendering using continuous collision detection to derive the position and orientation of the god object. However, they cannot guarantee to meet the time budget; therefore they use asynchronous update processes. Kolesnikov and Zefran [123] presented an analytical approximation of the penetration depth with additional considerations of the rotational motion.

Despite simplifications of temporal constraints, most often geometric simplifications were used. Many 6 DOF haptic rendering approaches are based on the Voxmap Pointshell (VPS) method [151]. The main idea is to divide the virtual environment into a dynamic object that is allowed to move freely through the virtual space and static objects that are fixed in the world. The static environment is discretized into a set of voxels, whereas the dynamic object is described by a set of points that represents its surface (see Fig. 2.5). During query time, for each of these points it is determined with a simple boolean test, whether it is located in a filled volume element or not. Today, voxelization can be efficiently computed using the GPU [42, 179, 198].

Many extensions for the classical VPS algorithms have been proposed: for instance, the use of distance fields instead of simple boolean voxmaps [152] or an additional voxel hierarchy for the use of temporal coherence [153], since also recent computer hardware can perform only a few thousands intersection tests in 1 millisecond. Prior and Haines [183] described a proximity agent method to reduce

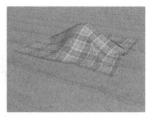

Fig. 2.6 Deformable objects like cloth require special algorithms, because pre-computed data structures become invalid after the deformation. Moreover, collision between parts of the object itself may occur

the number of collision tests for multiple object pairs in collaborative virtual environments. Renz et al. [190] presented extensions to the classic VPS, including optimizations to force calculation in order to increase its stability. Barbič and James [13] developed a distance-field-based approach that can handle contacts between rigid objects and reduced deformable models at haptic rates. Later they extended their approach to cover also deformable versus deformable contacts [14]. Ruffaldi et al. [193] described an implicit sphere tree based on an octree that represents the volumetric data. However, even these optimizations cannot completely avoid the limits of VPS, namely aliasing effects and huge memory consumption.

Other authors use level-of-detail techniques to simplify the complexity of large polygonal models [145]. Otaduy and Lin [172] presented a sensation preserving simplification algorithm and a collision detection framework that adaptively selects a LOD. Later, they added a linearized contact model using contact clustering [170]. Another idea is to combine low-resolution geometric objects along with texture images that encode the surface details [173]. Kim et al. [112] also clustered contacts based on their spatial proximity to speed up a local penetration depth estimation using an incremental algorithm. Johnson et al. [99] approximated the penetration depth by extending their normal cone approach. Glondu et al. [67] developed a method for very large environments using a neighborhood graph: for objects that are closer to the haptic probe they used the LOD.

2.5 Collision Detection for Deformable Objects

Usually, collision detection algorithms rely on pre-computed data structures like BVHs. This works fine, as long as the geometry of the objects does not change, i.e. if the objects are rigid. However, our world consists not only of rigid objects but includes a lot of deformable objects, like cloth (see Fig. 2.6). Consequently, a realistic simulation should also be able to handle deformable models. Beside cloth simulation, popular deformable applications include character animation, surgery simulation, and fractures.

An additional challenge for collision detection of deformable objects is the possibility that parts of one object intersect other parts of the same object, the so-called

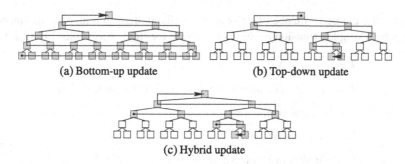

(a) Bottom-up update   (b) Top-down update

(c) Hybrid update

Fig. 2.7 Different updating strategies for BVHs

self-collisions. Actually, BVHs can easily be employed to find self-collisions by simply checking the BVH of an object against itself and rejecting collisions between adjacent primitives [229]. Additionally, techniques like hierarchies of normal cones [184] or power diagrams [77] can be used for further acceleration.

Since BVHs have proven to be very efficient for rigid objects, and, moreover, they can easily be extended to self-collision detection, researchers also want to use them for deformable objects. As the BVHs become invalid after deformations, several approaches have been published to handle this problem: the easiest method is to rebuild the BVH from scratch after each deformation. Unfortunately, it turns out that a complete rebuild is computationally too expensive. Even modern GPU acceleration cannot guarantee real-time performance for BVH construction in reasonably complex scenes [132]. Some authors reduced the rebuild to interesting regions. For example, Smith et al. [202] used a lazy reconstruction of an octree for all primitives in the overlap region, or they keep a more complex data structure like a full octree and simply reinsert all primitives in the leaves in each frame [61]. Other approaches completely avoid hierarchies but used regular spatial subdivision data structures like uniform grids [224, 252]. Spatial hashing helps to reduce the high memory requirements of uniform grids [219]. However, choosing the right grid size remains an unsolved problem due to the inherent "teapot in a stadium" problem [82].

Another method is to avoid the complete rebuild by simply updating the BVs of a pre-computed BVH after deformations. Bergen [225] stated that updating is about ten times faster compared to a complete rebuild of an AABB hierarchy, and as long as the topology of the object is conserved, there is no significant performance loss in the collision check compared to rebuilding. Basically, there exist two main techniques for updating a BVH: bottom-up and top-down. Bottom-up updates start by refitting the BVs of the primitives and merge them upwards with the root of the tree. This can be done efficiently for AABB trees [229] and sphere trees [21]. However, during a collision query usually not all of these BVs are visited. Hence a lot of work may be done on updates that are not required. A simple strategy to reduce the number of updated BVs is to update them on-line, when they are in fact visited during a traversal. This requires the traversal of all primitives placed under a BV. This is the typical top-down approach [127]. Of course, this raises the question: Which of the two methods is better?

Basically, the performance of deformable collision detection algorithms can be derived by a simple extension of the cost function for rigid objects (see Eq. (2.1)):

$$T = N_v C_v + N_p C_p + N_u C_u \quad \text{with}$$

$T = $ Total cost of testing a pair of models for intersection

$N_v = $ Number of BV Tests

$C_v = $ Cost of a BV Test

$N_p = $ Number of Primitive Tests   (2.2)

$C_p = $ Cost of a Primitive Test

$N_u = $ Number of BV Updates

$C_u = $ Cost of a BV Update

Usually, N_u is higher for the bottom-up update than for the top-down approach. On the other hand, C_u is higher for the top-down method. Consequently, there is no definite answer to the question. Actually, according to Larsson and Akenine-Möller [127], if many deep nodes in a tree are reached, it gives a better overall performance to update the AABBs in a tree bottom-up. In simple cases, however, with only a few deep nodes visited in a collision test, the top-down update performs better. As a compromise, the authors proposed a hybrid updating strategy: for a tree with depth n, initially the first $\frac{n}{2}$ should be updated bottom-up. The lower nodes should be updated top-down on the fly during collision traversal (see Fig. 2.7). Mezger et al. [155] accelerated the update by omitting the update process for several time steps. Therefore, the BVs are inflated by a certain distance, and as long as the enclosed polygon does not move farther than this distance, the BV does not need to be updated.

If specific information about the underlying deformation scheme or the geometric objects is available, additional updating techniques can be used for further acceleration. For instance, Larsson and Akenine-Möller [128] proposed a method for morphing objects, where the objects are constructed by interpolation between some morphing targets: one BVH is constructed for each of the morph targets so that the corresponding nodes contain exactly the same vertices. During running time, the current BVH can be constructed by interpolating the BVs. Spillmann et al. [206] presented a fast sphere tree update for meshless objects undergoing geometric deformations that also supports level-of-detail collision detection. Lau et al. [131] described a collision detection framework for deformable NURBS surfaces using AABB hierarchies. They reduce the number of updates by searching for special deformation regions. Guibas et al. [77] used cascade verification in a sphere tree for deformable necklaces. Sobottka et al. [205] extended this approach to hair simulation using AABBs and k-DOPs [204].

Refitting BVHs works as long as the objects do not deform too much, that is, when the accumulated overlap of the refitted BVs is not too large. This problem arises for example in simulations of fracturing objects. In this case, a complete or partial rebuild of the BVH may increase the running time significantly. Larsson and Akenine-Möller [129] proposed an algorithm that can handle highly dynamic breakable objects efficiently: they start a refitting bottom-up update at the BVs in the separation list and use a simple volume heuristic to detect degenerated sub-trees that must be completely rebuilt. Otaduy et al. [174] used a dynamic re-structuring of a balanced AVL-AABB tree. Tang et al. [215] described a two-level BVH for breakable objects based on mesh connectivity and bounds on the primitives' normals.

2.5.1 Excursus: GPU-Based Methods

Popular methods for real-time simulation of deformable objects like mass–spring systems [136, 160], but also multi-body simulations [48, 216], can be easily parallelized. Consequently, they are perfectly suited for modern GPU architectures. Hence, it is obvious to develop also collision detection schemes that work directly on the graphics hardware instead of copying data back and forth between main memory and GPU memory.

Actually, GPU-based algorithms have been proposed for all parts of the collision detection pipeline: the broad-phase Le Grand [135], Liu et al. [143], the narrow-phase Chen et al. [28], Greß et al. [76] and even for the primitive tests [73, 240].

The first approaches relied on the fixed-function graphics pipeline of at least OpenGL 1.6 and used image space techniques. For instance, Knott and Pai [119] implemented a ray-casting algorithm based on frame buffer operations to detect static interferences between polyhedral objects. Heidelberger et al. [86] described an algorithm for computation of layered depth images using depth and stencil buffers.

Later, the fixed function pipelines had been replaced by programmable vertex and fragment processors. This also changed the GPU collision detection algorithms: for example, Zhang and Kim [258] performed massively parallel pairwise intersection tests of AABBs in a fragment shader. Kolb et al. [122] used shaders for the simulation of large particle systems, including collisions between the particles.

Today, GPU processors are freely programmable via APIs such as OpenCL or CUDA. This further improves the flexibility of GPU-based collision detection algorithms, like the approach by Pan and Manocha [176] that uses clustering and collision-packet traversal or the method based on linear complementary programming for convex objects by Kipfer [114].

Moreover, several special hardware designs to accelerate collision detection were developed [6, 186]. With the Ageia PhysX card [38], one saw a special hardware card even managing to enter the market. But due to increasing performance and flexibility of GPUs it seems that special physics processing hardware has become obsolete.

Fig. 2.8 Ray tracing
supports a wide variety of
optical effects like reflections,
refractions, and shadows

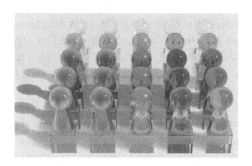

2.6 Related Fields

Of course, data structures for the acceleration of geometric queries are not restricted
to collision detection. They are also widely used in ray tracing (see Sect. 2.6.1),
object recognition [199], 3D audio rendering [223, 234] or occlusion [242, 254],
view frustum [31] and backface culling [253]. Moreover, they accelerate visibility
queries including hierarchical z-Buffers [74] and back-to-front [55] or front-to-back
[69] rendering via BSP-Trees. Geometric hierarchies help to index [79, 201] and
search [180] geometric databases efficiently, and they improve hardware tessellation
[161].

This small selection of very different applications and the large number of data
structures already presented just for the field of collision detection in the previous
sections suggests that there is available an almost uncountable number of different
approaches. A perfect geometric data structure would be one that can process every
imaginable geometric search query optimally. Unfortunately, such a data structure
does not—and maybe cannot—exist. Quite to the contrary, much research is con-
cerned with finding optimal data structures for each small sub-problem. However,
maintaining dozens of different optimized data structures in a simple virtual environment with ray tracing, sound rendering and collision detection could also be
very inefficient due to memory waste and the computational cost of hierarchy updates. Consequently, there is also a counter movement that proposes the use of more
general data structures [78].

2.6.1 Excursus: Ray Tracing

Basically, ray tracing is a rendering technique that realizes global illumination for
perfect reflections (see Fig. 2.8). Instead of scan converting all polygons in the
scene, as traditional renderers like OpenGL and DirectX do, a ray of light is traced
backward from the eye through the scene. If the ray hits an object, an additional
ray is shot to the light sources and moreover, reflected and refracted rays are further
traced recursively [238]. Consequently, the main challenge on tracing rays is to find
intersections between these rays and the scene. This problem is closely related to

collision detection where two objects are checked for intersection. Therefore, also the geometric acceleration data structures are very similar.

A complete overview of all existing data structures for ray tracing is far beyond the scope of this excursus. As a starting point we would like to refer the interested reader to the books and surveys of Hanrahan [83], Arvo and Kirk [5], Shirley and Morley [200], and Suffern [209]. In the following, we will briefly point out similarities and differences between ray tracing and collision detection and dwell on the open challenges.

Almost all data structures that were proposed for collision detection had been earlier applied to ray tracing. This includes non-hierarchical data structures like uniform grids [3, 57], as well as bounding volume hierarchies [104, 192]. However, a ray has to be tested for intersection with the whole scene, whereas during the collision detection process objects are checked for collision with other objects in the same scene. Therefore, the data structures for ray tracing are usually used at a *scene* level, while collision detection uses them on an *object* level. Consequently, other spatial subdivision data structures that are rarely used in collision detection, like octrees [196, 237] and kd-trees [59], which were originally developed for associative searches [16], became more popular for ray tracing [233].

However, these data structures are primarily designed for static scenes. If objects in the scene move or deform, the data structures have to be updated or rebuilt. As in collision detection for deformable objects, it is still a challenge to find the right updating strategy and a lot of recent work has been done on this problem recently [4, 244]. Moreover, even when using fast acceleration data structures, ray tracing is computational very expensive and is not applicable for real-time rendering on consumer hardware. However, the first GPU implementations that support parallel tracing of rays seem to be very promising [40, 91, 150, 181, 221].

References

1. Agarwal, P. K., Guibas, L. J., Har-Peled, S., Rabinovitch, A., & Sharir, M. (2000). Penetration depth of two convex polytopes in 3d. *Nordic Journal of Computing*, 7(3), 227–240. URL http://dl.acm.org/citation.cfm?id=642992.642999.
2. Albocher, D., Sarel, U., Choi, Y.-K., Elber, G., & Wang, W. (2006). Efficient continuous collision detection for bounding boxes under rational motion. In *ICRA* (pp. 3017–3022). New York: IEEE. URL http://dblp.uni-trier.de/db/conf/icra/icra2006.html.
3. Amanatides, J., & Woo, A. (1987). A fast voxel traversal algorithm for ray tracing. In *Eurographics 1987* (pp. 3–10).
4. Andrysco, N., & Tricoche, X. (2011). Implicit and dynamic trees for high performance rendering. In *Proceedings of graphics interface 2011, GI '11*, School of Computer Science, University of Waterloo, Waterloo, Ontario (pp. 143–150). Waterloo: Canadian Human-Computer Communications Society. ISBN 978-1-4503-0693-5. URL http://dl.acm.org/citation.cfm?id=1992917.1992941.
5. Arvo, J., & Kirk, D. (1989). A survey of ray tracing acceleration techniques. In A. S. Glassner (Ed.), *An introduction to ray tracing* (pp. 201–262). London: Academic Press Ltd. ISBN 0-12-286160-4. URL http://dl.acm.org/citation.cfm?id=94788.94794.

6. Atay, N., Lockwood, J. W., & Bayazit, B. (2005). A collision detection chip on reconfigurable hardware (Technical report). In *Proceedings of pacific conference on computer graphics and applications (pacific graphics)*.

7. Avila, R. S., & Sobierajski, L. M. (1996). A haptic interaction method for volume visualization. In *Proceedings of the 7th conference on visualization '96, VIS '96* (pp. 197-ff). Los Alamitos: IEEE Computer Society Press. ISBN 0-89791-864-9. URL http://dl.acm.org/citation.cfm?id=244979.245054.

8. Avril, Q., Gouranton, V., & Arnaldi, B. (2009). New trends in collision detection performance. In S. Richir & A. Shirai (Eds.), *Laval virtual VRIC'09 proceedings*, BP 0119, 53001 Laval Cedex, France, April 2009 (pp. 53–62).

9. Avril, Q., Gouranton, V., & Arnaldi, B. (2010). A broad phase collision detection algorithm adapted to multi-cores architectures. In S. Richir & A. Shirai (Eds.), *VRIC'10 proceedings*, April 2010.

10. Avril, Q., Gouranton, V., & Arnaldi, B. (2010). Synchronization-free parallel collision detection pipeline. In *ICAT 2010*, December 2010.

11. Avril, Q., Gouranton, V., & Arnaldi, B. (2011). Dynamic adaptation of broad phase collision detection algorithms. In *IEEE international symposium on virtual reality innovations*, March 2011.

12. Bandi, S., & Thalmann, D. (1995). An adaptive spatial subdivision of the object space for fast collision detection of animated rigid bodies. *Computer Graphics Forum, 14*(3), 259–270. URL http://dblp.uni-trier.de/db/journals/cgf/cgf14.html#BandiT95.

13. Barbič, J., & James, D. L. (2007). Time-critical distributed contact for 6-dof haptic rendering of adaptively sampled reduced deformable models. In *2007 ACM SIGGRAPH / eurographics symposium on computer animation*, August 2007.

14. Barbič, J., & James, D. L. (2008). Six-dof haptic rendering of contact between geometrically complex reduced deformable models. *IEEE Transactions on Haptics, 1*(1), 39–52.

15. Barequet, G., Chazelle, B., Guibas, L. J., Mitchell, J. S. B., & Tal, A. (1996). Boxtree: a hierarchical representation for surfaces in 3d. *Computer Graphics Forum, 15*(3), 387–396. URL http://dblp.uni-trier.de/db/journals/cgf/cgf15.html#BarequetCGMT96.

16. Bentley, J. L. (1975). Multidimensional binary search trees used for associative searching. *Communications of the ACM, 18*(9), 509–517. doi:10.1145/361002.361007. URL http://doi.acm.org/10.1145/361002.361007.

17. Bentley, J. L., & Friedman, J. H. (1979). Data structures for range searching. *ACM Computing Surveys, 11*(4), 397–409. doi:10.1145/356789.356797. URL http://doi.acm.org/10.1145/356789.356797.

18. Bicchi, A., Buss, M., Ernst, M. O., & Peer, A. (Eds.) (2008). *Springer tracts in advanced robotics (STAR): Vol. 45. The sense of touch and its rendering: progresses in haptics research*. Berlin: Springer.

19. Bonner, S., & Kelley, R. B. (1988). A representation scheme for rapid 3-d collision detection. In *IEEE international symposium on intelligent control* (pp. 320–325).

20. Bradshaw, G., & O'Sullivan, C. (2004). Adaptive medial-axis approximation for sphere-tree construction. *ACM Transactions on Graphics, 23*(1), 1–26. doi:10.1145/966131.966132. URL http://doi.acm.org/10.1145/966131.966132.

21. Brown, J., Sorkin, S., Bruyns, C., Latombe, J.-C., Montgomery, K., & Stephanides, M. (2001). Real-time simulation of deformable objects: tools and application. In *COMP. ANIMATION*.

22. Cameron, S. (1997). Enhancing gjk: computing minimum and penetration distances between convex polyhedra. In *Proceedings of international conference on robotics and automation* (pp. 3112–3117).

23. Canny, J. (1984). *Collision detection for moving polyhedra* (Technical report). Massachusetts Institute of Technology, Cambridge, MA, USA.

24. Chang, C.-T., Gorissen, B., & Melchior, S. (2011). Fast oriented bounding box optimization on the rotation group so(3,ℝ). *ACM Transactions on Graphics, 30*(5), 122:1–122:16. doi:10.1145/2019627.2019641. URL http://doi.acm.org/10.1145/2019627.2019641.

25. Chang, J.-W., & Kim, M.-S. (2009). Technical section: efficient triangle-triangle intersection test for obb-based collision detection. *Computer Graphics, 33*(3), 235–240. doi:10.1016/j.cag.2009.03.009.

26. Chazelle, B. (1984). Convex partitions of polyhedra: a lower bound and worst-case optimal algorithm. *SIAM Journal on Computing, 13*(3), 488–507. doi:10.1137/0213031.

27. Chen, J.-S., & Li, T.-Y. (1999). *Incremental 3D collision detection with hierarchical data structures.* November 22. URL http://citeseer.ist.psu.edu/356263.html; http://bittern.cs.nccu.edu.tw/li/Publication/pdf/vrst98.pdf.

28. Chen, W., Wan, H., Zhang, H., Bao, H., & Peng, Q. (2004). Interactive collision detection for complex and deformable models using programmable graphics hardware. In *Proceedings of the ACM symposium on virtual reality software and technology, VRST '04* (pp. 10–15). New York: ACM. ISBN 1-58113-907-1. doi:10.1145/1077534.1077539. URL http://doi.acm.org/10.1145/1077534.1077539.

29. Chin, F., & Wang, C. A. (1983). Optimal algorithms for the intersection and the minimum distance problems between planar polygons. *IEEE Transactions on Computers, 32*(12), 1203–1207. doi:10.1109/TC.1983.1676186.

30. Choi, Y.-K., Chang, J.-W., Wang, W., Kim, M.-S., & Elber, G. (2009). Continuous collision detection for ellipsoids. *IEEE Transactions on Visualization and Computer Graphics, 15*(2), 311–324. URL http://www.ncbi.nlm.nih.gov/pubmed/19147893.

31. Clark, J. H. (1976). Hierarchical geometric models for visible surface algorithms. *Communications of the ACM, 19*(10), 547–554. doi:10.1145/360349.360354. URL http://doi.acm.org/10.1145/360349.360354.

32. Cohen, J. D., Lin, M. C., Manocha, D., & Ponamgi, M. (1995). I-collide: an interactive and exact collision detection system for large-scale environments. In *Proceedings of the 1995 symposium on interactive 3D graphics, I3D '95* (pp. 189-ff). New York: ACM. ISBN 0-89791-736-7. doi:10.1145/199404.199437. URL http://doi.acm.org/10.1145/199404.199437.

33. Coming, D. S., & Staadt, O. G. (2007). Stride scheduling for time-critical collision detection. In *Proceedings of the 2007 ACM symposium on virtual reality software and technology, VRST '07* (pp. 241–242). New York: ACM. ISBN 978-1-59593-863-3. doi:10.1145/1315184.1315240. URL http://doi.acm.org/10.1145/1315184.1315240.

34. Coming, D. S., & Staadt, O. G. (2008). Velocity-aligned discrete oriented polytopes for dynamic collision detection. *IEEE Transactions on Visualization and Computer Graphics, 14*(1), 1–12. doi:10.1109/TVCG.2007.70405.

35. Coumans, E. (2005). *Continuous collision detection and physics* (Technical report). Sony Computer Entertainment. August.

36. Coumans, E. (2012). *Bullet physics library.* http://bulletphysics.com.

37. Coutinho, M. G. (2001). *Dynamic simulations of multibody systems.* London: Springer. ISBN 0-387-95192-X.

38. Davis, C., Hegde, M., Schmid, O. A., Maher, M., & Bordes, J. P. (2003). System incorporating physics processing unit 1.

39. Dingliana, J., & O'Sullivan, C. (2000). Graceful degradation of collision handling in physically based animation. *Computer Graphics Forum, 19*(3), 239–247 (Proc. of EUROGRAPHICS 2000).

40. Djeu, P., Hunt, W., Wang, R., Elhassan, I., Stoll, G., & Razor, W. R. M. (2011). An architecture for dynamic multiresolution ray tracing. *ACM Transactions on Graphics, 30*(5), 115:1–115:26. doi:10.1145/2019627.2019634. URL http://doi.acm.org/10.1145/2019627.2019634.

41. Dobkin, D. P., Hershberger, J., Kirkpatrick, D. G., & Suri, S. (1993). Computing the intersection-depth of polyhedra. *Algorithmica, 9*(6), 518–533.

42. Dong, Z., Chen, W., Bao, H., Zhang, H., & Peng, Q. (2004). Real-time voxelization for complex polygonal models. In *Proceedings of the computer graphics and applications, 12th pacific conference, PG '04* (pp. 43–50). Washington: IEEE Computer Society. ISBN 0-7695-2234-3. URL http://dl.acm.org/citation.cfm?id=1025128.1026026.

43. Eberly, D. H. (2003). *Game physics*. New York: Elsevier Science Inc. ISBN 1558607404.
44. Eckstein, J., & Schömer, E. (1999). Dynamic collision detection in virtual reality applications. In V. Skala (Ed.), *WSCG'99 conference proceedings*. URL citeseer.ist.psu.edu/eckstein99dynamic.html.
45. Edelsbrunner, H., & Maurer, H. A. (1981). On the intersection of orthogonal objects. *Information Processing Letters*, *13*(4/5), 177–181. URL http://dblp.uni-trier.de/db/journals/ipl/ipl13.html#EdelsbrunnerM81.
46. Ehmann, S. A., & Lin, M. C. (2001). Accurate and fast proximity queries between polyhedra using convex surface decomposition. *Computer Graphics Forum*, *20*(3), 500–510 (Proc. of EUROGRAPHICS 2001).
47. El-Far, N. R., Georganas, N. D., & El Saddik, A. (2007). Collision detection and force response in highly-detailed point-based hapto-visual virtual environments. In *Proceedings of the 11th IEEE international symposium on distributed simulation and real-time applications, DS-RT '07* (pp. 15–22). Washington: IEEE Computer Society. ISBN 0-7695-3011-7. doi:10.1109/DS-RT.2007.17.
48. Elsen, E., Houston, M., Vishal, V., Darve, E., Hanrahan, P., & Pande, V. (2006). N-body simulation on gpus. In *Proceedings of the 2006 ACM/IEEE conference on supercomputing, SC '06*, New York: ACM. ISBN 0-7695-2700-0. doi:10.1145/1188455.1188649. URL http://doi.acm.org/10.1145/1188455.1188649.
49. Ericson, C. (2004). *The Morgan Kaufmann series in interactive 3-D technology: Real-time collision detection*. San Francisco: Morgan Kaufmann Publishers Inc. ISBN 1558607323.
50. Fahn, C.-S., & Wang, J.-L. (1999). Efficient time-interupted and time-continuous collision detection among polyhedral. *Journal of Information Science and Engineering*, *15*(6), 769–799.
51. Fares, C., & Hamam, A. (2005). Collision detection for rigid bodies: a state of the art review. In *GraphiCon*.
52. Faure, F., Barbier, S., Allard, J., & Falipou, F. (2008). Image-based collision detection and response between arbitrary volumetric objects. In *ACM siggraph/eurographics symposium on computer animation, SCA*, Dublin, Irlande. July 2008.
53. Figueiredo, M., Oliveira, J., Araujo, B., & Madeiras, J. (2010). An efficient collision detection algorithm for point cloud models. In *Proceedings of graphicon*.
54. Fisher, S., & Lin, M. C. (2001). Deformed distance fields for simulation of non-penetrating flexible bodies. In *Proceedings of the eurographic workshop on computer animation and simulation* (pp. 99–111). New York: Springer. ISBN 3-211-83711-6. URL http://dl.acm.org/citation.cfm?id=776350.776360.
55. Fuchs, H., Kedem, Z. M., & Naylor, B. F. (1980). On visible surface generation by a priori tree structures. *SIGGRAPH Computer Graphics*, *14*(3), 124–133. doi:10.1145/965105.807481. URL http://doi.acm.org/10.1145/965105.807481.
56. Fuhrmann, A., Sobotka, G., & Groß, C. (2003). Distance fields for rapid collision detection in physically based modeling. In *Proceedings of GraphiCon 2003* (pp. 58–65). URL http://citeseerx.ist.psu.edu/viewdoc/download?doi=10.1.1.107.4043&rep=rep1&type=pdf.
57. Fujimoto, A., Tanaka, T., & Iwata, K. (1986). Arts: Accelerated ray-tracing system. *IEEE Computer Graphics and Applications*, *6*(4), 16–26.
58. Funfzig, C., Ullrich, T., & Fellner, D. W. (2006). Hierarchical spherical distance fields for collision detection. *IEEE Computer Graphics and Applications*, *26*(1), 64–74. doi:10.1109/MCG.2006.17.
59. Fussell, D. S., & Subramanian, K. R. (1988). *Fast ray tracing using k-d trees* (Technical report). University of Texas at Austin, Austin, TX, USA.
60. Ganjugunte, S. K. (2007). A survey on techniques for computing penetration depth.
61. Ganovelli, F., & Dingliana, J. (2000). Buckettree: improving collision detection between deformable objects. In *Proceedings of SCCG2000: spring conference on computer graphics*, Budmerice (pp. 4–6).
62. Giang, T., & O'Sullivan, C. (2005). Closest feature maps for time-critical collision handling. In *International workshop on virtual reality and physical simulation (VRIPHYS'05)*, Novem-

ber (pp. 65–72). URL http://isg.cs.tcd.ie/cosulliv/Pubs/GiangVriphys.pdf.

63. Giang, T., & O'Sullivan, C. (2006). Virtual reality interaction and physical simulation: approximate collision response using closest feature maps. *Computer Graphics, 30*(3), 423–431. doi:10.1016/j.cag.2006.02.019.

64. Gibson, S. F. F. (1995). Beyond volume rendering: visualization, haptic exploration, and physical modeling of voxel-based objects. In *Proc. eurographics workshop on visualization in scientific computing* (pp. 10–24). Berlin: Springer.

65. Gilbert, E. G., Johnson, D. W., & Keerthi, S. S. (1988). A fast procedure for computing the distance between complex objects in three-dimensional space. *IEEE Journal of Robotics and Automation, 4*(2), 193–203.

66. Gilbert, E. G., & Ong, C. J. (1994). New distances for the separation and penetration of objects. In *ICRA* (pp. 579–586).

67. Glondu, L., Marchal, M., & Dumont, G. (2010). A new coupling scheme for haptic rendering of rigid bodies interactions based on a haptic sub-world using a contact graph. In *Proceedings of the 2010 international conference on haptics: generating and perceiving tangible sensations, part I, EuroHaptics'10* (pp. 51–56). Berlin: Springer. ISBN 3-642-14063-7, 978-3-642-14063-1. URL http://dl.acm.org/citation.cfm?id=1884164.1884173.

68. Goldsmith, J., & Salmon, J. (1987). Automatic creation of object hierarchies for ray tracing. *IEEE Computer Graphics and Applications, 7*(5), 14–20. doi:10.1109/MCG.1987.276983.

69. Gordon, D., & Chen, S. (1991). Front-to-back display of bsp trees. *IEEE Computer Graphics and Applications, 11*(5), 79–85. doi:10.1109/38.90569.

70. Gottschalk, S., Lin, M. C., & Manocha, D. (1996). Obbtree: a hierarchical structure for rapid interference detection. In *Proceedings of the 23rd annual conference on computer graphics and interactive techniques, SIGGRAPH '96* (pp. 171–180). New York: ACM. ISBN 0-89791-746-4. doi:10.1145/237170.237244. URL http://doi.acm.org/10.1145/237170.237244.

71. Gottschalk, S. (1997). Collision detection techniques for 3d models.

72. Gottschalk, S. A. (2000). *Collision queries using oriented bounding boxes*. PhD thesis, The University of North Carolina at Chapel Hill. AAI9993311.

73. Govindaraju, N. K., Knott, D., Jain, N., Kabul, I., Tamstorf, R., Gayle, R., Lin, M. C., & Manocha, D. (2005). Interactive collision detection between deformable models using chromatic decomposition. *ACM Transactions on Graphics, 24*(3), 991–999. URL http://dblp.uni-trier.de/db/journals/tog/tog24.html#GovindarajuKJKTGLM05.

74. Greene, N., Kass, M., & Miller, G. (1993). Hierarchical z-buffer visibility. In *Proceedings of the 20th annual conference on computer graphics and interactive techniques, SIGGRAPH '93* (pp. 231–238). New York: ACM. ISBN 0-89791-601-8. doi:10.1145/166117.166147. URL http://doi.acm.org/10.1145/166117.166147.

75. Gregory, A., Lin, M. C., Gottschalk, S., & Taylor, R. (1999). A framework for fast and accurate collision detection for haptic interaction. In *Proceedings of the IEEE virtual reality, VR '99* (p. 38). Washington: IEEE Computer Society. ISBN 0-7695-0093-5. URL http://dl.acm.org/citation.cfm?id=554230.835691.

76. Greß, A., Guthe, M., & Klein, R. (2006). Gpu-based collision detection for deformable parameterized surfaces. *Computer Graphics Forum, 25*(3), 497–506.

77. Guibas, L., Nguyen, A., Russel, D., & Zhang, L. (2002). Collision detection for deforming necklaces. In *Proceedings of the eighteenth annual symposium on computational geometry, SCG '02* (pp. 33–42). New York: ACM. ISBN 1-58113-504-1. doi:10.1145/513400.513405. URL http://doi.acm.org/10.1145/513400.513405.

78. Günther, J., Mannuß, F., & Hinkenjann, A. (2009). Centralized spatial data structures for interactive environments. In *Proceedings of workshop on software engineering and architectures for realtime interactive systems, in conjunction with IEEE virtual reality*. URL http://cg.inf.fh-bonn-rhein-sieg.de/basilic/Publications/2009/GMH09.

79. Günther, O. (1989). The design of the cell tree: an object-oriented index structure for geometric databases. In *ICDE* (pp. 598–605).

80. Guttman, A. (1984). R-trees: a dynamic index structure for spatial searching. *SIGMOD Record, 14*(2), 47–57. doi:10.1145/971697.602266. URL http://doi.acm.org/10.1145/

971697.602266.

81. Hachenberger, P. (2007). Exact Minkowksi sums of polyhedra and exact and efficient decomposition of polyhedra in convex pieces. In *Proceedings of the 15th annual European conference on algorithms, ESA'07* (pp. 669–680). Berlin: Springer. ISBN 3-540-75519-5. URL http://dl.acm.org/citation.cfm?id=1778580.1778642.

82. Haines, E. (1988). Spline surface rendering, and what's wrong with octrees. *Ray Tracing News, 1*.

83. Hanrahan, P. (1989). A survey of ray-surface intersection algorithms. In A. S. Glassner (Ed.), *An introduction to ray tracing* (pp. 79–119). London: Academic Press Ltd. ISBN 0-12-286160-4. URL http://dl.acm.org/citation.cfm?id=94788.94791.

84. Hasegawa, S., & Sato, M. (2004). Real-time rigid body simulation for haptic interactions based on contact volume of polygonal objects. *Computer Graphics Forum, 23*(3), 529–538.

85. He, T. (1999). Fast collision detection using quospo trees. In *Proceedings of the 1999 symposium on interactive 3D graphics, I3D '99* (pp. 55–62). New York: ACM. ISBN 1-58113-082-1. doi:10.1145/300523.300529. URL http://doi.acm.org/10.1145/300523.300529.

86. Heidelberger, B., Teschner, M., & Gross, M. (2004). Detection of collisions and self-collisions using image-space techniques. In *Proceedings of the 12th international conference in central Europe on computer graphics, visualization and computer vision'2004 (WSCG'2004)*, University of West Bohemia, Czech Republic, February (pp. 145–152).

87. Held, M. (1998). Erit: a collection of efficient and reliable intersection tests. *Journal of Graphics Tools, 2*(4), 25–44. URL http://dl.acm.org/citation.cfm?id=763345.763348.

88. Held, M., Klosowski, J. T., & Mitchell, J. S. B. (1996). Collision detection for fly-throughs in virtual environments. In *Proceedings of the twelfth annual symposium on computational geometry, SCG '96* (pp. 513–514). New York: ACM. ISBN 0-89791-804-5. doi:10.1145/237218.237428. URL http://doi.acm.org/10.1145/237218.237428.

89. Ho, C.-H., Basdogan, C., & Srinivasan, M. A. (1999). Efficient point-based rendering techniques for haptic display of virtual objects. *Presence: Teleoperators & Virtual Environments, 8*(5), 477–491. doi:10.1162/105474699566413.

90. Hoang, T. (1998). *Convex analysis and global optimization. Nonconvex optimization and its applications*. Dordrecht: Kluwer Academic Publishers. ISBN 9780792348184. URL http://books.google.co.uk/books?id=hVkJc2IRDdcC.

91. Horn, D. R., Sugerman, J., Houston, M., & Hanrahan, P. (2007). Interactive k-d tree gpu raytracing. In *Proceedings of the 2007 symposium on interactive 3D graphics and games, I3D '07* (pp. 167–174). New York: ACM. ISBN 978-1-59593-628-8. doi:10.1145/1230100.1230129. URL http://doi.acm.org/10.1145/1230100.1230129.

92. Hubbard, P. M. (1996). Approximating polyhedra with spheres for time-critical collision detection. *ACM Transactions on Graphics, 15*(3), 179–210.

93. Hutter, M. (2007). Optimized continuous collision detection for deformable triangle meshes. *Computer, 15*(1–3), 25–32. URL http://citeseerx.ist.psu.edu/viewdoc/download?doi=10.1.1.85.1140&rep=rep1&type=pdf.

94. Izadi, S., Kim, D., Hilliges, O., Molyneaux, D., Newcombe, R., Kohli, P., Shotton, J., Hodges, S., Freeman, D., Davison, A., & Fitzgibbon, A. (2011). Kinectfusion: real-time 3d reconstruction and interaction using a moving depth camera. In *Proceedings of the 24th annual ACM symposium on user interface software and technology, UIST '11* (pp. 559–568). New York: ACM. ISBN 978-1-4503-0716-1. doi:10.1145/2047196.2047270. URL http://doi.acm.org/10.1145/2047196.2047270.

95. James, D. L., & Pai, D. K. (2004). Bd-tree: output-sensitive collision detection for reduced deformable models. In *ACM SIGGRAPH 2004 papers, SIGGRAPH '04* (pp. 393–398). New York: ACM. doi:10.1145/1186562.1015735. URL http://doi.acm.org/10.1145/1186562.1015735.

96. Je, C., Tang, M., Lee, Y., Lee, M., & Kim, Y. J. (2012). Polydepth: real-time penetration depth computation using iterative contact-space projection. *ACM Transactions on Graphics, 31*(1), 5:1–5:14. doi:10.1145/2077341.2077346. URL http://doi.acm.org/10.1145/2077341.2077346.

97. Jimenez, P., Thomas, F., & Torras, C. (2000). 3d collision detection: a survey. *Computers & Graphics, 25*, 269–285.

98. Johnson, D. E., & Cohen, E. (1998). A framework for efficient minimum distance computations. In *Proc. IEEE intl. conf. robotics and automation* (pp. 3678–3684).

99. Johnson, D. E., Willemsen, P., & Cohen, E. (2005). 6-dof haptic rendering using spatialized normal cone search. In *Transactions on visualization and computer graphics* (p. 2005).

100. Jolliffe, I. T. (2002). *Principal component analysis.* Berlin: Springer. ISBN 0387954422.

101. Ju, M.-Y., Liu, J.-S., Shiang, S.-P., Chien, Y.-R., Hwang, K.-S., & Lee, W.-C. (2001). Fast and accurate collision detection based on enclosed ellipsoid. *Robotica, 19*(4), 381–394. doi:10.1017/S0263574700003295.

102. Kallay, M. (1984). The complexity of incremental convex hull algorithms in r^d. *Information Processing Letters, 19*(4), 197.

103. Kamat, V. V. (1993). A survey of techniques for simulation of dynamic collision detection and response. *Computers & Graphics, 17*(4), 379–385.

104. Kay, T. L., & Kajiya, J. T. (1986). Ray tracing complex scenes. *SIGGRAPH Computer Graphics, 20*(4), 269–278. doi:10.1145/15886.15916. URL http://doi.acm.org/10.1145/15886.15916.

105. Kim, B., & Rossignac, J. (2003). Collision prediction for polyhedra under screw motions. In *ACM symposium in solid modeling and applications* (pp. 4–10). New York: ACM Press.

106. Kim, D., Heo, J.-P., & Yoon, S.-e. (2009). Pccd: parallel continuous collision detection. In *SIGGRAPH '09: posters, SIGGRAPH '09* (pp. 50:1–50:1). New York: ACM. doi:10.1145/1599301.1599351. URL http://doi.acm.org/10.1145/1599301.1599351.

107. Kim, J.-P., Lee, B.-C., Kim, H., Kim, J., & Ryu, J. (2009). Accurate and efficient cpu/gpu-based 3-dof haptic rendering of complex static virtual environments. *Presence: Teleoperators & Virtual Environments, 18*(5), 340–360. doi:10.1162/pres.18.5.340.

108. Kim, Y.-J., Oh, Y.-T., Yoon, S.-H., Kim, M.-S., & Elber, G. (2011). Coons bvh for freeform geometric models. In *Proceedings of the 2011 SIGGRAPH Asia conference, SA '11* (pp. 169:1–169:8). New York: ACM. ISBN 978-1-4503-0807-6. doi:10.1145/2024156.2024203. URL http://doi.acm.org/10.1145/2024156.2024203.

109. Kim, Y. J., Lin, M. C., & Manocha, D. (2002). DEEP: dual-space expansion for estimating penetration depth between convex polytopes. In *ICRA* (pp. 921–926). New York: IEEE. ISBN 0-7803-7273-5.

110. Kim, Y. J., Otaduy, M. A., Lin, M. C., & Manocha, D. (2002). *Fast penetration depth computation using rasterization hardware and hierarchical refinement* (Technical report). Department of Computer Science, University of North Carolina. URL ftp://ftp.cs.unc.edu/pub/publications/techreports/02-014.pdf.

111. Kim, Y. J., Otaduy, M. A., Lin, M. C., & Manocha, D. (2002). Fast penetration depth computation for physically-based animation. In *Proceedings of the 2002 ACM SIGGRAPH/eurographics symposium on computer animation, SCA '02* (pp. 23–31). New York: ACM. ISBN 1-58113-573-4. doi:10.1145/545261.545266. URL http://doi.acm.org/10.1145/545261.545266.

112. Kim, Y. J., Otaduy, M. A., Lin, M. C., & Manocha, D. (2003). Six-degree-of-freedom haptic rendering using incremental and localized computations. *Presence: Teleoperators & Virtual Environments, 12*(3), 277–295. doi:10.1162/105474603765879530.

113. Kim, Y. J., Lin, M. C., & Manocha, D. (2004). Incremental penetration depth estimation between convex polytopes using dual-space expansion. *IEEE Transactions on Visualization and Computer Graphics, 10*(2), 152–163. doi:10.1109/TVCG.2004.1260767.

114. Kipfer, P. (2007). LCP algorithms for collision detection using CUDA. In H. Nguyen (Ed.), *GPUGems 3* (pp. 723–739). Reading: Addison-Wesley.

115. Klein, J., & Zachmann, G. (2003). Adb-trees: controlling the error of time-critical collision detection. In T. Ertl, B. Girod, G. Greiner, H. Niemann, H.-P. Seidel, E. Steinbach, & R. Westermann (Eds.), *Vision, modeling and visualisation 2003* (pp. 37–46). Berlin: Akademische Verlagsgesellschaft Aka GmbH. ISBN 3-89838-048-3.

116. Klein, J., & Zachmann, G. (2004). Point cloud collision detection. In M.-P. Cani & M. Slater (Eds.), *Computer graphics forum (Proc. EUROGRAPHICS)*, Grenoble, France, Aug. 30–Sep. 3 (Vol. 23, pp. 567–576). URL http://www.gabrielzachmann.org/.
117. Klein, J., & Zachmann, G. (2005). Interpolation search for point cloud intersection. In *Proc. of WSCG 2005*, University of West Bohemia, Plzen, Czech Republic, January 31–February 7 (pp. 163–170). ISBN 80-903100-7-9. URL http://www.gabrielzachmann.org/.
118. Klosowski, J. T., Held, M., Mitchell, J. S. B., Sowizral, H., & Zikan, K. (1998). Efficient collision detection using bounding volume hierarchies of k-dops. *IEEE Transactions on Visualization and Computer Graphics*, 4(1), 21–36. doi:10.1109/2945.675649.
119. Knott, D., & Pai, D. (2003). Cinder: collision and interference detection in real–time using graphics hardware. URL citeseer.ist.psu.edu/knott03cinder.html.
120. Kobbelt, L., & Botsch, M. (2004). A survey of point-based techniques in computer graphics. *Computers & Graphics*, 28(6), 801–814.
121. Kockara, S., Halic, T., Iqbal, K., Bayrak, C., & Rowe, R. (2007). Collision detection: a survey. In *SMC* (pp. 4046–4051). New York: IEEE.
122. Kolb, A., Latta, L., & Rezk-Salama, C. (2004). Hardware-based simulation and collision detection for large particle systems. In *Proceedings of the ACM SIGGRAPH/EUROGRAPHICS conference on graphics hardware, HWWS '04* (pp. 123–131). New York: ACM. ISBN 3-905673-15-0. doi:10.1145/1058129.1058147. URL http://doi.acm.org/10.1145/1058129.1058147.
123. Kolesnikov, M., & Zefran, M. (2007). Energy-based 6-dof penetration depth computation for penalty-based haptic rendering algorithms. In *IROS* (pp. 2120–2125).
124. Krishnan, S., Gopi, M., Lin, M., Manocha, D., & Pattekar, A. (1998). Rapid and accurate contact determination between spline models using shelltrees.
125. Krishnan, S., Pattekar, A., Lin, M. C., & Manocha, D. (1998). Spherical shell: a higher order bounding volume for fast proximity queries. In *Proceedings of the third workshop on the algorithmic foundations of robotics on robotics: the algorithmic perspective, WAFR '98* (pp. 177–190). Natick: A. K. Peters, Ltd. ISBN 1-56881-081-4. URL http://dl.acm.org/citation.cfm?id=298960.299006.
126. Larsen, E., Gottschalk, S., Lin, M. C., & Manocha, D. (1999). *Fast proximity queries with swept sphere volumes*, November 14. URL http://citeseer.ist.psu.edu/408975.html; ftp://ftp.cs.unc.edu/pub/users/manocha/PAPERS/COLLISION/ssv.ps.
127. Larsson, T., & Akenine-Möller, T. (2001). Collision detection for continuously deforming bodies. In *Eurographics 2001, short presentations* (pp. 325–333). Geneve: Eurographics Association. URL http://www.mrtc.mdh.se/index.php?choice=publications&id=0354.
128. Larsson, T., & Akenine-Möller, T. (2003). Efficient collision detection for models deformed by morphing. *The Visual Computer*, 19(2–3), 164–174. URL http://www.mrtc.mdh.se/index.phtml?choice=publications&id=0551.
129. Larsson, T., & Akenine-Möller, T. (2006). A dynamic bounding volume hierarchy for generalized collision detection. *Computer Graphics*, 30(3), 450–459. doi:10.1016/j.cag.2006.02.011.
130. Larsson, T., & Akenine-Möller, T. (2009). Bounding volume hierarchies of slab cut balls. *Computer Graphics Forum*, 28(8), 2379–2395. URL http://dblp.uni-trier.de/db/journals/cgf/cgf28.html#LarssonA09.
131. Lau, R. W. H., Chan, O., Luk, M., & Li, F. W. B. (2002). Large a collision detection framework for deformable objects. In *Proceedings of the ACM symposium on virtual reality software and technology, VRST '02* (pp. 113–120). New York: ACM. ISBN 1-58113-530-0. doi:10.1145/585740.585760. URL http://doi.acm.org/10.1145/585740.585760.
132. Lauterbach, C., Garland, M., Sengupta, S., Luebke, D. P., & Manocha, D. (2009). Fast bvh construction on gpus. *Computer Graphics Forum*, 28(2), 375–384. URL http://dblp.uni-trier.de/db/journals/cgf/cgf28.html#LauterbachGSLM09.
133. Lauterbach, C., Mo, Q., & Manocha, D. (2010). gproximity: hierarchical gpu-based operations for collision and distance queries. *Computer Graphics Forum*, 29(2), 419–428. URL http://dblp.uni-trier.de/db/journals/cgf/cgf29.html#LauterbachMM10.

134. LaValle, S. M. (2006). *Planning algorithms*. Cambridge: Cambridge University Press. Available at http://planning.cs.uiuc.edu/.

135. Le Grand, S. (2008). Broad-phase collision detection with CUDA. In *GPU gems 3* (pp. 697–721). URL http://http.developer.nvidia.com/GPUGems3/gpugems3_ch32.html.

136. Leon, C. A. D., Eliuk, S., & Gomez, H. T. (2010). Simulating soft tissues using a gpu approach of the mass-spring model. In B. Lok, G. Klinker, & R. Nakatsu (Eds.), *VR* (pp. 261–262). New York: IEEE. ISBN 978-1-4244-6258-2.

137. Leutenegger, S. T., Edgington, J. M., & Lopez, M. A. (1997). *Str: a simple and efficient algorithm for r-tree packing* (Technical report). Institute for Computer Applications in Science and Engineering (ICASE).

138. Lien, J.-M., & Amato, N. M. (2008). Approximate convex decomposition of polyhedra and its applications. *Computer Aided Geometric Design*, *25*(7), 503–522. doi:10.1016/j.cagd.2008.05.003.

139. Lin, M. C., & Canny, J. F. (1991). A fast algorithm for incremental distance calculation. In *IEEE international conference on robotics and automation* (pp. 1008–1014).

140. Lin, M. C., & Gottschalk, S. (1998). Collision detection between geometric models: a survey. In *Proc. of IMA conference on mathematics of surfaces* (pp. 37–56).

141. Lin, M. C., Otaduy, M., Lin, M. C., & Otaduy, M. (2008). *Haptic rendering: foundations, algorithms and applications*. Natick: A. K. Peters, Ltd. ISBN 1568813325.

142. Lin, Y.-T., & Li, T.-Y. (2006). A time-budgeted collision detection method. In *ICRA* (pp. 3029–3034). New York: IEEE.

143. Liu, F., Harada, T., Lee, Y., & Kim, Y. J. (2010). Real-time collision culling of a million bodies on graphics processing units. *ACM Transactions on Graphics*, *29*(6), 154:1–154:8. doi:10.1145/1882261.1866180. URL http://doi.acm.org/10.1145/1882261.1866180.

144. Liu, J.-S., Kao, J.-I., & Chang, Y.-Z. (2006). Collision detection of deformable polyhedral objects via inner-outer ellipsoids. In *IROS* (pp. 5600–5605). New York: IEEE. URL http://dblp.uni-trier.de/db/conf/iros/iros2006.html#LiuKC06.

145. Liu, M., Wang, D., & Zhang, Y. (2010). A novel haptic rendering algorithm for stable and precise 6-dof virtual assembly. In *Proceedings of the ASME 2010 world conference on innovative virtual reality, WINVR2010* (pp. 1–7).

146. Luebke, D. (2003). *The Morgan Kaufmann series in computer graphics and geometric modeling. Level of detail for 3D graphics*. San Francisco: Morgan Kaufmann. ISBN 9781558608382. URL http://books.google.de/books?id=CB1N1aaoMloC.

147. Luque, R. G., Comba, J. L. D., & Freitas, C. M. D. S. (2005). Broad-phase collision detection using semi-adjusting bsp-trees. In *Proceedings of the 2005 symposium on interactive 3D graphics and games, I3D '05* (pp. 179–186). New York: ACM. ISBN 1-59593-013-2. doi:10.1145/1053427.1053457. URL http://doi.acm.org/10.1145/1053427.1053457.

148. Massie, T. H., & Salisbury, K. J. (1994). Phantom haptic interface: a device for probing virtual objects. *American Society of Mechanical Engineers, Dynamic Systems and Control Division (Publication) DSC*, *55*(1), 295–299.

149. Mazhar, H. (2009). Gpu collision detection using spatial subdivision with applications in contact dynamics. In *ASME IDETC conference*.

150. McGuire, M., & Luebke, D. (2009). Hardware-accelerated global illumination by image space photon mapping. In *Proceedings of the conference on high performance graphics 2009, HPG '09* (pp. 77–89). New York: ACM. ISBN 978-1-60558-603-8. doi:10.1145/1572769.1572783. URL http://doi.acm.org/10.1145/1572769.1572783.

151. McNeely, W. A., Puterbaugh, K. D., & Troy, J. J. (1999). Six degrees-of-freedom haptic rendering using voxel sampling. *ACM Transactions on Graphics*, *18*(3), 401–408 (SIGGRAPH 1999).

152. McNeely, W. A., Puterbaugh, K. D., & Troy, J. J. (2005). Advances in voxel-based 6-dof haptic rendering. In *ACM SIGGRAPH 2005 courses, SIGGRAPH '05*. New York: ACM. doi:10.1145/1198555.1198606. URL http://doi.acm.org/10.1145/1198555.1198606.

153. McNeely, W. A., Puterbaugh, K. D., & Troy, J. J. (2006). Voxel-based 6-dof haptic rendering improvements. *Hapticse: The Electronic Journal of Haptics Research*, *3*(7).

154. Mendoza, C., & O'Sullivan, C. (2006). Interruptible collision detection for deformable objects. *Computer Graphics*, *30*(3), 432–438. doi:10.1016/j.cag.2006.02.018.
155. Mezger, J., Kimmerle, S., & Etzmuß, O. (2003). Hierarchical techniques in collision detection for cloth animation. *Journal of WSCG*, *11*(2), 322–329.
156. Mirtich, B. (1998). Efficient algorithms for two-phase collision detection. In K. Gupta & A. P. del Pobil (Eds.), *Practical motion planning in robotics: current approaches and future directions* (pp. 203–223). New York: Wiley.
157. Mirtich, B. (1998). V-clip: fast and robust polyhedral collision detection. *ACM Transactions on Graphics*, *17*(3), 177–208. doi:10.1145/285857.285860. URL http://doi.acm.org/10.1145/285857.285860.
158. Mirtich, B. (2000). Timewarp rigid body simulation. In *Proceedings of the 27th annual conference on computer graphics and interactive techniques, SIGGRAPH '00* (pp. 193–200). New York: ACM Press/Addison-Wesley Publishing Co. ISBN 1-58113-208-5. doi:10.1145/344779.344866.
159. Möller, T. (1997). A fast triangle-triangle intersection test. *Journal of Graphics Tools*, *2*(2), 25–30. URL http://dl.acm.org/citation.cfm?id=272317.272320.
160. Mosegaard, J., Herborg, P., & Sørensen, T. S. (2005). A GPU accelerated spring mass system for surgical simulation. *Studies in Health Technology and Informatics*, *111*, 342–348. URL http://view.ncbi.nlm.nih.gov/pubmed/15718756.
161. Munkberg, J., Hasselgren, J., Toth, R., & Akenine-Möller, T. (2010). Efficient bounding of displaced Bezier patches. In *Proceedings of the conference on high performance graphics, HPG '10* (pp. 153–162). Aire-la-Ville: Eurographics Association. URL http://dl.acm.org/citation.cfm?id=1921479.1921503.
162. Naylor, B. F. (1992). Interactive solid geometry via partitioning trees. In *Proceedings of the conference on graphics interface '92* (pp. 11–18). San Francisco: Morgan Kaufmann Publishers. ISBN 0-9695338-1-0. URL http://dl.acm.org/citation.cfm?id=155294.155296.
163. NVIDIA (2012). *Nvidia physx*. http://www.nvidia.com/object/nvidia_physx.html.
164. O'Brien, J. F., & Hodgins, J. K. (1999). Graphical modeling and animation of brittle fracture. In *Proceedings of the 26th annual conference on computer graphics and interactive techniques, SIGGRAPH '99* (pp. 137–146). New York: ACM Press/Addison-Wesley Publishing Co. ISBN 0-201-48560-5. doi:10.1145/311535.311550.
165. Ong, C. J., Huang, E., & Hong, S.-M. (2000). A fast growth distance algorithm for incremental motions. *IEEE Transactions on Robotics*, *16*(6), 880–890.
166. O'Rourke, J. (1984). *Finding minimal enclosing boxes* (Technical Report). Johns Hopkins Univ., Baltimore, MD.
167. Ortega, M., Redon, S., & Coquillart, S. (2007). A six degree-of-freedom god-object method for haptic display of rigid bodies with surface properties. *IEEE Transactions on Visualization and Computer Graphics*, *13*(3), 458–469. doi:10.1109/TVCG.2007.1028.
168. O'Sullivan, C., & Dingliana, J. (1999). Real-time collision detection and response using sphere-trees.
169. O'Sullivan, C., & Dingliana, J. (2001). Collisions and perception. *ACM Transactions on Graphics*, *20*(3), 151–168. doi:10.1145/501786.501788. URL http://doi.acm.org/10.1145/501786.501788.
170. Otaduy, M. A., & Lin, M. C. (2006). *A modular haptic rendering algorithm for stable and transparent 6-dof manipulation*. URL http://ieeexplore.ieee.org/lpdocs/epic03/wrapper.htm?arnumber=1668258.
171. Otaduy, M. A., & Lin, M. C. (2003). CLODs: Dual hierarchies for multiresolution collision detection. In *Symposium on geometry processing* (pp. 94–101).
172. Otaduy, M. A., & Lin, M. C. (2005). Sensation preserving simplification for haptic rendering. In *ACM SIGGRAPH 2005 courses, SIGGRAPH '05*. New York: ACM. doi:10.1145/1198555.1198607. URL http://doi.acm.org/10.1145/1198555.1198607.
173. Otaduy, M. A., Jain, N., Sud, A., & Lin, M. C. (2004). *Haptic rendering of interaction between textured models* (Technical report). University of North Carolina

Chapel Hill, April 13. URL http://citeseer.ist.psu.edu/638785.html; ftp://ftp.cs.unc.edu/pub/publications/techreports/04-007.pdf.

174. Otaduy, M. A., Chassot, O., Steinemann, D., & Gross, M. (2007). Balanced hierarchies for collision detection between fracturing objects. In *Virtual reality conference, IEEE* (pp. 83–90). New York: IEEE. URL http://doi.ieeecomputersociety.org/10.1109/VR.2007.352467.

175. Page, F., & Guibault, F. (2003). Collision detection algorithm for nurbs surfaces in interactive applications. In *Canadian conference on electrical and computer engineering, 2003. IEEE CCECE 2003*, May 2003 (Vol. 2, pp. 1417–1420). doi:10.1109/CCECE.2003.1226166.

176. Pan, J., & Manocha, D. (2012). Gpu-based parallel collision detection for fast motion planning. *The International Journal of Robotics Research, 31*(2), 187–200. doi:10.1177/0278364911429335.

177. Pan, J., Chitta, S., & Manocha, D. (2011). Probabilistic collision detection between noisy point clouds using robust classification. In *International symposium on robotics research*, Flagstaff, Arizona, 08/2011. URL http://www.isrr-2011.org/ISRR-2011//Program_files/Papers/Pan-ISRR-2011.pdf.

178. Pan, J., Chitta, S., & Manocha, D. (2012). Proximity computations between noisy point clouds using robust classification. In *RGB-D: advanced reasoning with depth cameras*, Los Angeles, California, 06/2012. URL http://www.cs.washington.edu/ai/Mobile_Robotics/rgbd-workshop-2011/.

179. Pantaleoni, J. (2011). Voxelpipe: a programmable pipeline for 3d voxelization. In *Proceedings of the ACM SIGGRAPH symposium on high performance graphics, HPG '11* (pp. 99–106). New York: ACM. ISBN 978-1-4503-0896-0. doi:10.1145/2018323.2018339. URL http://doi.acm.org/10.1145/2018323.2018339.

180. Park, S.-H., & Ryu, K. (2004). Fast similarity search for protein 3d structure databases using spatial topological patterns. In F. Galindo, M. Takizawa, & R. Traunmüller (Eds.), *Lecture notes in computer science: Vol. 3180. Database and expert systems applications* (pp. 771–780). Berlin: Springer. doi:10.1007/978-3-540-30075-5_74.

181. Parker, S. G., Bigler, J., Dietrich, A., Friedrich, H., Hoberock, J., Luebke, D., McAllister, D., McGuire, M., Morley, K., Robison, A., & Stich, M. (2010). Optix: a general purpose ray tracing engine. *ACM Transactions on Graphics, 29*(4), 66:1–66:13. doi:10.1145/1778765.1778803. URL http://doi.acm.org/10.1145/1778765.1778803.

182. Ponamgi, M., Manocha, D., & Lin, M. C. (1995). Incremental algorithms for collision detection between solid models. In *Proceedings of the third ACM symposium on solid modeling and applications, SMA '95* (pp. 293–304). New York: ACM. ISBN 0-89791-672-7. doi:10.1145/218013.218076. URL http://doi.acm.org/10.1145/218013.218076.

183. Prior, A., & Haines, K. (2005). The use of a proximity agent in a collaborative virtual environment with 6 degrees-of-freedom voxel-based haptic rendering. In *Proceedings of the first joint eurohaptics conference and symposium on haptic interfaces for virtual environment and teleoperator systems, WHC '05* (pp. 631–632). Washington: IEEE Computer Society. ISBN 0-7695-2310-2. doi:10.1109/WHC.2005.137.

184. Provot, X. (1997). Collision and self-collision handling in cloth model dedicated to design garments. In *Proc. graphics interface '97* (pp. 177–189).

185. Quinlan, S. (1994). Efficient distance computation between non-convex objects. In *Proceedings of international conference on robotics and automation* (pp. 3324–3329).

186. Raabe, A., Bartyzel, B., Anlauf, J. K., & Zachmann, G. (2005). Hardware accelerated collision detection—an architecture and simulation results. In *Proceedings of the conference on design, automation and test in Europe, DATE '05* (Vol. 3, pp. 130–135). Washington: IEEE Computer Society. ISBN 0-7695-2288-2. doi:10.1109/DATE.2005.167.

187. Redon, S., Kheddar, A., & Coquillart, S. (2000). An algebraic solution to the problem of collision detection for rigid polyhedral objects. In *Proceedings 2000 ICRA millennium conference IEEE international conference on robotics and automation symposia proceedings cat No00CH37065*, April (Vol. 4, pp. 3733–3738). URL http://ieeexplore.ieee.org/lpdocs/epic03/wrapper.htm?arnumber=845313.

188. Redon, S., & Lin, C. M. (2006). A fast method for local penetration depth computation. *Journal of Graphics Tools*. URL http://hal.inria.fr/inria-00390349.

189. Redon, S., Kheddar, A., & Coquillart, S. (2002). Fast continuous collision detection between rigid bodies. *Computer Graphics Forum*, *21*(3), 279–287. URL http://dblp. uni-trier.de/db/journals/cgf/cgf21.html#RedonKC02.

190. Renz, M., Preusche, C., Potke, M., Kriegel, H.-P., & Hirzinger, G. (2001). Stable haptic interaction with virtual environments using an adapted voxmap-pointshell algorithm. In *Proc. eurohaptics* (pp. 149–154).

191. Roussopoulos, N., & Leifker, D. (1985). Direct spatial search on pictorial databases using packed r-trees. In *Proceedings of the 1985 ACM SIGMOD international conference on management of data, SIGMOD '85* (pp. 17–31). New York: ACM. ISBN 0-89791-160-1. doi:10.1145/318898.318900. URL http://doi.acm.org/10.1145/318898.318900.

192. Rubin, S. M., & Whitted, T. (1980). A 3-dimensional representation for fast rendering of complex scenes. In *Proceedings of the 7th annual conference on computer graphics and interactive techniques, SIGGRAPH '80* (pp. 110–116). New York: ACM. ISBN 0-89791-021-4. doi:10.1145/800250.807479. URL http://doi.acm.org/10.1145/800250.807479.

193. Ruffaldi, E., Morris, D., Barbagli, F., Salisbury, K., & Bergamasco, M. (2008). Voxel-based haptic rendering using implicit sphere trees. In *Proceedings of the 2008 symposium on haptic interfaces for virtual environment and teleoperator systems, HAPTICS '08* (pp. 319–325). Washington: IEEE Computer Society. ISBN 978-1-4244-2005-6. doi:10.1109/HAPTICS.2008.4479964.

194. Ruspini, D. C., Kolarov, K., & Khatib, O. (1997). The haptic display of complex graphical environments. In *Proceedings of the 24th annual conference on computer graphics and interactive techniques, SIGGRAPH '97* (pp. 345–352). New York: ACM Press/Addison-Wesley Publishing Co. ISBN 0-89791-896-7. doi:10.1145/258734.258878.

195. Salisbury, K., Conti, F., & Barbagli, F. (2004). Haptic rendering: introductory concepts. *IEEE Computer Graphics and Applications*, *24*, 24–32. URL http://doi.ieeecomputersociety. org/10.1109/MCG.2004.10030.

196. Samet, H. (1989). Implementing ray tracing with octrees and neighbor finding. *Computers & Graphics*, *13*, 445–460.

197. Schneider, P. J., & Eberly, D. (2002). *Geometric tools for computer graphics*. New York: Elsevier Science Inc. ISBN 1558605940.

198. Schwarz, M., & Seidel, H.-P. (2010). Fast parallel surface and solid voxelization on gpus. In *ACM SIGGRAPH Asia 2010 papers, SIGGRAPH ASIA '10* (pp. 179:1–179:10). New York: ACM. ISBN 978-1-4503-0439-9. doi:10.1145/1866158.1866201. URL http://doi.acm.org/10.1145/1866158.1866201.

199. Selinger, A., & Nelson, R. C. (1999). A perceptual grouping hierarchy for appearance-based 3d object recognition. *Computer Vision and Image Understanding*, *76*(1), 83–92. doi:10.1006/cviu.1999.0788.

200. Shirley, P., & Morley, R. K. (2003). *Realistic ray tracing* (2nd ed.). Natick: A. K. Peters, Ltd. ISBN 1568811985.

201. Six, H.-W., & Widmayer, P. (1992). Spatial access structures for geometric databases. In B. Monien & Th. Ottmann (Eds.), *Lecture notes in computer science: Vol. 594. Data structures and efficient algorithms* (pp. 214–232). Berlin: Springer. ISBN 978-3-540-55488-2. doi:10.1007/3-540-55488-2_29.

202. Smith, A., Kitamura, Y., Takemura, H., & Kishino, F. (1995). A simple and efficient method for accurate collision detection among deformable polyhedral objects in arbitrary motion. In *Proceedings of the virtual reality annual international symposium VRAIS'95* (p. 136). Washington: IEEE Computer Society. ISBN 0-8186-7084-3. URL http://dl.acm.org/citation.cfm?id=527216.836015.

203. Smith, R. (2012). *Open dynamics engine*. http://www.ode.org.

204. Sobottka, G., & Weber, A. (2005). Efficient bounding volume hierarchies for hair simulation. In *The 2nd workshop in virtual reality interactions and physical simulations (VRIPHYS '05)*, November.

205. Sobottka, G., Varnik, E., & Weber, A. (2005). Collision detection in densely packed fiber assemblies with application to hair modeling. In H. R. Arabnia (Ed.), *The 2005 international conference on imaging science, systems, and technology: computer graphics (CISST'05)* (pp. 244–250). Athens: CSREA Press. ISBN 1-932415-64-5.

206. Spillmann, J., Becker, M., & Teschner, M. (2007). Efficient updates of bounding sphere hierarchies for geometrically deformable models. *Journal of Visual Communication and Image Representation, 18*(2), 101–108. doi:10.1016/j.jvcir.2007.01.001.

207. Stewart, D., & Trinkle, J. C. (1996). An implicit time-stepping scheme for rigid body dynamics with coulomb friction. *International Journal for Numerical Methods in Biomedical Engineering, 39*, 2673–2691.

208. Su, C.-J., Lin, F., & Ye, L. (1999). A new collision detection method for csg-represented objects in virtual manufacturing. *Computers in Industry, 40*(1), 1–13. doi:10.1016/S0166-3615(99)00010-X.

209. Suffern, K. (2007). *Ray tracing from the ground up*. Natick: A. K. Peters, Ltd. ISBN 1568812728.

210. Taeubig, H., & Frese, U. (2012). A new library for real-time continuous collision detection. In *Proceedings of the 7th German conference on robotics (ROBOTIK-2012)*, May 21–22. Munich, Germany. Frankfurt am Main: VDE.

211. Tang, C., Li, S., & Wang, G. (2011). Fast continuous collision detection using parallel filter in subspace. In *Symposium on interactive 3D graphics and games, I3D '11* (pp. 71–80). New York: ACM. ISBN 978-1-4503-0565-5. doi:10.1145/1944745.1944757. URL http://doi.acm.org/10.1145/1944745.1944757.

212. Tang, M., Kim, Y. J., & Manocha, D. (2009). C2a: controlled conservative advancement for continuous collision detection of polygonal models. In *Proceedings of international conference on robotics and automation*.

213. Tang, M., Lee, M., & Kim, Y. J. (2009). Interactive Hausdorff distance computation for general polygonal models. In *ACM SIGGRAPH 2009 papers, SIGGRAPH '09* (pp. 74:1–74:9). New York: ACM. ISBN 978-1-60558-726-4. doi:10.1145/1576246.1531380. URL http://doi.acm.org/10.1145/1576246.1531380.

214. Tang, M., Manocha, D., Otaduy, M. A., & Tong, R. (2012). Continuous penalty forces. *ACM Transactions on Graphics, 31*(4) (Proc. of ACM SIGGRAPH). URL http://www.gmrv.es/Publications/2012/TMOT12.

215. Tang, M., Tang, M., Curtis, S., Yoon, S.-E., Yoon, S.-E., & Manocha, D. (2008). *Iccd: interactive continuous collision detection between deformable models using connectivity-based culling*. URL http://www.ncbi.nlm.nih.gov/pubmed/19423880.

216. Tasora, A., Negrut, D., & Anitescu, M. (2009). Gpu-based parallel computing for the simulation of complex multibody systems with unilateral and bilateral constraints: an overview.

217. Tavares, D. L. M., & Comba, J. L. D. (2007). *Broad-phase collision detection using Delaunay triangulation* (Technical report). Universidade Federal do Rio Grande do Sul (UFRGS).

218. Teschner, M., Kimmerle, S., Heidelberger, B., Zachmann, G., Raghupathi, L., Fuhrmann, A., Cani, M.-P., Faure, F., Magnenat-Thalmann, N., Strasser, W., & Volino, P. (2005). Collision detection for deformable objects. *Computer Graphics Forum, 24*(1), 61–81. doi:10.1111/j.1467-8659.2005.00829.x.

219. Teschner, M., Heidelberger, B., Müller, M., Pomerantes, D., & Gross, M. H. (2003). Optimized spatial hashing for collision detection of deformable objects. In *Proc. 8th international fall workshop vision, modeling, and visualization (VMV 2003)* (pp. 47–54).

220. Thompson, T. V. II., Johnson, D. E., & Cohen, E. (1997). Direct haptic rendering of sculptured models. In *Proceedings of the 1997 symposium on interactive 3D graphics, I3D '97* (pp. 167–176). New York: ACM. ISBN 0-89791-884-3. doi:10.1145/253284.253336. URL http://doi.acm.org/10.1145/253284.253336.

221. Torres, R., Martín, P. J., & Gavilanes, A. (2009). Ray casting using a roped bvh with cuda. In *Proceedings of the 2009 spring conference on computer graphics, SCCG '09* (pp. 95–102). New York: ACM. ISBN 978-1-4503-0769-7. doi:10.1145/1980462.1980483. URL http://doi.acm.org/10.1145/1980462.1980483.

222. Tropp, O., Tal, A., & Shimshoni, I. (2006). A fast triangle to triangle intersection test for collision detection. *Computer Animation and Virtual Worlds, 17*(5), 527–535. URL http://doi.wiley.com/10.1002/cav.115.

223. Tsingos, N., Dachsbacher, C., Lefebvre, S., & Dellepiane, M. (2007). Instant sound scattering. In *Rendering techniques (Proceedings of the eurographics symposium on rendering).* URL http://www-sop.inria.fr/reves/Basilic/2007/TDLD07.

224. Turk, G. (1989). *Interactive collision detection for molecular graphics* (Technical report). University of North Carolina at Chapel Hill. URL http://citeseerx.ist.psu.edu/viewdoc/summary?doi=10.1.1.93.4927.

225. van den Bergen, G. (1998). Efficient collision detection of complex deformable models using aabb trees. *Journal of Graphics Tools, 2*(4), 1–13. URL http://dl.acm.org/citation.cfm?id=763345.763346.

226. Van den Bergen, G. (1999). A fast and robust gjk implementation for collision detection of convex objects. *Journal of Graphics Tools, 4*(2), 7–25. URL http://dl.acm.org/citation.cfm?id=334709.334711.

227. van den Bergen, G. (2001). Proximity queries and penetration depth computation on 3D game objects. In *Proceedings of game developers conference 2001*, San Jose, CA, March.

228. Van Den Bergen, G. (2004). *The Morgan Kaufmann series in interactive 3D technology. Collision detection in interactive 3D environments.* San Francisco: Morgan Kaufman Publishers. ISBN 9781558608016. URL http://books.google.com/books?id=E-9AsqZCTSEC.

229. Volino, P., & Magnenat Thalmann, N. M. (1995). Collision and self-collision detection: efficient and robust solutions for highly deformable surfaces. In *Computer animation and simulation '95* (pp. 55–65). Berlin: Springer.

230. Von Herzen, B., Barr, A. H., & Zatz, H. R. (1990). Geometric collisions for time-dependent parametric surfaces. In *Proceedings of the 17th annual conference on computer graphics and interactive techniques, SIGGRAPH '90* (pp. 39–48). New York: ACM. ISBN 0-89791-344-2. doi:10.1145/97879.97883. URL http://doi.acm.org/10.1145/97879.97883.

231. Voronoi, G. (1908). Nouvelles applications des paramètres continus à la théorie des formes quadratiques. Deuxième mémoire. Recherches sur les parallélloèdres primitifs. *Journal für die Reine und Angewandte Mathematik (Crelles Journal), 134*, 198–287. doi:10.1515/crll.1908.134.198.

232. Wald, I. (2007). On fast construction of sah-based bounding volume hierarchies. In *Proceedings of the 2007 IEEE symposium on interactive ray tracing, RT '07* (pp. 33–40). Washington: IEEE Computer Society. ISBN 978-1-4244-1629-5. doi:10.1109/RT.2007.4342588.

233. Wald, I., & Havran, V. (2006). On building fast kd-trees for ray tracing, and on doing that in o(n log n). In *Symposium on interactive ray tracing* (pp. 61–69). URL http://doi.ieeecomputersociety.org/10.1109/RT.2006.280216.

234. Wand, M. (2004). *Point-based multi-resolution rendering.* PhD thesis, Department of computer science and cognitive science, University of Tübingen.

235. Weghorst, H., Hooper, G., & Greenberg, D. P. (1984). Improved computational methods for ray tracing. *ACM Transactions on Graphics, 3*(1), 52–69.

236. Welzl, E. (1991). Smallest enclosing disks (balls and ellipsoids). In *Results and new trends in computer science* (pp. 359–370). Berlin: Springer.

237. Whang, K.-Y., Song, J.-W., Chang, J.-W., Kim, J.-Y., Cho, W.-S., Park, C.-M., & Song, I.-Y. (1995). Octree-r: an adaptive octree for efficient ray tracing. *IEEE Transactions on Visualization and Computer Graphics, 1*, 343–349. URL http://doi.ieeecomputersociety.org/10.1109/2945.485621.

238. Whitted, T. (1980). An improved illumination model for shaded display. *Communications of the ACM, 23*(6), 343–349. doi:10.1145/358876.358882. URL http://doi.acm.org/10.1145/358876.358882.

239. Wong, S.-K. (2011). Adaptive continuous collision detection for cloth models using a skipping frame session. *Journal of Information Science and Engineering, 27*(5), 1545–1559.

240. Wong, W. S.-K., & Baciu, G. (2005). Gpu-based intrinsic collision detection for deformable surfaces. *Computer Animation and Virtual Worlds, 16*(3–4), 153–161. doi:10.1002/cav.104.

241. Woulfe, M., Dingliana, J., & Manzke, M. (2007). Hardware accelerated broad phase collision detection for realtime simulations. In J. Dingliana & F. Ganovelli (Eds.), *Proceedings of the 4th workshop on virtual reality interaction and physical simulation (VRIPHYS 2007)* (pp. 79–88). Aire-la-Ville: Eurographics Association. URL https://www.cs.tcd.ie/~woulfem/publications/paper2007/.

242. Yilmaz, T., & Gudukbay, U. (2007). Conservative occlusion culling for urban visualization using a slice-wise data structure. *Graphical Models, 69*(3–4), 191–210. doi:10.1016/j.gmod.2007.01.002.

243. Yoon, S.-E., Salomon, B., Lin, M., & Manocha, D. (2004). Fast collision detection between massive models using dynamic simplification. In *Proceedings of the 2004 eurographics/ACM SIGGRAPH symposium on geometry processing, SGP '04* (pp. 136–146). New York: ACM. ISBN 3-905673-13-4. doi:10.1145/1057432.1057450. URL http://doi.acm.org/10.1145/1057432.1057450.

244. Yoon, S.-E., Curtis, S., & Manocha, D. (2007). Ray tracing dynamic scenes using selective restructuring. In *ACM SIGGRAPH 2007 sketches, SIGGRAPH '07*. New York: ACM. doi:10.1145/1278780.1278847. URL http://doi.acm.org/10.1145/1278780.1278847.

245. Zachmann, G. (1998). Rapid collision detection by dynamically aligned dop-trees. In *Proceedings of the virtual reality annual international symposium, VRAIS '98* (p. 90). Washington: IEEE Computer Society. ISBN 0-8186-8362-7. URL http://dl.acm.org/citation.cfm?id=522258.836122.

246. Zachmann, G. (2000). *Virtual reality in assembly simulation—collision detection, simulation algorithms, and interaction techniques*. Dissertation, Darmstadt University of Technology, Germany, May.

247. Zachmann, G. (2001). Optimizing the collision detection pipeline. In *Proc. of the first international game technology conference (GTEC)*, January.

248. Zachmann, G. (2002). Minimal hierarchical collision detection. In *Proceedings of the ACM symposium on virtual reality software and technology, VRST '02* (pp. 121–128). New York: ACM. ISBN 1-58113-530-0. doi:10.1145/585740.585761. URL http://doi.acm.org/10.1145/585740.585761.

249. Zachmann, G., & Langetepe, E. (2003). Geometric data structures for computer graphics. In *Proc. of ACM SIGGRAPH. ACM transactions of graphics*, 27–31 July. URL http://www.gabrielzachmann.org/.

250. Zachmann, G., Teschner, M., Kimmerle, S., Heidelberger, B., Raghupathi, L., & Fuhrmann, A. (2005). Real-time collision detection for dynamic virtual environments. In *Tutorial #4, IEEE VR*, Bonn, Germany, 12–16 March. Washington: IEEE Computer Society.

251. Zeiller, M. (1993). Collision detection for objects modelled by csg. In T. K. S. Murthy, J. J. Conner, S. Hernandez, & H. Power (Eds.), *Visualization and intelligent design in engineering and architecture*, April. Amsterdam: Elsevier Science Publishers. ISBN 1853122270. URL http://www.cg.tuwien.ac.at/research/publications/1993/zeiller-1993-coll/.

252. Zhang, D., & Yuen, M. M. F. (2000). Collision detection for clothed human animation. In *Pacific conference on computer graphics and applications* (p. 328). URL http://doi.ieeecomputersociety.org/10.1109/PCCGA.2000.883956.

253. Zhang, H., & Hoff, K. E. III. (1997). Fast backface culling using normal masks. In *Proceedings of the 1997 symposium on interactive 3D graphics, I3D '97* (pp. 103-ff). New York: ACM. ISBN 0-89791-884-3. doi:10.1145/253284.253314. URL http://doi.acm.org/10.1145/253284.253314.

254. Zhang, H., Manocha, D., Hudson, T., & Hoff, K. E. III. (1997). Visibility culling using hierarchical occlusion maps. In *Proceedings of the 24th annual conference on computer graphics and interactive techniques, SIGGRAPH '97* (pp. 77–88). New York: ACM Press/Addison-Wesley Publishing Co. ISBN 0-89791-896-7. doi:10.1145/258734.258781.

255. Zhang, L., Kim, Y. J., & Manocha, D. (2007). A fast and practical algorithm for generalized penetration depth computation. In *Robotics: science and systems conference (RSS07)*.

256. Zhang, L., Kim, Y. J., & Manocha, D. (2007). C-dist: efficient distance computation for rigid and articulated models in configuration space. In *Proceedings of the*

2007 ACM symposium on solid and physical modeling, SPM '07 (pp. 159–169). New York: ACM. ISBN 978-1-59593-666-0. doi:10.1145/1236246.1236270. URL http://doi. acm.org/10.1145/1236246.1236270.

257. Zhang, L., Kim, Y. J., Varadhan, G., & Manocha, D. (2007). Generalized penetration depth computation. *Computer Aided Design, 39*(8), 625–638. doi:10.1016/j.cad.2007.05.012.

258. Zhang, X., & Kim, Y. J. (2007). Interactive collision detection for deformable models using streaming aabbs. *IEEE Transactions on Visualization and Computer Graphics, 13*(2), 318–329. doi:10.1109/TVCG.2007.42.

259. Zhang, X., Lee, M., & Kim, Y. J. (2006). Interactive continuous collision detection for non-convex polyhedra. *The Visual Computer, 22*(9), 749–760. doi:10.1007/s00371-006-0060-0.

260. Zhang, X., Redon, S., Lee, M., & Kim, Y. J. (2007). Continuous collision detection for articulated models using Taylor models and temporal culling. In *ACM SIGGRAPH 2007 papers, SIGGRAPH '07*. New York: ACM. doi:10.1145/1275808.1276396. URL http://doi.acm.org/10.1145/1275808.1276396.

261. Zhu, X., Ding, H., & Tso, S. K. (2004). A pseudodistance function and its applications. *IEEE Transactions on Robotics, 20*(2), 344–352.

262. Zilles, C. B., & Salisbury, J. K. (1995). A constraint-based god-object method for haptic display. In *Proceedings of the international conference on intelligent robots and systems, IROS '95* (Vol. 3, p. 3146). Washington: IEEE Computer Society. ISBN 0-8186-7108-4. URL http://dl.acm.org/citation.cfm?id=846238.849727.

Part II
Algorithms and Data Structures

Chapter 3
Kinetic Data Structures for Collision Detection

As already seen in the previous chapter, bounding volume hierarchies for geometric objects are widely employed in many areas of computer science to accelerate geometric queries. These acceleration data structures are used in computer graphics for ray-tracing, occlusion culling, geographical databases and collision detection, to name but a few. Usually, a bounding volume hierarchy is constructed in a pre-processing step, which is suitable as long as the objects are rigid.

However, deformable objects play an important role, e.g. for creating virtual environments in medical applications, entertainment, and virtual prototyping. If the object deforms, the pre-processed hierarchy becomes invalid. In order to still use this well-known method for deforming objects as well, it is necessary to update the hierarchies after the deformation happens.

Most current techniques do not make use of the temporal and spatial coherence of simulations and just update the hierarchy by brute-force at every time step or they simply restrict the kind of deformation in some way in order to avoid the time consuming per-frame update of all bounding volumes.

On the one hand, we all know that motion in the physical world is normally continuous. So, if animation is discretized by very fine time intervals, a brute-force approach to the problem of updating BVHs would need to do this at each of these points in time. On the other hand, changes in the *combinatorial* structure of a BVH only occur at discrete points in time. Therefore, we propose to utilize an event-based approach to remedy this unnecessary frequency of BVH updates.

In accordance to this observation, we present two new algorithms to update hierarchies in a more sensitive way: we only make an update if it is necessary. In order to determine exactly when it is necessary, we use the framework of kinetic data structures (KDS). To use this kind of data structures, it is required that a *flight-plan* is given for every vertex. This flightplan may change during the motion, maybe by user interaction or physical events (like collisions). Many deformations caused by simulations satisfy these constraints, including keyframe animations and many other animation schemes.

Parts of this work has been previously published in [21] and [23].

R. Weller, *New Geometric Data Structures for Collision Detection and Haptics*,
Springer Series on Touch and Haptic Systems, DOI 10.1007/978-3-319-01020-5_3,
© Springer International Publishing Switzerland 2013

In the following, we first present a kinetization of a tree of axis aligned bounding boxes and show that the associated update algorithm is optimal in the number of BV updates (this means that each AABB hierarchy which performs fewer updates must be invalid at some point of time). Moreover, we prove an asymptotic lower bound on the total number of update operations in the worst case which holds for every BVH updating strategy. This number is independent from the length of the animation sequence under certain conditions. In order to reduce the number of update operations, we propose a kinetization of the BoxTree. A BoxTree is a special case of an AABB where we store only two splitting axes per node. On account of this we can reduce the overall number of events.

Additionally, we present the results of a comparison to the running times of hierarchical collision detection based on our novel kinetic BVHs and conventional bottom-up updating, respectively. This general technique of kinetic BVHs is available for all applications which use bounding volume hierarchies, but our main aim is their application to collision detection of deformable objects.

Virtually all simulations of deforming objects, like surgery simulation or computer games, require collision detection to be performed in order to avoid the simulated objects to penetrate themselves or each other. For example, in cloth simulations, we have to avoid penetrations between the cloth and the body, but also between the wrinkles of the cloth itself.

Most current techniques use bounding volume hierarchies in order to quickly cull parts of the objects that cannot intersect. In addition to the required BVH updates, another problem arises when using BVHs for self-collision detection: two adjacent sub-areas are always colliding by contact along their borders. In consequence, checking BVHs against themselves for self-collision results in a large number of false positive tests. Moreover, using swept-volumes and lazy updating methods for continuous collision detection results in very large BVs and hence more false positive tests.

In order to avoid all the problems mentioned above, we propose a new event-based approach for continuous collision detection of deformable objects. Analogously to the changes in the combinatorial structure of the BVH, also collisions only occur at *discrete* points in time. Exploiting this observation, we have developed the novel *kinetic Separation-List*, which enables continuous inter- and intra-object collision detection for arbitrary deformations such that checks between bounding volumes and polygons are done only when necessary, i.e. when changes in the moving front really occur.

This way, the continuous problem of continuous collision detection is reduced to the discrete problem of determining exactly those points in time when the combinatorial structure of our kinetic Separation-List changes. The kinetic Separation-List is based on the kinetic AABB-Tree and extends the same principle to collision detection between pairs of objects. We maintain the combinatorial structure of a Separation-List of a conventional recursion tree.

As a natural consequence of this event-based approach collisions are detected automatically in the right chronological order, so there is no further ordering required like in many other approaches. Therefore, our kinetic Separation-List is well suited for collision response.

In the following, we will restrict our discussion to polygonal meshes, but it should become obvious that our data structures can, in principle, handle all objects for which we can build a bounding volume hierarchy, including polygon soups, point clouds, and NURBS models. Our algorithms are even flexible enough for handling insertions or deletions of vertices or edges in the mesh during running-time.

3.1 Recap: Kinetic Data Structures

In this section we start with a quick recap of the kinetic data structure framework and its terminology.

The kinetic data structure framework is a framework for designing and analyzing algorithms for objects (e.g. points, lines, polygons) in motion, which was invented by Basch et al. [5]. The KDS framework leads to event-based algorithms that sample the state of different parts of the system only as often as necessary for a special task. This task can be for example maintaining the convex hull [6], a heap [10], a sorted list [1] or the closest pair [4] of a set of moving points.

There also exist first approaches of collision detection using kinetic data structures. For instance Erickson et al. [13] described a KDS for collision detection between two convex polygons by using a so-called boomerang hierarchy. Agarwal et al. [3] and Speckmann [19] developed a KDS using pseudo triangles for a decomposition of the common exterior of a set of simple polygons for collision. Basch et al. [7] tracked a separating polygonal line between a pair of simple polygons and Guibas et al. [15] used a KDS for the separating plane between rigid objects. However, all these approaches are limited to two dimensions or very simple objects. Simultaneously to our approach, Coming and Staadt [9] presented a kinetic version of the Sweep-and-Prune algorithm. But this method is limited to broad-phase collision detection.

However, these are just a few examples of tasks that can be efficiently solved using the framework of kinetic data structures. Guibas [14] presents further examples. In the terminology of KDS these tasks are called the *attribute* of the KDS.

Usually, a KDS consists of a set of elementary conditions, called *certificates*, which prove altogether the correctness of its attribute. Those certificates can fail as a result of the motion of the objects. These certificate failures, the so-called *events*, are placed in an *event-queue*, ordered according to their earliest failure time. If the attribute changes at the time of an event, the event is called *external*, otherwise the event is called *internal*. Thus sampling of time is not fixed but determined by the failure of certain conditions.

As an example, we can assume the bounding box of a set of moving points in the plane. The bounding box is the attribute we are interested in. It is generated by four points $P^t_{\{max,min\},\{x,y\}}$ which have the maximum and minimum x- and y-values at a certain time point t. For every inner point P^t_i we have $P^t_i[x] < P^t_{max,x}[x]$, $P^t_i[y] < P^t_{max,x}[y]$, $P^t_i[x] > P^t_{min,x}[x]$ and $P^t_i[y] > P^t_{min,y}[y]$. These four simple inequations are the certificates in our example. If an inner point moves out of the bounding box,

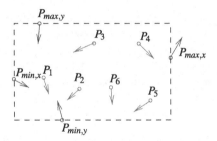

Fig. 3.1 Assume a set of moving points in the plane. $P_{\{max,min\},\{x,y\}}$ is for the current bounding volume of this points. At some time, P_5 will become smaller than $P_{min,y}$, and this causes an event

due to its motion, e.g. $P_i^{t_2}[x] > P_{max,x}^{t_2}[x]$, this causes an external event at the point of time $t + \Delta t$ when $P_i^{t+\Delta t}[x] = P_{max,x}^{t+\Delta t}[x]$ (see Fig. 3.1). If $P_i^t[x] > P_j^t[x]$ and $P_i^{t_3}[x] < P_j^{t_3}[x]$ for points that are not in $P_{\{max,min\},\{x,y\}}^t$, this causes an internal event.

We measure the quality of a KDS by four criteria: compactness, responsiveness, locality, and efficiency. In detail:

- A KDS is *compact* if it requires only little space.
- A KDS is *responsive* if we can update it quickly in case of a certificate failure.
- A KDS is called *local* if one object is involved in not too many events. This guarantees that we can adjust changes in the flightplan of the objects quickly.
- And finally, a KDS is *efficient* if the overhead of internal events with respect to external events is reasonable.

A proof that the example KDS described above fulfills all four quality criteria can be found in Agarwal et al. [2]. We will continue to describe our new kinetic data structures for hierarchies of objects.

3.2 Kinetic Bounding Volume Hierarchies

In our case, the objects are a set of m polygons with n vertices. Every vertex p_i has a flightplan $f_{p_i}(t)$. This might be a chain of line segments in case of a keyframe animation or algebraic motions in case of physics-based simulations. The flightplan is assumed to use $O(1)$ space and the intersection between two flightplans can be computed in $O(1)$ time. The flightplan of a vertex may change during simulation by user interaction or physical phenomena, including collisions. In this case we have to update all events the vertex is involved with.

The attribute is a valid BVH for a set of moving polygons. An event will occur, when a vertex moves out of its BV.

The kinetic data structures we will present have some properties in common, which will be described as follows.

They all use an event-queue for which we use an AVL-Tree, because with this data structure we can insert and delete events as well as extract the minimum in time $O(\log k)$ where k is the total number of events.

Both kinetic hierarchies, the kinetic AABB as well as the kinetic BoxTree, run within the same framework for kinetic updates, which is explained in Algorithm 3.1.

Algorithm 3.1 Simulation Loop

---

while *simulation runs* **do**
    calc time t of next rendering
    e ← min events in event-queue
    while *e.timestamp* < t **do**
        processEvent(e)
        e ← min events in event-queue
    check for collisions
    render scene

3.2.1 Kinetic AABB-Tree

In this section, we present a kinetization of the well known AABB tree. We build the tree by any algorithm which can be used for building static BVHs and store for every node of the tree the indices of these points that determine the bounding box. For our analysis of the algorithms it is only required that the height of the BVH is logarithmic in the number of polygons.

After building the hierarchy, we traverse the tree again to find the initial events.

3.2.1.1 Kinetization of the AABB-Tree

Actually, there are three kinds of different events:

- *Leaf event*: Assume that P_1 realizes the BVs maximum along the x-axis. A leaf event happens, when the x-coord of one of the other points P_2 or P_3 becomes larger than $P_{1,x}$ (see Fig. 3.2).
- *Tree event*: Let K be an inner BV with its children K_l and K_r; and $P_2 \in K_r$ is the current maximum of K on the x-axis. A tree event happens when the maximum of K_l becomes larger than P_2 (see Fig. 3.3). Analogously, tree events are generated for the other axis and the minima.
- *Flightplan-update event*: Every time a flightplan of a point changes we get a flightplan-update event.

So after the initialization we have stored six events with each BV. In addition, we put the events in the event queue sorted by their time stamps.

During run time, we perform an update according to Algorithm 3.1 before each collision check. In order to keep the BV hierarchy valid, we have to handle the events as follows:

- *Leaf event*: Assume in a leaf BV B, realized by the vertices P_1, P_2, and P_3, that the maximum extent along the x-axis has been realized by P_2. With the current event, P_1 takes over, and becomes larger than $P_2[x]$. In order to maintain the validity of the BV hierarchy, in particular, we have to associate P_1 to the max x extent of B. In addition, we have to compute a new event. This means that we

Fig. 3.2 When P_1 becomes
larger than the current
maximum vertex P_2, a leaf
event will happen

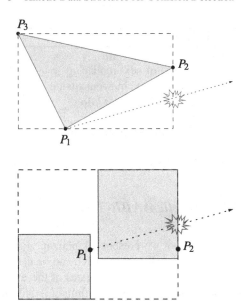

Fig. 3.3 When P_1, the
maximum of the left
child-box, becomes larger
than the overall maximum
vertex P_2, a tree event will
happen

have to compute all the intersections of the flightplans of all other vertices in B
with P_1 in the xt-plane. An event for the pair with the earliest intersection time is
inserted into the event queue (see Fig. 3.4). But that is not necessarily sufficient
for keeping the BVH valid. In addition, we have to propagate this change in the
BVH to the upper nodes. Assume B to be the right son of its father V, so we
have to check whether P_2 had been the maximum of V too. In this case, we have
to replace P_2 by the new maximum P_1. Moreover, the corresponding event of
V is not valid anymore because it was computed with P_2. So we have to delete
this event from the event-queue and compute a new event between P_1 and the
maximum of the left son of V. Similarly we have to proceed up the BVH until we
find the first predecessor $\overline{V}$ with $\max_x\{\overline{V}\} \neq P_2$, or until we reach the root. In the
first case we only have to compute another event between $\max_x\{\overline{V}\}$ and P_1 and
stop the recursion (see Fig. 3.5).

- *Tree event*: Let K be an inner node of the BVH and P_2 be the maximum along
  the x-axis. Assume further that P_2 is also the maximum of the left son. When a

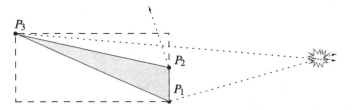

Fig. 3.4 To keep the hierarchy valid when a leaf event happens, we have to replace the old maximum P_2 by the new maximum P_1, and compute the time, when one of the other vertices of the
polygon, P_2 or P_3, will become larger than P_1. In this example this will be P_3

Fig. 3.5 In case of a tree-
and a leaf event, we have to
propagate the change to upper
BVs in the hierarchy. After
replacing the old maximum
P_2 by the new maximum P_1
in the lower left box, we have
to compute the event between
P_1 and P_3, which is the
maximum of the father

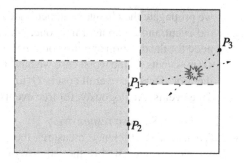

tree event happens, P_2 will be replaced by P_1, which is the maximum of the right
son of K (see Fig. 3.5). In addition, we have to compute a new event between P_1
and P_2 and propagate the change to the upper nodes in the BVH in the same way
as described above for the leaf event.

- *Flightplan-update event*: When the flightplan of a vertex changes, we have to
  update all the time stamps of those events it is involved with.

3.2.1.2 Analysis of the Kinetic AABB-Tree

For measuring the theoretical performance of our algorithm we use the four criteria
of quality defined for every KDS.

Moreover, we have to prove that our data structure is a valid BVH even if the
object deforms. Therefore, we need the following definition.

Definition 3.1 We call a kinetic AABB-Tree *valid* if every node in the tree is a
bounding volume for all polygons in its sub-tree.

Then we get the following theorem:

Theorem 3.2 *The kinetic AABB-Tree is compact, local, responsive, and efficient.
Furthermore, if we update the BVHs in the manner described above, then the tree is
valid at every point of time.*

We start with the proof of the first part of the theorem.

- *Compactness*: For a BVH we need $O(m)$ BVs. With every BV we store at most
  six tree or leaf events. Therefore, we need a space of $O(m)$ overall. Thus, our
  KDS is *compact*.
- *Responsiveness*: We have to show that we can handle certificate failures quickly.
  Therefore, we view the different events separately.

  – Leaf events: In the case of a leaf event we have to compute new events for
    all points in the polygon. Thus, the responsiveness depends on the number of
    vertices per polygon. If this number is bounded we have costs of $O(1)$. When

we propagate the change to upper nodes in the hierarchy, we have to delete an old event and compute a new one, which causes costs of $O(\log m)$ per inner node for the deletion and insertion in the event-queue, since the queue contains $O(m)$ events. In the worst case we have to propagate the changes until we reach the root. Thus the overall cost is $O(\log^2 m)$ for a leaf event.

– Tree events: Analogously, for tree events we get costs of $O(\log^2 m)$.

Thus the KDS is also *responsive*.

- *Efficiency*: The efficiency measures the ratio of the *inner* to the *outer* events. Since we are interested in the validity of the whole hierarchy, each event is an inner event because each event provokes a real change of our attribute. So the *efficiency* is automatically given.
- *Locality*: The locality measures the number of events one vertex is participating in. For sake of simplicity, we assume that the degree of every vertex is bounded. Thus, every vertex can participate in $O(\log m)$ events. Therefore, a flightplan update can cause costs of $O(\log^2 m)$. Consequently, the KDS is *local*.

We show the second part of the theorem by induction over time.

After the creation of the hierarchy, the BVH is apparently valid. The validity will be violated for the first time, when the combinatorial structure of the BVH changes; this means that a vertex flies out of its BV.

In the case of a leaf, every vertex in the enclosed polygon could be considered to such an event. The initial computation of the leaf events guarantees that there exists an event for the earliest time point this can happen. For the inner nodes, it is sufficient to consider only the extremal vertices of their children: Assume a BV B with P_1 maximum of the left son B_{left} along the x-axis and P_2 maximum of the right son B_{right} along the x-axis. This means that all vertices in B_{left} have smaller x-coords than P_1 and all vertices in B_{right} have smaller x-coords than P_2. Thus, the maximum of B along the x-axis must be $\max\{P_1, P_2\}$. Assume w.l.o.g. P_1 is the maximum. The vertex P_{next}, which could become larger than P_1, could be either P_2, or a vertex of a BV in a lower level in the hierarchy becomes invalid before an event at B could occur. Assume P_{next} is in the right sub-tree, then P_{next} must become larger than P_2 and therefore B_{right} has become invalid sometime before. If P_{next} is in the left sub-tree, it must become larger than P_1 and thus B_{left} has become invalid before.

Summarizing, we get a valid BVH after the initialization, and the vertex which will violate the validity of the BVH for the first time triggers an event.

We still have to show that the hierarchy stays valid after an event happens and that the next vertex which violates the validity also triggers an event.

- *Leaf event:* Assume B the affected leaf and P_2 becomes larger than P_1, which is the current maximum of B. As described above, we replace P_1 by P_2. Therefore, B stays valid. Furthermore, we check for all other vertices in the polygon, which is the next to become larger than P_2 and store an event for that vertex, for which this happens first. This guarantees that we will find the next violation of the validity of this BV correctly.

In addition, all predecessors of B on the path up to the root which have P_1 as maximum become invalid too. Due to the algorithm described above, we replace all occurrences of P_1 on this path by P_2. Thus, BVH stays valid. The recomputation of the events on the path to the root ensures that the vertex which will violate the validity provokes a suitable event.

- *Tree event:* Assume B the affected inner node. When an event happens, e.g. P_2 becomes larger than P_1, which is the current maximum of B, we once again replace P_1 by P_2 and therefore B stays valid. For the computation of the new event it is sufficient to consider only the two child BVs of B as described above. The propagation to the upper nodes happens analogously to the tree event.
- *Flightplan-update event:* Actually, a flightplan-update event does not change the combinatorial structure of the BVH. Therefore, the BVH stays valid after such an event happens. However, it is possible that the error times of some certificate failures change. To ensure that we find the next violation of the BVH, we have to recompute all affected events.

Recapitulating, we have shown that we have a valid BVH after the initialization and the first vertex that violates the validity provokes an event. If we update the hierarchy as described above, it stays valid after an event happens and we compute the next times when an event can happen correctly.

Note that by this theorem the BVH is valid at *every* time point, not only at the moments when we check for a collision as is the case with most other update algorithms like bottom-up or top-down approaches.

3.2.1.3 Optimality of the Kinetic AABB-Tree

In the previous section, we have proven that our kinetic AABB-Tree can be updated efficiently. Since there are no internal events, we would also like to determine the overall number of events for a whole animation sequence in order to estimate the running-time of the algorithm more precisely. Therefore, we prove the following theorem:

Theorem 3.3 *Given n vertices P_i, we assume that each pair of flightplans, $f_{P_i}(t)$ and $f_{P_j}(t)$, intersect at most s times. Then, the total number of events is in nearly $O(n \log n)$.*

We consider all flightplans along each coordinate axis separately (see Fig. 3.6). We reduce the estimation of the number of events on the computation of the upper envelope of a number of curves in the plane. This computation can be done by an algorithm using a combination of divide-and-conquer and sweep-line for the merge step. The sweep-line events are the sections of the sub-envelopes (we call them the *edge events*) and intersections between the two sub-envelopes (which we call the *intersection events*). Obviously, each sweep-line event corresponds to an update in our kinetic BVH.

Fig. 3.6 The flightplans are functions f_1 (*dashed*) and f_2 (*dotted*) in the xt-plane and similarly in the yt- and zt-planes. The function $\max(f_1, f_2)$ (*continuous*) determines the upper envelope of f_1 and f_2

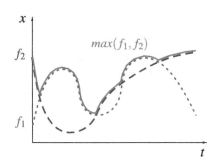

The total number of sweep-line events depends on s. We define $\lambda_s(n)$ as the maximum number of edges for the upper envelope of n functions, whereas two of these functions intersect at most s times.

For the number of edge events we get

$$2\lambda_s\left(\left\lceil\frac{n}{2}\right\rceil\right) \leq \lambda_s(n) \tag{3.1}$$

since the two sub-envelopes are envelopes of $\lceil\frac{n}{2}\rceil$ flightplans.

Furthermore, we get a new edge in the envelope for every intersection event. Obviously, this can be at most $\lambda_s(n)$. Therefore, we can estimate the total number of events by the following recursive equation:

$$T(2) = C$$

$$T(n) \leq 2T\left(\frac{n}{2}\right) + C\lambda_s(n) \tag{3.2}$$

for some constant C. Overall we get

$$T(n) \leq \sum_{i=0}^{\log n} 2^i C\lambda_s\left(\frac{n}{2^i}\right) \tag{3.3}$$

In order to resolve the inequality we have to know more about $\lambda_s(n)$. Actually, $\lambda_s(n)$ can be characterized in a purely combinatorial manner without knowledge about the geometrical structure of the functions that form the upper envelope. Therefore, we use the definition of *Davenport–Schinzel sequences* [11]. Originally developed for the analysis of linear differential equations, today such Davenport–Schinzel sequences are widely used in computational geometry. For some alphabet Γ with n letters a word in Γ is called *Davenport–Schinzel sequence* if the number of times any two letters may appear in alternation is at least s and the word has maximum length. Obviously, the length of such a Davenport–Schinzel sequence matches $\lambda_s(n)$.

A total analysis of $\lambda_s(n)$ would exceed the scope of this chapter. Therefore, we will concentrate on employing a few specific features of $\lambda_s(n)$ but we will omit the proofs. We refer the interested reader to Sharir and Agarwal [18] to look up the proofs and many other interesting things about Davenport–Schinzel sequences.

One special characteristic of $\lambda_s(n)$ is

Theorem 3.4 *For all $s, n \geq 1$ we have $2\lambda_s(n) \leq \lambda_s(2n)$.*

With this theorem we can solve the recursive equation and get

Theorem 3.5 *For the computation of the upper envelope of n functions we need at most $O(\lambda_s(n)\log n)$ events.*

Furthermore, it is true that $\lambda_s(n)$ behaves almost linearly; more precisely $\lambda_s(n) \in O(n \log^* n)$ where $\log^* n$ is the smallest number m for which the mth iteration of the logarithm is smaller than 1. For example, $\log^* n \leq 5$ for all $n \leq 10^{20000}$.

Moreover, it can be shown that the problem of computing the upper envelope is in $\Theta(n \log n)$ by reducing it to a sorting problem (see [18] for details). Altogether this proves that our algorithm is optimal in the worst case.

This demonstrates one of the strengths of the kinetic AABB-Tree: with classical update strategies like bottom-up, we need $O(kn)$ updates, where k is the number of queries. However, with our kinetic BVH, we can reduce this to nearly $O(n \log n)$ updates in the worst case. Furthermore, it is completely independent of the number of frames the animation sequence consists of (or, the frame rate), provided the number of intersections of the flightplans depends only on the length of the sequence in "wall clock time" and not on the number of frames.

Moreover, our kinetic AABB-Tree is updated only if the vertices that realize the BVs change; if all BVs in the BVH are still realized by the same vertices after a deformation step, nothing is done. As an extreme example, consider a translation or a scaling of all vertices. A brute-force update would need to update all BVs—in our kinetic algorithm nothing needs to be done, since no events occur. Conversely, the kinetic algorithm never performs more updates than the brute-force update, even if only a small number of vertices has moved.

3.2.2 Kinetic BoxTree

The kinetic AABB-Tree needs up to six events for each BV. In order to reduce the total number of events we kinetized another kind of BVH, the BoxTree [22], which uses less memory than the kinetic AABB-Tree. The main idea of a BoxTree is to store only two splitting planes per node instead of six values for the extents of the box. Hence, the BoxTree can be considered as a lazy version of a kd-Tree. To turn this into a KDS we proceed as follows:

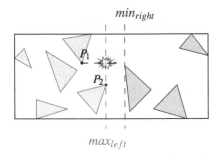

Fig. 3.7 If a vertex in the left sub-tree becomes larger than the point P_2 that realizes its current maximum $\max_{\text{left}}$, a tree event will happen. Similarly, we get an event for the right sub-tree, if a point in it becomes smaller than its current minimum $\min_{\text{right}}$

3.2.2.1 Kinetization of the BoxTree

In the pre-processing step we build a BoxTree as proposed by [22], but similarly to the kinetization of the AABB tree, we do not store real values for the splitting planes. Instead, we store that vertex for each plane that realizes it (see Fig. 3.7). We continue with the initialization of the events.

There are only two kinds of events:

• *Tree event*: Assume B is an inner node of the hierarchy with splitting plane $e \in \{x, y, z\}$ and assume further $\min_B$ is the minimum of the right sub-tree (or $\max_B$ the maximum of the left sub-tree). A tree event happens, when a vertex of the right sub-tree becomes smaller than $\min_B$ with regard to the splitting axis e, or a vertex of the left sub-tree becomes larger than $\max_B$ (see Fig. 3.7).

• *Flightplan-update event*: Every time if the flightplan of a vertex changes, a flightplan-update event happens.

During running-time, we perform an update according to Algorithm 3.1 before each collision check. For keeping the BVH valid we have to handle the events as described in the following:

• *Tree event* Let K be the node, where the tree event happens and let P_{new} be the vertex in the left sub-tree of K that becomes larger than the current maximum $K_{\max}$.

  In this case we have to replace $K_{\max}$ by P_{new} and compute a new event for this node. The computation of a new event is more complicated than in the case of a kinetic AABB-Tree. This is because of the number of possibilities of different splitting planes and because of the fact that the extents of the BVs are given implicitly.

  For simplicity, we first assume that all BVs have the same splitting axis. In this case we have to look for event candidates, i.e. vertices, which can become larger than the maximum, in a depth-first search manner (see Fig. 3.8). Note that we do not have to look in the left sub-tree of the left sub-tree because those vertices would generate an earlier event stored with one of the nodes in the sub-tree.

  If more than one splitting axis is allowed, we first have to search for the nodes with the same splitting axis (see Fig. 3.9).

  In both cases, we have to propagate the change to the upper nodes: First we have to search a node above K in the hierarchy with the same splitting axis. If its

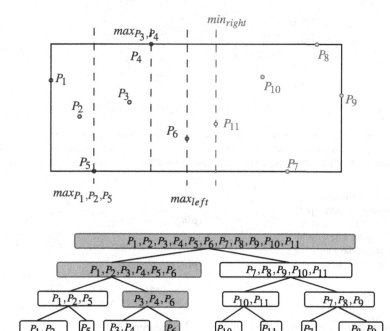

Fig. 3.8 In order to compute a new event for max$_{\text{left}}$, we have to look which vertex can become larger than max$_{\text{left}}$, which is recently realized with P_6. In the first level, this could be either the maximum of the left sub-tree, the vertex P_5, or any vertex in the right sub-tree of node (P_1, P_2, P_3, P_4, P_5, P_6). On the next level it could be the maximum of the left sub-tree of node (P_3, P_4, P_6), and thus the vertex P_4, and all vertices in the right sub-tree, which only contains P_6

maximum is also K_{max}, we have to replace it and compute a new event for this node. We have to continue recursively until we reach a node O with the same splitting axis but $O_{\text{max}} \neq K_{\text{max}}$ or until we reach the root.

- *Flightplan-update event:* If the flightplan of a point changes, we have to update all events it is involved with. Therefore, we once again start at the leaves and propagate it to the upper nodes.

3.2.2.2 Analysis of the Kinetic BoxTree

In order to show the performance of the algorithm, we have to show the four quality criteria for KDS again.

Theorem 3.6 *The kinetic BoxTree is compact, local, and efficient. The responsiveness holds only in the one-dimensional case. Furthermore, if we use the strategies described above to update the BVH, we get a valid BVH at every point of time.*

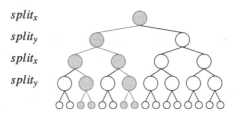

$split_x$
$split_y$
$split_x$
$split_y$

Fig. 3.9 If more than one splitting axis is allowed, we have to search for the next level with the same splitting axis, when we want to look for the next candidates for an event. We have to visit the red marked nodes when we compute a new event for the root box

Fig. 3.10 In the worst case, all levels have the same split axis, except of the root. If we want to compute a new event for the root, we have to traverse the whole tree

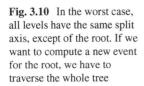

$split_x$
$split_y$
$split_y$
$split_y$

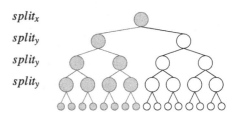

We start with the proof of the first part of the theorem.

- *Compactness*: We need space of $O(m)$ for storing the kinetic BoxTree. In addition, we get at most two events per node, so we have $O(m)$ events in total. So the kinetic BoxTree is *compact*.
- *Efficiency*: Since we are interested in the validity of the whole hierarchy and every event leads to a real change of the combinatorial structure of the hierarchy, our KDS is also *efficient*.
- *Locality*: Assuming the tree is not degenerated, one polygon can be involved in at most $O(\log m)$ events. Consequently, the KDS is local.
- *Responsiveness*: Not so straightforward is the responsiveness of our KDS, which is due to the costly computation of new events, where we have to descend the tree in dfs-manner. If all nodes have the same splitting axis, the computation of a new event costs at most $O(\log m)$ because of the length of a path from the root to a leaf in the worst case. Deletion and insertion of an event in the event-queue generate costs of $O(\log m)$ and in the worst case we have to propagate the change up to the root BV. Therefore, the overall cost for computing an event is $O(m \log^2 m)$ and thus the KDS is *responsive* in the one-dimensional case. But if the other nodes are allowed to use other split-axes too, it could be much more expensive. Assume that the root BV has the x-axis as split-axis and all other nodes have y as split-axis (see Fig. 3.10). If an event appears at the root, we have to traverse the whole tree to compute the next event. So we have total costs of $O(m \log m)$ and, thus, the KDS is not responsive. However, we can simply avoid this problem by defining a maximum number of tree-levels for the appearance of the same splitting axis.

The total number of events is nearly in $O(n \log n)$, which follows analogously to the kinetic AABB-Tree.

Fig. 3.11 Kinetic Interval
DOP: We inflate each point
by a certain amount

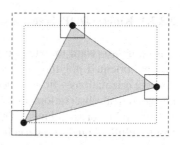

We show the second part of the theorem by induction over time. W.l.o.g. we restrict ourselves to prove it only for the maxima, the arguments for the minima following analogously. After building the BVH we have a valid hierarchy. It can become invalid if a vertex P gets larger along some axis than the maximum of some inner node K, i.e. if a tree event happens. Since we calculate the tree events for every inner node correctly, we will recognize the first time when the hierarchy becomes invalid.

We still have to show that the hierarchy stays valid after an event happens and that we find the next event as well.

If a tree events happens, this means some vertex P becomes larger than the maximum K_{max} of a node K, we have to replace all occurrences of K_{max} on the way from K to the root box by P and recalculate the events. This guarantees that the hierarchy is still valid and we will find the next violation of the validity of the BVH correctly.

In the case of a flightplan-update event, the validity of the BVH does not change, but the error times of the events may change. Thus we have to recompute the times for all events the vertex is involved with.

Summarizing, the hierarchy is valid after initialization and the first violation of the validity is stored as event in the BVH. After an event happens, the hierarchy is valid again and it is guaranteed that we find the next violation of the validity. Thus, the BVH is valid at every point of time.

Recapitulating, we have a second KDS for fast updating a BVH which uses fewer events than the kinetic AABB-Tree, but the computation of one single event is more complicated.

3.2.3 Dead Ends

During the development of our kinetic data structures we also ran into some dead ends that looked promising at first sight, either in theory or in practice. In their implementation it turned out that their drawbacks predominate their advantages. However, in this section we will give a short overview on these dead end data structures and provide descriptions on their specific disadvantages.

3.2.3.1 Kinetic DOP-Tree

It is straightforward to extend the kinetic AABB-Tree to additional axis by using discrete oriented polytopes. Obviously, these k-DOPs—k denotes the number of discrete orientations—fit the objects more tightly than ordinary AABBs. Moreover, all theoretical observations that hold for the kinetic AABB-Tree (see Sect. 3.2.1) are also valid for such kinetic DOP-Trees. Consequently, such a kinetic DOP-Tree would fulfill all quality criteria for a good KDS. Unfortunately, in practice the devil is hidden in the asymptotic notation.

It is clear that the number of events increases with an increasing number of discrete orientations. Moreover, the computation of the events becomes more complicated because we need an additional projection on the DOPs' orientations. However, this projection is not only required for the event determination but also during the queries. Actually, the bounding boxes of the kinetic AABB are stored implicitly. During a bounding box test we re-construct the AABBs explicitly by looking up their actual values. Hence, the re-construction of a DOP during queries requires the computation of an additional dot product for each orientation.

We have implemented a prototypical version of the kinetic DOP-Tree. But the results show that the disadvantages predominate the tighter fitting bounding volumes. In all cases, the kinetic DOP-Tree performed significantly slower than the kinetic AABB-Tree.

3.2.3.2 Kinetic Interval DOP-Tree

The Kinetic DOP-Tree was an attempt to increase the tightness of the bounding volume. Unfortunately, the advantages of the tighter BVs where overcompensated by the increasing number of events. Consequently, we also developed another strategy that *reduces* the number of the events at the cost of *worse fitting* BVs.

The basic idea relies on a method that was firstly proposed by Mezger et al. [17] (see also Sect. 2.5): He inflated the BVs by a certain distance. As long as the enclosed polygon does not move farther that this distance, the BV need not to be updated. In this section we will present an event-based kinetic version of this approach, which we call *kinetic Interval-DOP-Tree*.

Basically, we enclose each vertex by a small BV. Actually, we used an AABB or a DOP of higher degree (see Fig. 3.11). Based on these inflated BVs we build a BVH. Besides the flightplan-update event which is defined similarly to the other kinetic BVHs, there exists only one other type of event—the Point Event. A point event happens each time when a vertex escapes its surrounding BV (see Fig. 3.12). In this case we simply move the inflated BV into the direction where the event has happened (see Fig. 3.13). Moreover, we have to propagate the changes to the upper levels of the hierarchy.

Obviously, we get $O(n)$ events for an object that consists of n vertices. Each vertex is associated to exactly one event. In case of an event, we have to move the BV and propagate the change. If the BVH is balanced, this can be done in time

Fig. 3.12 A point event
happens if a point leaves its
enclosing inflated BV

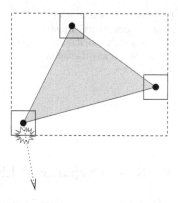

$O(\log n)$ in the worst case. Summarizing, our Kinetic Interval DOP-Tree is compact, local and responsive.

Surprisingly, if we define the attribute like for the kinetic AABB-Tree and the kinetic BoxTree as the validity of the BVH, we cannot prove the efficiency. This is simply because a point event does not necessarily change the BV of its corresponding triangle (see Fig. 3.14). What is even worse: there may be an unlimited amount of such events. We can simply avoid this problem if we define the validity of the BVH on a *per point* instead of a *per triangle* level. In this case, each event changes the attribute and we get the efficiency. Obviously, this extended BVH is also a valid BVH for the whole object.

However, in our prototypical implementation we recognized many more events for the kinetic Interval DOP-Tree than for the kinetic AABB-Tree in all our test scenarios. Moreover, the traversal during query time is more time consuming because of the worse fitting bounding volumes. Consequently, we measured a running-time that is more than two times slower than that of our kinetic AABB-Tree or our kinetic BoxTree.

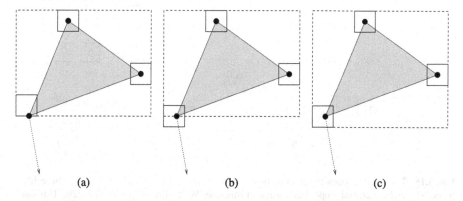

(a) (b) (c)

Fig. 3.13 When a point event occurs (**a**), we move into the appropriate direction (**b**) and recompute the BV (**c**). Moreover, we have to propagate the change in the hierarchy

Fig. 3.14 An oscillation of
point P_1 between its current
position and $\tilde{P}_1$ will throw
events without any change in
the hierarchy

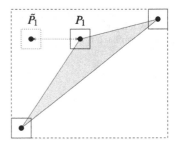

3.3 Kinetic Separation-List

So far, the kinetic AABB-Tree utilizes the temporal and thus combinatorial coherence only for the updates of individual hierarchies. In this section we will describe a novel KDS specifically for detecting collisions between pairs of objects.

3.3.1 Kinetization of the Separation-List

Our so-called *kinetic Separation-List* builds on the kinetic AABB-Tree and utilizes an idea described by [8] for rigid bodies. Given two kinetic AABB-Trees of two objects O_1 and O_2, we traverse them once for the initialization of the kinetic incremental collision detection. Thereby, we get a list, the so-called *Separation-List*, of overlapping BVs in the BV test tree (BVTT) (see Fig. 3.15). We call the pairs of BVs in the Separation-List *nodes*. This list contains three different kinds of nodes: those which contain BVs that do not overlap (we will call them the *inner nodes*), leaves in the BVTT, where the BV pairs do not overlap (the *non-overlapping leaves*), and

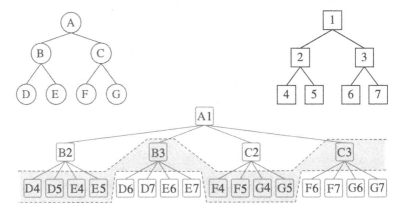

Fig. 3.15 The simultaneous traversal of two BVHs results in a BVTT (see Fig. 2.4). Those BV pairs, where the traversal stops, build a list in this tree. We call it the *Separation-List*. This list consists of inner nodes, whose BVs do not overlap (B, 3) and leaf nodes, where the BVs are leaves in the BVH that do either overlap or not

Fig. 3.16 BV-overlap event:
If the BVs B_1 and B_2 move
so that they begin to overlap,
we get a *BV-overlap event*

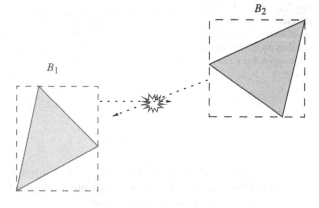

Fig. 3.17 Fathers-do-not-
overlap event: Currently, the
BV pairs (b_l, c_l), (b_l, c_r),
(b_r, c_l) and (b_r, c_r) are in the
Separation-List. If their father
BVs B and C do not overlap
anymore, e.g. because the
point P_1 that realizes the
maximum of B becomes
smaller than the minimum of
C, we get a *fathers-do-not-
overlap event*

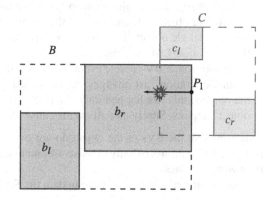

finally, leaf nodes in the BVTT that contain pairs of overlapping BVs, the so-called
overlapping leaves.

During run time, this list configuration changes at discrete points in time, when
one of the following events occurs.

- *BV-overlap event*: This event happens when the pair of BVs of a node in the
  Separation-List which did not overlap so far now do. Thus, this event can happen
  only at inner nodes and non-overlapping leaves (see Fig. 3.16).
- *Fathers-do-not-overlap event*: This event happens, if the BVs of a father of an
  inner node or a non-overlapping leaf in the BVTT do not overlap anymore (see
  Fig. 3.17). These could be inner nodes or non-overlapping leaves.
- *Leaves-do-not-overlap event*: The fathers-do-not-overlap event cannot occur to
  overlapping leaves, because if their fathers do not overlap, then the leaves cannot
  overlap in the first place. Therefore, we introduce the leaves-do-not-overlap event.
- *Polygons-collide event*: A collision between two triangles can only happen in
  overlapping leaves. If a non-overlapping leaf turns into an overlapping leaf, we
  have to compute the collision time and insert an adequate event into the event
  queue.

Fig. 3.18 If the flightplan of P_2^C changes, this has no effect on the Separation-List, and thus no BV-change event will happen due to this change

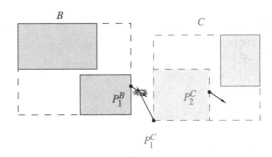

- *BV-change event*: Finally, we need an event that notes changes of the BV hierarchies. This event is somewhat comparable to flightplan updates of the kinetic AABB-Tree, but it is not exactly the same.

  This is so, because an object in the Separation-List is composed of two BVs of different objects O_1 and O_2 and the flightplans are attributes of the vertices of only one single object. Therefore, not every flightplan update of an object affects the Separation-List (see Fig. 3.18).

  In addition, a BV-change event happens if the combinatorial structure of a BV in the Separation-List changes. Since we use kinetic AABB-Trees as BVH for the objects, this can happen only if a tree event or a leaf event in the BVH of an object happens. Surely, not all events cause changes at the Separation-List.

Assuming that the BVs of the object do not overlap at the beginning of the simulation, the Separation-List only consists of one node, which contains the root BVs of the two hierarchies.

During running-time we have to update the Separation-List every time one of the above events happens according to the following cases:

- *BV-overlap event*: Let K be the inner node with BVs V_1 of object O_1 and V_2 of object O_2. Here, we need to distinguish two cases:

  – Node K is inner node: In order to keep the Separation-List valid after the event happened we have to delete K from it and insert the child nodes from the BVTT instead. This means that if V_1 has the children V_{1L} and V_{1R}, and V_2 has the children V_{2L} and V_{2R} we have to put four new nodes, namely (V_{1L}, V_{2L}), (V_{1L}, V_{2R}), (V_{1R}, V_{2L}) and (V_{1R}, V_{2R}) into the list. Then we have to compute the next time point t, when (V_1, V_2) do not overlap. Furthermore, we have to compute the times t_i for the new nodes when they will overlap. If $t_i < t$ we put a BV-overlap event in the queue, otherwise a father-do-not-overlap event.

  – Node K is a not overlapping leaf: In this case we just have to turn the node into an overlapping leaf and compute the next leaves-do-not-overlap event (see Fig. 3.19).

- *Fathers-do-not-overlap event*: In this case we have to delete the corresponding node from the Separation-List and insert its father from the BVTT instead. Furthermore, we have to compute the new fathers-do-not-overlap event and BV-overlap event for the new node and insert the one which will happen first into the event queue (see Fig. 3.20).

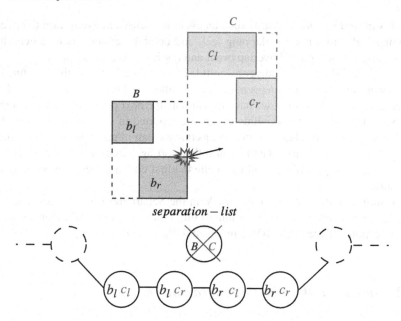

Fig. 3.19 The BV-overlap event is somewhat the opposite of the fathers-do-not-overlap event (see Fig. 3.20): If the BVs B and C begin to overlap, we have to remove the corresponding node from the Separation-List and insert their child BVs (b_l, c_l), (b_l, c_r), (b_r, c_l), and (b_r, c_r) instead

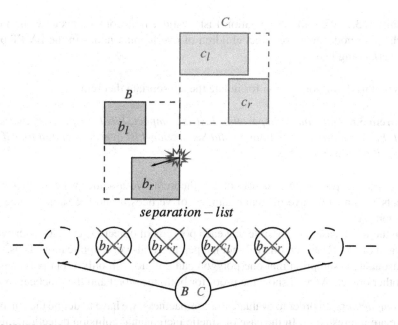

Fig. 3.20 If a fathers-do-not-overlap event happens, that means that B and C do not overlap anymore, and we have to remove their child BVs (b_l, c_l), (b_l, c_r), (b_r, c_l), and (b_r, c_r) from the Separation-List and insert the new node (B, C) instead

- *Leaves-do-not-overlap event*: If such an event happens we have to turn the over-lapping leaf into a non-overlapping leaf, and compute either a new fathers-do-not-overlap event or a BV-overlap event and put it into the event queue.
- *Polygons-collide event*: A polygons-collide event does not change the structure of the Separation-List. Such an event must be handled by the collision response. But after the collision response we have to compute the next polygons-collide event.

  Note that the polygons-collide events are reported in the correct order to the collision response module, and this means that the pair of polygons which collides first is also reported first. There is no other sorting required as it is by normal bottom-up strategies if we want to handle the first collision between two frames foremost.
- *BV-change event*: If something in a BV in the Separation-List changes, e.g. the fligthplan of a vertex or the maximum or minimum vertex of a BV, then we have to recompute all events the BV is involved with.

3.3.2 Analysis of the Kinetic Separation-List

Analogously to the theorems on the kinetic AABB-Tree and the kinetic BoxTree, we get a similar theorem for the kinetic incremental collision detection. First we have to define the "validity" of a Separation-List.

Definition 3.7 We call a Separation-List "valid", if it contains exactly the non-overlapping nodes that are direct children of overlapping nodes in the BVTT plus the overlapping leaves.

With this definition we can formulate the appropriate theorem.

Theorem 3.8 *Our kinetic Separation-List is compact, local, responsive, and efficient. Furthermore, we maintain a valid Separation-List at every point in time if we update it as described above.*

In order to prove the first part of the theorem, we assume, w.l.o.g., that both objects O_1 and O_2 have the same number of vertices n and the same number of polygons m.

In the worst case it is possible that each polygon of object O_1 collides with every polygon of O_2. However, this will not happen in a real-world application. Thus, it is a reasonable assumption that one polygon can collide with only $O(1)$ polygons of the other object. We will show the proof for both, the worst and the practical case.

- *Compactness*: In order to evaluate the compactness, we have to define the attribute we are interested in. In the case of kinetic incremental collision detection, this is the Separation-List. Thus, the size of a proof of correctness of the attribute may have size $O(n^2)$ in the worst case and $O(n)$ in the practical case.

For every node in the Separation-List, we store one event in the event queue, which will be at most $O(n^2)$ in the worst, respectively $O(n)$ in the practical case in total.

Furthermore, for every BV we have to store the nodes in the Separation-List in which it is participating; that could be at most $O(n^2)$ in the worst case or rather $O(n)$ in the practical case, too. Summarizing, the storage does not exceed the asymptotic size of the proof of correctness and, thus, the data structure is *compact*.

- *Responsiveness*: We will show the responsiveness for the four kinds of events separately.

  – Leaves-do-not-overlap event: The structure of the Separation-List does not change if such an event happens. We just have to declare the node as not overlapping leaf and compute a new event which costs time $O(1)$. The insertion into the event queue of the new event could be done in $O(\log n)$.
  – BV-overlap event: The insertion of a new node into the Separation-List and deletion of the old node needs time $O(\log n)$. In addition we have to delete the links from the old BV to the old node in the Separation-List and insert the new ones. If we organize this list of links as an AVL-tree, we get a cost of $O(\log n)$.
  – Fathers-do-not-overlap event: The deletion of nodes and events takes a time of $O(\log n)$ again.
  – BV-change event: When this kind of event happens, the structure of our Separation-List does not change. We just have to recompute the event of the affected node. The insertion and deletion of an event costs $O(\log n)$.

  Overall, our data structure is *responsive* in all cases.

- *Efficiency*: To determine the efficiency is a bit more complicated because it is not immediately obvious which events we should treat as inner and which as outer events. Clearly, leaves-do-not-overlap events, BV-overlap events and fathers-do-not-overlap events cause a real change of the attribute—the Separation-List—so these events are outer events. But classifying the BV-change events is more difficult. Those which occur due to flightplan updates clearly do not count, because they happen due to user interactions and could not be counted in advance. But there are also BV-change events which happen due to changes of the BV hierarchies and they could be regarded as inner events.

  Since we use the kinetic AABB-Tree there are at most $O(n \log n)$ events in one single BVH. One BV could be involved with n nodes in the Separation-List. So there are $O(n^2 \log n)$ inner events in the worst case.

  On the other hand, there may be $\Omega(n^2)$ outer events and thus the KDS is still *responsive*, even if we treat the BV-change events as inner events.

  In a reasonable case we have at most $O(n \log n)$ inner events from the kinetic AABB-Tree and $O(n)$ outer events in the Separation-List. Consequently, our KDS is also responsive in this case.

- *Locality*: We also have to be careful when showing the locality of our data structure. The objects of our kinetic data structure are the nodes in the Separation-List, not the single BVs in the kinetic AABB hierarchies. Each node is involved with only $O(1)$ events and, thus, our kinetic Separation-List is trivially *local*.

Otherwise, if the flightplan of one single BV changes this could cause $O(n)$ BV-change events in the kinetic Separation-List, because one BV could participate $O(n)$ nodes in the worst case. However, this is to be compared to $O(n^2)$ total nodes in our kinetic Separation-List small and, moreover, in the reasonable case there are at most $O(1)$ nodes affected by a flightplan update. Summarized, our kinetic Separation-List can be updated efficiently in all cases if a flightplan update happens.

In order to show the second part of the theorem, we use induction over time once more.

Obviously, after the first collision check we get a valid Separation-List. The hierarchy becomes invalid if either the BVs of an inner node or of a not overlapping leaf do not overlap anymore or if the fathers of one of this kind of nodes do not overlap anymore.

Furthermore, it could happen that the BVs of an overlapping leaf do not overlap anymore. During initialization we compute these points of time as events and store them sorted by time in the event queue. Thus, we will notice the first point in time when the hierarchy becomes invalid.

We have to show that the Separation-List is updated correctly if an event happens and that the next point in time when it becomes invalid provokes an event.

- *BV-overlap event*: If a BV-overlap event happens, the Separation-List becomes invalid because the BVs of an inner node overlap. To repair the defect we have to remove the node from the list and replace it by its four children. In order to determine the next time when one of this new nodes becomes invalid we have to calculate the events and insert them into the event queue.
- *Fathers-do-not-overlap event*: In case of a fathers-do-not-overlap event the list becomes invalid because the BVs of a node K overlapped before and do not overlap anymore. Thus, K is not the deepest node in the hierarchy whose BVs do not overlap. So, K must be replaced by its parent node VK.

  The hierarchy can become invalid at node VK the next time if the BVs of VK overlap or the predecessor of VK do not overlap anymore. So we have to compute what happens first and generate an event and insert it into the event queue. This guarantees that we will find the next time that VK becomes invalid.
- *Leaves-do-not-overlap event*: A leaves-do-not-overlap event does not affect the validity of the Separation-List. It is sufficient to turn the node into a not overlapping leaf.

  In order to recognize the next point of time that this node may violate the validity we have to look if either a BV-overlap event or a fathers-do-not-overlap event will happen first for this node and insert the corresponding event into the event queue.
- *BV-change event*: A BV-change event does not affect the validity of the Separation-List. But it is necessary to recompute the event times for the corresponding BVs in the list.

Overall, the validity of the hierarchy is guaranteed at all points of time.

If we want to check for a collision at any time, we only have to test the primitives in the overlapping leaves for collision.

Though our data structure fulfills all quality criteria of a kinetic data structure, the bounds of the used storage $O(n^2)$ or update costs of $O(n)$ for flightplan updates of one single vertex do not seem to be very promising. On the other hand these are worst-case scenarios and only hold if all polygons of one object overlap with all polygons of another object. This case does not happen in real-world applications. In most applications the number of overlapping polygons could be shown to be nearly linear (see also Sect. 6.2). Our experiments in the results section of this chapter show that the kinetic Separation-List performs very well in practical cases and that the running-time is up to 50 times faster compared to other approaches.

3.3.3 Self-collision Detection

BVHs are also used for self-collision detection. In general, collisions and self-collisions are detected in the same way. If two different objects are tested for collisions, their BVHs are checked against each other. Analogously, self-collisions of an object are performed by testing one BVH against itself. The main problem which arises when using this method in combination with discrete time sampling algorithms is the problem of adjacency: the BVs of adjacent polygons always overlap.

Therefore, approaches which are not using temporal and spatial coherence have to descent from the root of the BVTT down to all neighbors of a polygon at every query time. These are $O(n \log n)$ BV overlap tests, even if there is not a single pair of colliding polygons.

Our kinetic Separation-List avoids the problem of adjacency. For self-collision tests we also test the BVH against itself, but we do this only one time for the initialization. During run time, pairs of adjacent BVs stay all the time in the Separation-List and their parents will never be checked for collision as with most other approaches.

3.3.4 Implementation Details

In this section we describe some implementation details of our kinetic Separation-List which differ in several points from the basic algorithms described above. Algorithm 3.2 shows the basic simulation loop.

First of all, it is not necessary to store the Separation-List explicitly. Instead, it is sufficient to link only the two colliding BVs in the kinetic AABB-Tree. Therefore, we use a simple list for every BV in the kinetic AABB hierarchy and store pointers to the colliding BVs in the other hierarchy. It is sufficient, to use a list, even if we have to delete or insert some pointers when an event appears, because in real-world scenarios the degree of vertices is bounded and, thus, a single BV does not collide with too many other BVs in the BVTT.

Algorithm 3.2 Simulation Loop

---

while *simulation runs* **do**
    determine time t of next rendering
    $e \leftarrow$ min event in event queue
    while $e.timestamp < t$ **do**
        processEvent(e)
        if $e = $ *Polygons-Collide event* **then**
            collision response
        $e \leftarrow$ min event in event queue
    render scene

Moreover, if a fathers-do-not-overlap event happens we do not simply add the father of the affected BVs into our Separation-List, because in most cases the fathers of the fathers do not overlap either. Instead, we ascend in the hierarchy to the highest pair of BVs which does not overlap and then delete all its children that are in the Separation-List. Note that the data structure is not responsive anymore if we proceed like this, because in the worst case, we have a cost of $O(n^2)$ for one single event. However, if we simply proceed as described in the section before, we would have to process $O(n^2)$ events. Thus, the overall complexity is still the same. Equivalently, we do not insert just the children if a BV-overlap event happens. Instead, we descent directly to the deepest non-overlapping nodes in the BVHs.

For the event queue we use a Fibonacci heap. With this data structure we can efficiently insert, delete, and update events.

3.3.4.1 Continuous Primitive Intersection Test

The *polygons-collide event* requires two continuously moving polygons to be checked for intersection. In our implementation we used a continuous triangle intersection test according to the tests described in Eckstein and Schömer [12]. In this section we will give a short sketch of the basic ideas.

We break the triangle test into several sub-tests that can be computed more efficiently than testing a pair of triangles as a whole. In detail, we test vertices and faces and the edges separately for intersection. Overall, this results in three vertex/face- and nine edge/edge-tests for each pair of triangles.

A necessary condition for a vertex/face intersection is that the point is located in the triangles' plane (see Fig. 3.21). This means that

$$\big(q(t) - p_1(t)\big) \cdot n(t) = 0 \tag{3.4}$$

With $n(t) = (p_2(t) - p_1(t)) \times (p_3(t) - p_1(t))$ this results in a cubic equation that has to be solved for t. Moreover, we have to test if $q(t)$ is really located inside the triangle, e.g. by computing the barycentric coordinates.

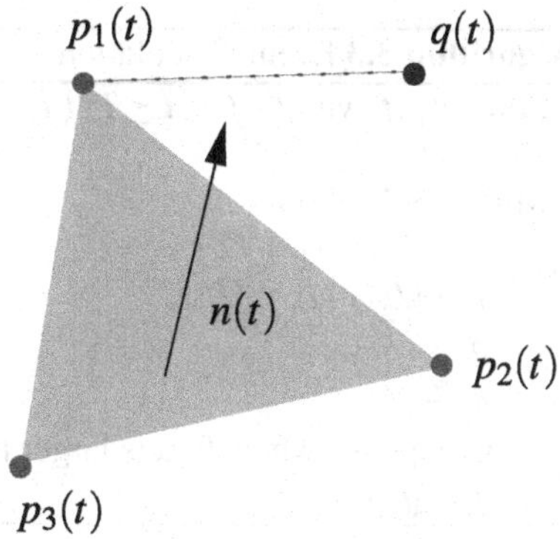

Fig. 3.21 Continuous
vertex/face-test: As a
pre-condition of an
intersection, $q(t)$ has to be
located in the triangles plane,
i.e. $(q(t) - p_1(t)) \cdot n(t) = 0$

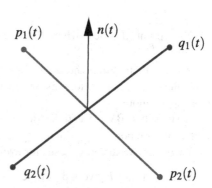

Fig. 3.22 Continuous
edge/edge-test: As a
pre-condition of an
intersection, both lines
$(p_1(t), p_2(t))$ and
$(q_1(t), q_2(t))$ have to be
located in the same plane

Similarly, we get a necessary condition for an edge/edge-intersection: both lines
must be located in the same plane (see Fig. 3.22). We get the equation

$$(q_1(t) - p_1(t)) \cdot n(t) = 0 \tag{3.5}$$

with $n(t) = (p_2(t) - p_1(t)) \times (q_2(t) - q_1(t))$. Again, we get a cubic equation and
we additionally have to apply a validity test that checks if the edges really intersect.

Summarizing, for both kinds of intersection tests—vertex/face and edge/edge—
we first have to find a point in time where four points are co-planar by solving a
cubic equation. Next, we have to check for validity at the time of co-planarity.

3.4 Event Calculation

The calculation of the events depends on the motion of the objects. At first we
assume a linear motion of the vertices.

In the kinetic AABB-Tree we get an event if a vertex P becomes larger than another vertex Q along some axis. Therefore, the computation of an event corresponds
to line intersection tests in 2D.

More precisely, assume that we have two vertices P and Q with velocity vectors
p and q, respectively. At point in time t we have $P_x(t) < Q_x(t)$. In order to get

---

Algorithm 3.3 Event Calculation

Compute f with $l \cdot f \leq t \leq l \cdot (f+1)$

$\bar{t} = l \cdot (f+1)$

while $t > l \cdot f$ **do**

    $\bar{p} = P_{l \cdot (f+1)} - P_{l \cdot f}$

    $\bar{q} = Q_{l \cdot (f+1)} - Q_{l \cdot f}$

    $p_f = \frac{\bar{p}}{l}$

    $q_f = \frac{\bar{q}}{l}$

    Compute $\bar{t}$ when P gets larger than Q

    $f = f + 1$

---

the next point of time $\bar{t}$ when P becomes larger than Q along the x-axis, we get $\bar{t} = \frac{Q_x(t) - P_x(t)}{p_x - q_x}$.

If $\bar{t} < 0$, there will be no event.

In the kinetic Separation-List we get events if two BVs begin to overlap or do not overlap anymore.

Assume two BVs A and B with extreme points $P^A_{i\max}$ and $P^B_{i\max}$, respectively, and minimum points $P^A_{i\min}$ and $P^B_{i\max}$, respectively, with $i \in \{x, y, z\}$ at time t.

There are two different cases for events:

- Assume A and B overlap at time t and we want to get the point of time $\bar{t}$ when they do not overlap anymore. Surely, A and B do not overlap $\Leftrightarrow$ there exists an axis $i \in \{x, y, z\}$ with $P^A_{i\max}(\bar{t}) < P^B_{i\min}(\bar{t})$ or $P^B_{i\max}(\bar{t}) < P^A_{i\min}(\bar{t})$.

  Thus, we have to compute the points of time $\bar{t}_i$ for every axis $i \in \{x, y, z\}$ when $P^A_{i\max}$ becomes smaller than $P^B_{i\min}$ and $P^B_{i\max}$ becomes smaller than $P^A_{i\min}$. We generate an event for the minimum of these $\bar{t}_i$.

- If A and B do not overlap at time t, we have to look for the time $\bar{t}$ when they overlap. A and B overlap $\Leftrightarrow$ $P^A_{i\max}(\bar{t}) \geq P^B_{i\min}(\bar{t})$ and $P^B_{i\max}(\bar{t}) \geq P^A_{i\min}(\bar{t})$ for all axes $i \in \{x, y, z\}$.

  Thus we have to compute the points of time $\bar{t}_i$ for all $i \in \{x, y, z\}$, when $P^A_{i\min}$ becomes smaller than $P^B_{i\max}$ and $P^B_{i\min}$ gets smaller than $P^A_{i\max}$ too. We generate an event for the maximum of the $\bar{t}_i$.

We tested our algorithms with keyframe animations. Between two keyframes we interpolated linearly. Therefore, we get paths of line segments as motion of the vertices.

Assume that we have k keyframes $K_0, \ldots, K_k$. Let l be the number of interpolated frames between two keyframes. We want to compute for the vertices P and Q with positions $P(t)$ and $Q(t)$, respectively, when the next event between these points will happen, i.e. when P will become larger along the x-axis than Q.

Therefore, we first have to determine the actual keyframe K_f with $l \cdot f \leq t \leq l \cdot (f + 1)$. We get the recent velocity p_f and q_f for the two vertices by $p_f = P(l \cdot (f + 1)) - P(l \cdot f)$ and $q_f = Q(l \cdot (f + 1)) - Q(l \cdot f)$.

Algorithm 3.4 Check{*BV a of object A, BV b object B*}

---

if *overlap (a, b)* **then**
　　if *a and b are leaves* **then**
　　　　test_primitives(a, b)
　　else
　　　　forall *children a[i] of a* **do**
　　　　　　forall *children b[j] of b* **do**
　　　　　　　　Check(a[i], b[j])
else
　　　return

Now we can compute time $\bar{t}$ when P gets larger than Q as described in the previous section. If $\bar{t} \leq m \cdot (f + 1)$ we get the event for P and Q. But if $\bar{t} > l \cdot (f + 1)$ we have to look at the next keyframe whether the paths of P and Q intersects and so on (see Algorithm 3.3). Thus, we have to compute k line intersections for one single event in the worst case.

3.5 Results

We implemented our algorithms in C++ and tested the performance on a PC running Linux with a 3.0 GHz Pentium IV with 1 GB of main memory. We used two different types of test scenarios, keyframe animations and simple velocity fields with linear motion.

In order to test the updating performance of the kinetic hierarchies, we used three different keyframe animations. The first one shows a tablecloth falling on a table. We tested this scene with several resolutions of the cloth, ranging from 2k to 16k faces. This scene shows the behavior of our algorithms under heavy deformation. The two other keyframe scenarios show typical cloth animations. The first one shows a male avatar with shirt in resolutions of from 32k to 326k deforming triangles, the other one a female avatar with a dress having from 65k to 580k deforming triangles (see Fig. 3.23).

In order to measure the speed of updates when the flightplan changes, we used a benchmark with two expanding spheres. We assign a velocity vector which points away from the midpoint to each point of a sphere, so that the spheres expand regularly. When they collide, the velocity vectors of the colliding triangles are reversed. We tested this scene with resolutions from 2k to 40k triangles.

Additionally, we implemented a typically recursive static collision detection algorithm (see Algorithm 3.4) in order to compare the overall performance of the Kinetic AABB-Tree and the Kinetic BoxTree. Because we are primarily interested in the speed of the updates we did not include self-collision detection. Moreover, we compared the performance of our algorithms with a bottom-up updating strategy. The plots in Figs. 3.24–3.39 show some results of our measurements.

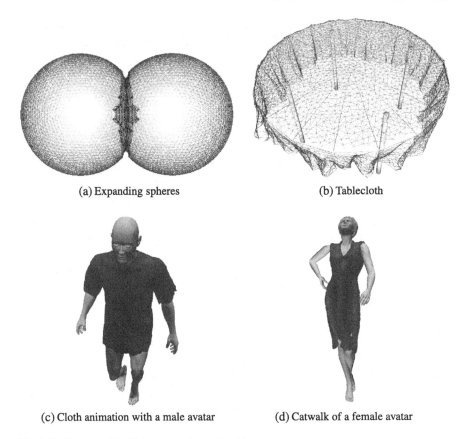

(a) Expanding spheres

(b) Tablecloth

(c) Cloth animation with a male avatar

(d) Catwalk of a female avatar

Fig. 3.23 Scenes with which we tested our algorithms

First, we consider the number of events. In the high-resolution tablecloth scene
we have about 400 events per frame and have to update only 1000 values for the
kinetic AABB-Tree and even fewer for the kinetic BoxTree (see Fig. 3.24). In contrast, the bottom-up approach has to update 60 000 values. For the Catwalk scene,
we found similar values (see Fig. 3.28). Since the computation costs for an event are
relatively high, this results in an overall speed-up of a factor of about 5 for updating the kinetic AABB-Tree (see Fig. 3.25). The number of events increases almost
linearly with the number of polygons, which supports our lower bound for the total
number of events of nearly $O(n \log n)$ (see Fig. 3.26).

The diagram also shows that we need fewer events for the kinetic BoxTrees, but
the proper collision check takes more time since the kinetic BoxTree is susceptible
to deformations.

A high amount of flightplan updates does not affect the performance of our kinetic hierarchies; they are still up to 5 times faster than the bottom-up updates (see
Fig. 3.27).

Fig. 3.24 Tablecloth scene: Average number of events and updates per frame. The kinetic BoxTree has, as expected, the smallest total number of events and the smallest number of total updates per event

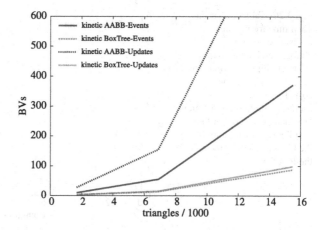

Fig. 3.25 Tablecloth scene: The total number of updates is significantly smaller than the updates required by the bottom-up strategy

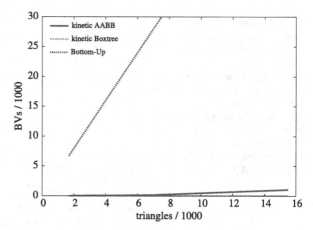

In the cloth animation scenes the gain of the kinetic data structures is highest, because the objects undergo less deformation than the tablecloth. Consequently, we have to perform fewer events. In this scenarios we see a performance gain of a factor about 10 (see Figs. 3.29, 3.31 and 3.32). From Theorem 3.3, it is clear that this factor increases with the number of interpolated frames between two keyframes. This is so, because the performance of the event based kinetic data structures only depends on the number of keyframes and not on the total length of the scene (see Fig. 3.30).

Overall, the kinetic AABB-Tree performs best and the running time of the updating operations is independent from the sampling frequency. This means, for example, that if we want to render a scene in slow motion—maybe 10 times slower—the costs for updating are still the same while they increase for the bottom-up update by a factor of 10.

In order to evaluate the performance of our kinetic Separation-List we re-used the tablecloth scene (see Fig. 3.23(b)) and the male cloth animation scene (see Fig. 3.23(c)). Moreover, we added a new scene with single swirling cloth in resolutions of 4K to 33K deforming polygons (see Fig. 3.33). We used this scene in

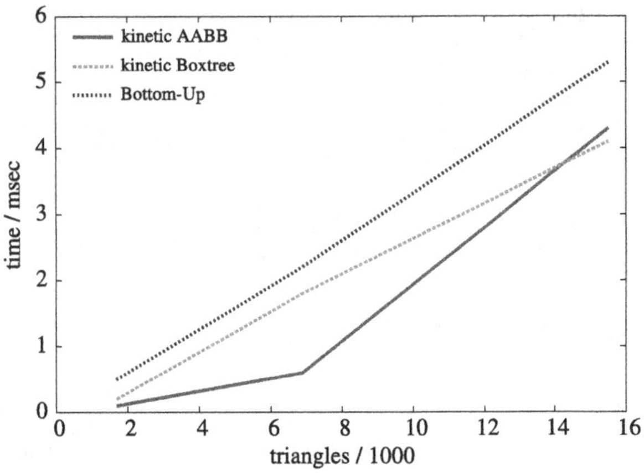

Fig. 3.26 Tablecloth scene:
Total time for updates and
collision detection.
Unfortunately, due to the
relatively high deformation of
the tablecloth and the high
costs for the
event-computation, the gain is
less than expected, but there
is still a significant gain for
the kinetic AABB-Tree and
the BoxTree

Fig. 3.27 Expanding spheres
scene: Average total time for
the updates and the collision
checks. This scene seems to
be more appropriate for the
KDSs than the tablecloth
scene, despite the high
amount of flightplan updates.
The gain of the kinetic data
structures compared to the
bottom-up approach is more
than a factor of 5

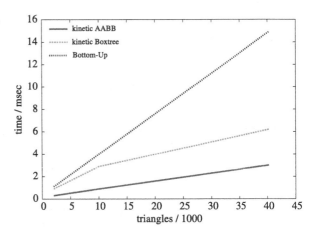

order to stress our algorithm: it contains very heavy deformation of the cloth and
many self-collisions.

We compared the performance of our kinetic Separation-List with a classical
swept-volume algorithm for continuous collision detection: we updated the hierarchy with a bottom-up updating strategy. For the proper collision check we constructed an AABB which encloses the BVs at the beginning and the end of the
frame.

First, we considered the number of events in our kinetic Separation-List compared to the number of checks the swept-volume algorithm has to perform. In the
high-resolution tablecloth scene we have about 500 events per frame with our kinetic data structure compared to several tens of thousands collision checks with the
swept-volume. Since the computational costs for an event are relatively high, this
results in an overall speed-up of about factor 50 for updating the kinetic Separation-
List (see Fig. 3.36). The number of events rises nearly linearly with the number of
polygons (see Fig. 3.37).

Fig. 3.28 Catwalk scene:
Average number of events
and updates. The ratio seems
to be nearly the same as in the
tablecloth scene

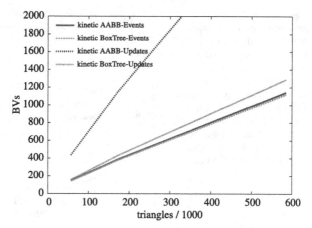

Fig. 3.29 Catwalk scene:
Updating times. In this scene
we have an overall gain of a
factor about 10 for the kinetic
AABB-Tree compared to the
bottom-up-update

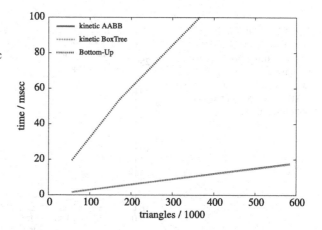

In the cloth animation scenes with the male avatar and the tablecloth the gain of
our kinetic data structures is highest, because the objects undergo less deformation
than the swirling cloth (see Figs. 3.38 and 3.39) and thus we have to compute and
handle fewer events. In these scenarios we see a performance gain of a factor up
to 50 compared to the swept-volume algorithm (see Fig. 3.34). This factor would
increase even further if the number of interpolated frames between two keyframes
were increased (see Fig. 3.35). This is because the performance of the event-based
kinetic data structures only depends on the number of keyframes and not on the total
length of the scene or the number of collision checks.

Overall the kinetic Separation-List performs best and the running time of the updating operations is independent from the sampling frequency. Moreover, the collisions are reported in the right order with our kinetic Separation-List. This is important for a correct collision response scheme. The collisions in the swept-volume
algorithms are reported in random order. If we would sort them the gain by our
algorithms would even increase.

Fig. 3.30 Male cloth animation scene: Average update time depending on the number of interpolated frames between two keyframes. Since the number of events only depends on the number of keyframes and not on the number of interpolated frames, so, the average update time decreases if we increase the total number of frames

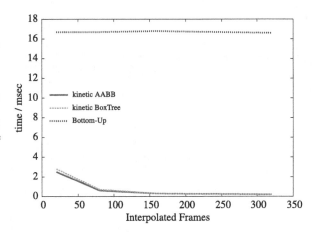

Fig. 3.31 Male cloth animation scene: Average updating time. In this scene we have an overall gain of a factor about 10 for the kinetic AABB-Tree compared to the bottom-up update

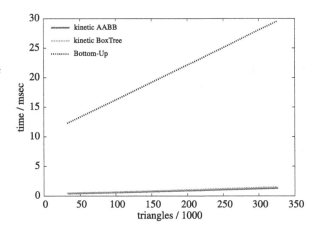

Fig. 3.32 Male cloth animation scene: Total time, this means the time for updates and the proper check time

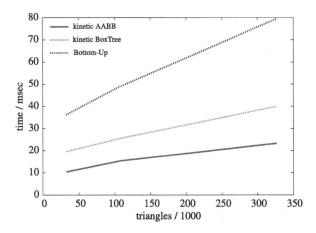

Fig. 3.33 The swirling cloth animation scene

Fig. 3.34 Male cloth animation scene: Average total time for updating the hierarchies and performing the inter- and intra-collision detection. We have an overall gain of about a factor of 20 with our kinetic Separation-List

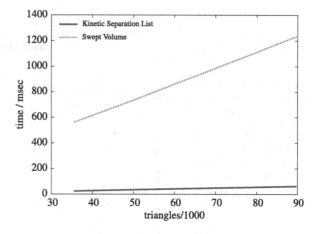

Fig. 3.35 Male cloth animation scene: Total time, including updating and collision check, in the resolution of 49K triangles, depending on the number of interpolated frames in-between two keyframes. Since the number of events only depends on the number of keyframes and not on the number of interpolated frames, the average update time decreases if we increase the total number of frames

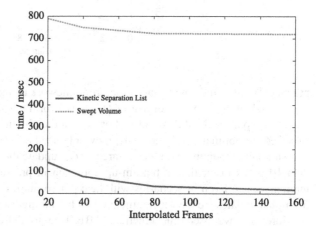

3.6 Conclusion and Future Work

We introduced two novel bounding volume hierarchies for updating a BVH over deformable objects fast and efficiently. We presented a theoretical and experimental analysis showing that our new algorithms are fast and efficient both in theory and in

Fig. 3.36 Tablecloth scene: Total time; this means updating the hierarchies and the time for the collision check including self-collision. The gain of our kinetic data structures is about a factor of 50

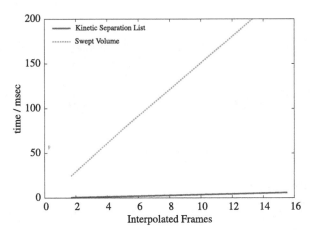

Fig. 3.37 Tablecloth scene: Number of events in our kinetic data structure compared to the number of collision checks we have to perform with the swept-volume algorithm. The number of events is significantly smaller. Note the different scales

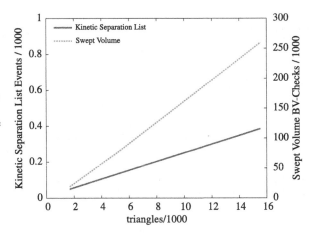

practice. We used the kinetic data structure framework to analyze our algorithms and we showed an upper bound of nearly $O(n \log n)$ for the updates that are required at most to keep a BVH valid. We also showed that the kinetic AABB-Tree and kinetic BoxTree are optimal in the sense that they only need to make $O(n \log n)$ updates.

Our kinetic bounding volume hierarchies can update the bounding volumes more than 10 times faster than a bottom-up approach in practically relevant cloth animation scenes. Even in scenarios with heavy deformations of the objects or many flightplan updates we have a significant gain by our algorithms.

Moreover, we used our kinetic AABB-Tree to define another kinetic data structure—the kinetic Separation-List—for continuous inter- and intra-collision detection between deformable objects, i.e. pairwise and self-collision detection. The algorithm gains its efficiency from the event-based approach.

It contains a discrete event-based part which updates only the combinatorial changes in the BVH and a continuous part which needs to compute only the time of future events after such a combinatorial change. Our algorithm is particularly

Fig. 3.38 Swirling cloth scene: Time for updating and self-collision check. Even in this worst-case scenario for our algorithm, we have a gain of a factor about 2 for our kinetic data structure. This depends on the higher number of events in this scenario

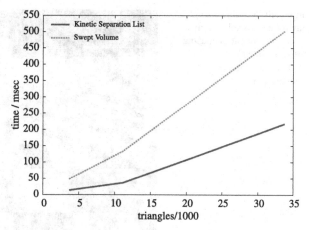

Fig. 3.39 Swirling cloth scene: Number of events for the kinetic Separation-List and the number of collision checks for the swept AABB approach. Again, note the different scales

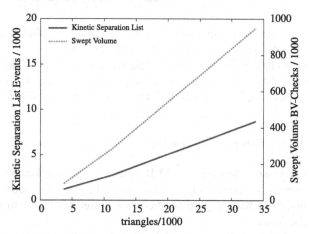

well-suited for animations where the deformation cannot be restricted in some way (such as bounded deformations). Our kinetic Separation-List is perfectly qualified for a stable collision response, because it naturally delivers the collisions ordered by time to the collision response module. In practically relevant cloth animation scenes our kinetic data structure can find collisions and self-collisions more than 50 times faster than a swept-volumes approach. Even in scenarios with heavy deformations of the objects we observed a significant gain by our algorithm.

3.6.1 Future Work

We believe that the kinetic data structures are a fruitful starting point for future work on collision detection for deformable objects.

Small changes could help to improve the performance of our kinetic data structures. For instance, the use of trees of higher order than binary trees could on the

Fig. 3.40 Sending a single
ray for each pixel in a ray
tracer may result in aliasing
artifacts, like the
checkerboard in the
background

one hand reduce the number of events, and on the other hand accelerate the propagation of events. Also the rebuild of parts of the BVHs in case of heavy deformations
could help to improve the running-time. In addition, it should be straightforward to
extend our novel algorithms to other primitives such as NURBS or point clouds and
to other applications like ray-tracing or occlusion culling.

3.6.1.1 Kinetic Ray-Tracing

Obviously, our kinetic AABB-Tree and also our kinetic BoxTree can be applied
directly to accelerating of ray-tracing of deformable scenes. However, in this para-
graph we will propose another event-based kinetic method that we will pursuit in
the future.

A typical ray tracer sends a single ray for each pixel through the scene. This
may result in aliasing artifacts (see Fig. 3.40). Therefore, advanced ray tracers send
not only a single ray but several rays for each pixel and in the end they interpolate
the results. Actually, a single pixel does not represent only a single ray—or several
rays—but the whole viewing frustum that is spanned by the pixel.

We will exploit this idea in our *kinetic ray tracer*. Basically, we will maintain a
sorted list of all primitives for each viewing frustum that is spanned by a single ray
(we call it the *pixel frustum*). Such an ordering can be easily realized with a kinetic
sorted list. Events will happen if two primitives change place. It is easy to prove the
four KDS quality criteria for this data structure.

Moreover, we propose an event-based 3D version of the Sutherland–Hodgman
polygon clipping algorithm [20] for each primitive. The basic principle is very easy:
A *subject polygon* is clipped consecutively against the spanning lines or, in 3D,
the spanning planes of the *clip polygon* (see Fig. 3.41). Events will happen if a
vertex passes through a spanning plane. Please note that this will also throw an
event in one or more pixel frusta in the neighborhood. A combined handling of
these simultaneous events will reduce the overall workload significantly.

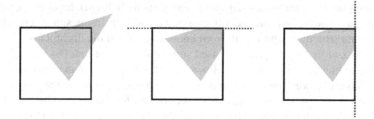

Fig. 3.41 The red polygon is clipped consecutively against the spanning lines of the clip polygon

During a query there is no explicit ray-shooting required any more. We simply have to collect the closest triangle or a set of closest triangles and combine their colors with respect to their sizes and their distances. This also allows an easy way to realize anti-aliasing.

Kinetic version of light buffers [16] or kinetic BSP-trees can be used for further speed-up or the recursive tracing of rays.

3.6.1.2 Parallel Kinetic Data Structures

The kinetic data structures for the pixel frusta of the kinetic ray tracer described above are widely independent from their neighbors. This allows a trivial parallelization.

However, we can also advance the concept of parallelization to deeper level for general kinetic data structures. Basically, a KDS relies on the consecutive handling of events that are stored in a global event-queue. An event stores the expiration time of a certificate. These certificates are elementary geometric conditions that prove altogether the correctness of an attribute. The *locality* of a KDS guarantees that these certificates are widely independent. This means that a single event does not affect too many changes in other certificates.

Consequently, we could parallelize a KDS on a *certificate* level. We just have to replace the global event-queue by a local event-queue for each certificate. Due to the locality of a KDS, the synchronization overhead should be relatively small.

3.6.1.3 Flightplans for Unknown Paths

A major drawback of kinetic data structures is the requirement of a flightplan. Actually, the more information is available about the flightplan, the more efficient is the KDS in practice. It is straightforward to derive such flightplans from keyframe animations. Our results show that the performance of our kinetic data structures increase with increasing number of interpolated frames between the keyframes.

However, in highly interactive scenes such as computer games or virtual reality applications, the interaction is determined by using physics-based simulation instead of pre-computed keyframe animations because of their higher level of flexibility. Physics-based simulations are usually computed for each frame separately. Hence, a kinetic data structure cannot gain from knowledge about the flightplans.

Therefore, at first sight, physics-based simulations do not seem to be well suited for the use in kinetic data structures. However, in the future we plan to integrate them anyway. Basically, we do not have to now the exact point in time when an event will happen, but it is sufficient to maintain a lower bound for the event. This means that we search a time interval where it is guaranteed that *no* event will happen.

Therefore, we can use e.g. larger time steps for the integration. However, larger time steps also result in a higher uncertainty. Consequently, we plan to analyze different integration schemes like explicit and implicit Euler and Runge–Kutta schemes, and so on, with respect to their error bounds. These error bounds will define a region that a particle cannot exceed during a certain time interval and, thus, defines a lower bound for the events.

References

1. Abam, M. A., & de Berg, M. (2007). Kinetic sorting and kinetic convex hulls. *Computational Geometry*, *37*(1), 16–26. doi:10.1016/j.comgeo.2006.02.004.
2. Agarwal, P. K., Guibas, L. J., Hershberger, J., & Veach, E. (1997). Maintaining the extent of a moving point set. In *Proceedings of the 5th international workshop on algorithms and data structures, WADS '97* (pp. 31–44). London: Springer. ISBN 3-540-63307-3. URL http://dl.acm.org/citation.cfm?id=645931.673046.
3. Agarwal, P. K., Basch, J., Guibas, L. J., Hershberger, J., & Zhang, L. (2002). Deformable free-space tilings for kinetic collision detection. I. *The International Journal of Robotics Research*, *21*(3), 179–198.
4. Agarwal, P. K., Kaplan, H., & Sharir, M. (2008). Kinetic and dynamic data structures for closest pair and all nearest neighbors. *ACM Transactions on Algorithms*, *5*(1), 4:1–4:37. doi:10.1145/1435375.1435379. URL http://doi.acm.org/10.1145/1435375.1435379.
5. Basch, J., Guibas, L., & Hershberger, J. (1997). Data structures for mobile data. In *SODA: ACM-SIAM symposium on discrete algorithms (A conference on theoretical and experimental analysis of discrete algorithms)*. URL citeseer.ist.psu.edu/145907.html.
6. Basch, J., Guibas, L. J., & Hershberger, J. (1999). Data structures for mobile data. *Journal of Algorithms*, *31*(1), 28.
7. Basch, J., Erickson, J., Guibas, L. J., Hershberger, J., & Zhang, L. (2004). Kinetic collision detection between two simple polygons. *Computational Geometry*, *27*(3), 211–235. doi:10.1016/j.comgeo.2003.11.001.
8. Chen, J.-S., & Li, T.-Y. (1999). *Incremental 3D collision detection with hierarchical data structures*. November 22. URL http://citeseer.ist.psu.edu/356263.html; http://bittern.cs.nccu. edu.tw/li/Publication/pdf/vrst98.pdf.
9. Coming, D., & Staadt, O. G. (2006). Kinetic sweep and prune for multi-body continuous motion. *Computers & Graphics*, *30*(3).
10. da Fonseca, G. D., & de Figueiredo, C. M. H. (2003). Kinetic heap-ordered trees: tight analysis and improved algorithms. *Information Processing Letters*, *85*(3), 165–169. doi:10.1016/S0020-0190(02)00366-6.
11. Davenport, H., & Schinzel, A. (1965). A combinatorial problem connected with differential equations. *American Journal of Mathematics*, *87*, 684–694.
12. Eckstein, J., & Schömer, E. (1999). Dynamic collision detection in virtual reality applications. In V. Skala (Ed.), *WSCG'99 conference proceedings*. URL citeseer.ist.psu.edu/eckstein99dynamic.html.

13. Erickson, J., Guibas, L. J., Stolfi, J., & Zhang, L. (1999). Separation-sensitive collision detection for convex objects. In *SODA '99: proceedings of the tenth annual ACM-SIAM symposium on discrete algorithms* (pp. 327–336). Philadelphia: Society for Industrial and Applied Mathematics. ISBN 0-89871-434-6.

14. Guibas, L. J. (1998). *Kinetic data structures—a state of the art report.* April 01. URL http://citeseer.ist.psu.edu/480263.html; http://graphics.stanford.edu/~guibas/g-kds.ps.

15. Guibas, L. J., Xie, F., & Zhang, L. (2001). Kinetic collision detection: algorithms and experiments. In *ICRA* (pp. 2903–2910).

16. Haines, E., & Greenberg, D. (1986). The light buffer: a shadow-testing accelerator. *IEEE Computer Graphics and Applications*, *6*, 6–16. URL http://doi.ieeecomputersociety.org/10.1109/MCG.1986.276832.

17. Mezger, J., Kimmerle, S., & Etzmuß, O. (2003). Hierarchical techniques in collision detection for cloth animation. *Journal of WSCG*, *11*(2), 322–329.

18. Sharir, M., & Agarwal, P. K. (1995). *Davenport–Schinzel sequences and their geometric applications.* Cambridge: Cambridge University Press. ISBN 9780521470254. URL http://books.google.de/books?id=HSZhIHxHXJAC.

19. Speckmann, B. (2001). *Kinetic data structures for collision detection.* PhD thesis, University of British Columbia. URL citeseer.ist.psu.edu/speckmann01kinetic.html.

20. Sutherland, I. E., & Hodgman, G. W. (1974). Reentrant polygon clipping. *Communications of the ACM*, *17*(1), 32–42. doi:10.1145/360767.360802. URL http://doi.acm.org/10.1145/360767.360802.

21. Weller, R., & Zachmann, G. (2006). Kinetic Separation-Lists for continuous collision detection of deformable objects. In *Third workshop in virtual reality interactions and physical simulation (Vriphys)*, Madrid, Spain, 6–7 November.

22. Zachmann, G. (2002). Minimal hierarchical collision detection. In *Proceedings of the ACM symposium on virtual reality software and technology, VRST '02* (pp. 121–128). New York: ACM. ISBN 1-58113-530-0. doi:10.1145/585740.585761. URL http://doi.acm.org/10.1145/585740.585761.

23. Zachmann, G., & Weller, R. (2006). Kinetic bounding volume hierarchies for deformable objects. In *ACM international conference on virtual reality continuum and its applications (VRCIA)*, Hong Kong, China, 14–17 June.

Chapter 4
Sphere Packings for Arbitrary Objects

Sphere packings have diverse applications in a wide spectrum of scientific and engineering disciplines: for example in automated radiosurgical treatment planning, investigation of processes such as sedimentation, compaction, and sintering, in powder metallurgy for three-dimensional laser cutting, in cutting different natural crystals, etc.; and the discrete element method is based on them.

In contrast, in the field of computer graphics sphere packings are hardly used.[1] This has two main reasons: first, computer graphics usually concentrates on the visual parts of the scene, i.e. the surface of the objects and not on what is behind. Secondly, computing sphere packings for arbitrary 3D objects is a highly non-trivial task [9]. Almost all algorithms that are designed to compute sphere packings are computationally very expensive and, therefore, they are restricted to very simple geometric objects like cubes or cylinders.

However, *volumetric* object representations also have their advantages. For instance, in physics-based simulations, the penetration volume is known to be the best measure for contact information that collision detection algorithms can provide [36]. Or take physics-based simulations of deformable objects, which sometimes require a prevention of the objects' volume. Within simple mass–spring systems it is hard to fulfil volume constraints, just because the volume is not really modeled. Algorithms that take the volume into account, e.g. the Finite-Element-Method (FEM) that relies on a volumetric tetrahedral representation of the objects, are computationally very expensive and hardly applicable to real-time scenarios. A representation of the objects' volumes by sphere packings could make the best out of both worlds: they could avoid the computational expense of FEM methods but preserve the volume during simulation by simply maintaining the non-overlap constraints (see Sect. 7.2).

---

[1] Actually, we know only two applications of sphere or circle packings in computer graphics: Shimada and Gossard [42] and Miller et al. [34] used uniform sphere packings to compute triangulated surfaces from other object representations like CSG or free form surfaces. Schiftner et al. [39] defined a new kind of triangle meshes that can be described by 2D circle packings. These triangle meshes can be used to construct very stable hexagonal surfaces.

Parts of this work have been previously published in [48] and [49].

R. Weller, *New Geometric Data Structures for Collision Detection and Haptics*, Springer Series on Touch and Haptic Systems, DOI 10.1007/978-3-319-01020-5_4, © Springer International Publishing Switzerland 2013

The pre-condition for these applications, however, is an efficient and stable method to compute sphere packings for arbitrary objects. In this chapter we will present two almost new methods that are able to compute polydisperse sphere packings. To our knowledge, such a method did not exist before.

The first method is based on a voxelization of the object. We greedily choose the centers of the voxels as potential centers of the spheres. The main drawback of this approach is exactly these fixed positions of the centers. If the object, or the voxelization, are not perfectly symmetric and aligned, it produces a lot of regular, small spheres close to the surface. During the collision detection (see Chap. 5) this can result in a noisy signal. Moreover, it is complicated to define the number of resulting spheres and the density of the packing in advance.

Therefore, we present a more flexible extension of this greedy voxel-based method, which is able to produce space-filling sphere packings. The basic idea is very simple and related to prototype-based approaches known from machine learning. Furthermore, this prototype-based approach directly leads to a version of our algorithm parallel to that we have implemented using CUDA. The theoretic analysis shows that our algorithm generates an approximation of the Apollonian diagram for arbitrary objects.

However, we will start with a short review of existing sphere-packing algorithms before we will explain our two new methods in more detail. Finally, we will briefly sketch how sphere packings can help to create entirely new solutions to fundamental problems in computer graphics: for instance, the segmentation and classification of 3D objects, real-time path planning in dynamic environments, 3D reconstruction from point clouds, and global illumination computation using photon mapping.

4.1 Related Work

For centuries, people have been fascinated by packing spheres into objects. Having started as a pure intellectual challenge in the time of Kepler [45], today there exist a wide variety of applications of sphere packings, reaching from the optimal composition of granular materials to automated neurosurgical treatment planning [21].

However, *the one and only* sphere-packing problem does not exist. In fact, as diverse as the fields of application is the number of *different* sphere-packing problems. Most sphere-packing problems turn out to be surprisingly complicated, but their solution has inspired researchers to mathematical,[2] but also lyrical[3] highlights over time. There are still a lot of open questions with respect to sphere packings,

---

[2]For instance, the proof of Kepler's conjecture was solved just a few years ago. This proof was, beside the 4-color theorem, one of the first proofs that was solved with the help of a computer [18].

[3]Soddy's "Kiss Precise" [43].

e.g. most parts of the sausage conjecture.[4] Moreover, there are interesting links between sphere-packing problems and other mathematical fields, like hyperbolic geometries, Lie algebras or monster groups [14].

Sphere-packing problems can be classified by several parameters, including the dispersity, the dimension, the orientation of the contacts between the spheres, etc. [51]. The focus of this chapter is the computation of space-filling polydisperse sphere packings for arbitrary objects and arbitrary object representations in any dimension. Because of the wide spectrum of different sphere-packing problems, we cannot provide a complete overview of all of them. We confine ourselves to recent and basic methods that are related to our problem definition or our approaches.

As an introduction to the general sphere-packing literature, including homogeneous sphere packings, we refer the interested reader to [4, 14, 28] or [21].

4.1.1 Polydisperse Sphere Packings

Polydisperse sphere packings are widely used and researched in material science and in simulations via the Discrete-Element method (DEM). Basically, there exist two different methods to construct polydisperse sphere packings: the *dynamic method* places a pre-defined distribution of spheres inside a given container and then changes the positions and the radii of the spheres until a required density is reached. To the contrary, the *geometric method* places the spheres one after another, following geometric rules. Usually, the geometric method performs better, but the quality of the sphere packing depends on the placement of the initial spheres.

However, both methods are restricted to very simple geometric containers like cubes or spheres. Especially existing dynamic algorithms can hardly be extended to arbitrary objects, because the dynamic simulation requires a time-consuming collision detection of the spheres with the surface of the object.

For instance, Schaertl and Sillescu [38] used a dynamic algorithm to simulate Brownian movements of spherical atoms. They start with a regular distribution of the spheres but allow an intersection. Then they start a simulation until an equilibrium state without overlaps is reached. Kansal et al. [24] presented a dynamic algorithm which they applied to the simulation of granular materials. It is an extension of the sphere-packing method by Lubachevsky and Stillinger [30]. Initially, they place the spheres in a non-overlapping state and let the radii of the spheres grow. Collisions were resolved using an event-based approach.

Azeddine Benabbou et al. [6] combined dynamic and geometric methods by using an advancing-front approach. In order to avoid large voids, they applied a dynamic point-relocation scheme that is based on weighted Delaunay triangulations.

---

[4]The sausage conjecture deals with the minimum volume of the convex hull for a packing of homogeneous spheres. For fewer than 56 spheres in 3D, this volume will be minimal if the spheres are ordered as a sausage [16]. Surprisingly, in 42 dimensions this is true independently of the number of spheres [28]. For other dimensions and other numbers of spheres this question is still open.

Another combined method was proposed by Herrmann et al. [20]. They used a generalization of the parking lot model: after an initial greedy filling, a dynamic compaction moves the spheres in order to make room for more insertions.

Jerier et al. [22] presented a purely geometric approach that is based on tetrahedral meshes and can be used to fill also arbitrary polygonal objects. The tetrahedra are used to compute isotropic hard-sphere clusters. Successive tetrahedrization of the voids allows to insert additional spheres. However, even with extensions that allow small intersections between the spheres as presented by Jerier et al. [23], this method is very time consuming.

There are also first approaches that support the parallel computation of polydisperse sphere packings. Kubach [27] presented an algorithm to solve the 3D knapsack problem for spheres in a cube. They compute several greedy solutions simultaneously with a master–slave approach. A non-parallel solution to this problem was proposed by Sutou and Dai [44]. They used a non-convex problem with quadratic constraints formulation.

4.1.2 Apollonian Sphere Packings

All the approaches described above try to solve some kind of optimization problem. This means that either the number or the size of the spheres is defined a priori. Real space-filling sphere packings potentially require an infinite number of spheres. They usually rely on fractal structures—the Apollonian sphere packings [4].

Such Apollonian sphere packings can be computed via an inversion algorithm [11]. Mahmoodi-Baram and Herrmann [31] presented an extension that uses other start parameters and can produce also other self-similar sphere packings. Packings like this are used in materials science to create very compact materials and to avoid micro fractures in the materials [19].

An important quality criterium is the density, which is closely related to the fractal dimension. An exact determination of the fractal dimension is still an open problem. Borkovec et al. [11] presented a numerical approximation of the fractal dimension. Mahmoodi-Baram and Herrmann [31] determined different densities for several start parameters of their inversion algorithm.

Closely related to Apollonian sphere packings are space-filling bearings. They are used to simulate the continental drift for instance [7]. Baram et al. [8] modified the inversion algorithm for the computation of complex bi-chromatic bearings for platonic solids. Classical Apollonian sphere packings require five colors.

However, all these algorithms are very time consuming and, moreover, they cannot be extended to arbitrary objects.

4.1.3 Sphere Packings for Arbitrary Objects

Sphere packings for arbitrary geometries are predominantly investigated in the field of radiosurgical treatment planning. Usually, the tumor region is represented by a polygonal model. A Gamma-Knife can shoot spherical beams inside this region. In order to avoid hot-spots, which are regions that are irradiated by several beams—they hold the risk of overdosage—but also in order to avoid regions that are not hit by a beam, it is essential to compute a good spherical covering of the tumor region.

This problem was firstly formulated as a min-max sphere packing by Wu [50]. In this problem formulation a set of spheres with different radii and a 3D region are predefined. The objective is to compute the minimum number of spheres that maximize the covered volume. According to Wang [47] there exists an optimal solution where the centers of the spheres are located on the medial axis of the 3D region. However, the greedy method is not optimal in each case [50]. Actually, Wang [46] proved the NP completeness of this problem, even if it is restricted to integer radii. Li and Ng [29] used a Monte-Carlo algorithm, but they can compute an optimal solution only for a few hundred spheres that are located inside a simple tetrahedron.

Wang [46] presented a simplification that allows arbitrary integer radii. They used a voxelization to approximate the objects' medial axis and an algorithm that explores the whole search-tree, even if they called it "dynamic programming". Consequently, their approach can be used only for very simple polygonal objects and a handful of spheres.

Anishchik and Medvedev [3] computed an explicit approximation of the objects' medial axis by using so called *Voronoi-S-Networks*. This yields a higher accuracy and delivers an estimation of density of the sphere packing.

4.1.4 Voronoi Diagrams of Spheres

Basically, the computation of sphere packings can be reduced to the successive computation of Voronoi diagrams for a set of spheres. Also our *Protosphere* algorithm is based on this idea. However, there is not much research on the computation of such generalized Voronoi diagrams, even if they are useful for the estimation of voids in complex proteins.

To our knowledge, there exist only two implementations that both use a very similar structure: a method presented by Anikeenko et al. [2], which was later extended by Medvedev et al. [33] and an algorithm that was described by Kim et al. [25]. Both approaches trace Voronoi edges between already computed Voronoi sites via edge tracing through a set of spheres. The main problem is to a lesser extent the construction of the Voronoi edges, which can be represented as quadratic Bezier patches [26], but rather the localization of the Voronoi sites.

A brute-force approach has a quadratic complexity [26]. Cho et al. [13] used geometric filters, called feasible regions, to accelerate the Voronoi site search. Manak and Kolingerova [32] extended this idea by using a 3D Delaunay triangulation of the spheres' centers. This allows a faster spherical region search.

In addition to their computational complexity, all these methods are restricted to sets of points and spheres. They cannot handle complex polyhedral objects or free form surfaces. A dense sampling of the object's surface as proposed by Agarwal et al. [1] results in inaccuracies [41] and higher running times [10].

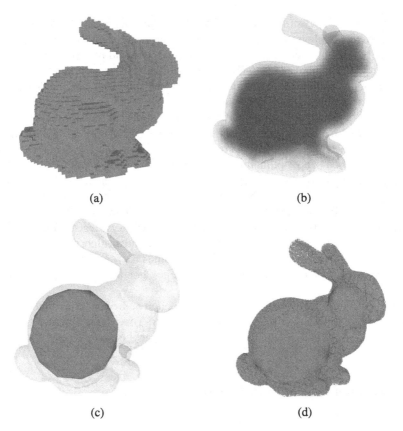

(a)   (b)

(c)   (d)

Fig. 4.1 The different stages of our sphere packing algorithm: First, we voxelize the object (**a**) and compute distances from the voxels to the closest triangle ((**b**); transparency = distance). Then we pick the voxel with the largest distance and put a sphere at its center (**c**). We proceed incrementally and, eventually, we obtain a dense sphere packing of the object (**d**)

4.2 Voxel-Based Sphere Packings

Almost all algorithms described in the previous section are designed to solve some kind of optimization problems. The reason for our interest in sphere packings was initially not the problem itself, but we needed sphere packings for arbitrary objects in order to implement our new data structure for volumetric collision detection, the *Inner Sphere Trees* (see Chap. 5). The only pre-condition for a sphere packing to be used in this data structure is that the sphere packing has to be *feasible*. Precisely stated, we call a sphere packing *feasible*, if all spheres are located *inside* an object, and if the spheres *do not overlap* each other.

Certainly, the object should be approximated well by the spheres, while their number should be small. But there are no constraints that restrict the number of spheres, the radii of the spheres or the volume that must be covered. Consequently,

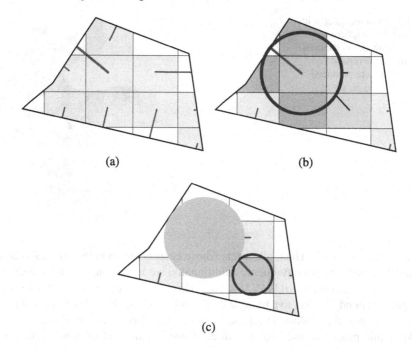

(a)   (b)

(c)

Fig. 4.2 This figure shows the first steps of the creation of the inner spheres. First, the object is voxelized (**a**). Additionally, we compute the shortest distance to the surface (marked as *lines*) for interior voxel centers (*filled*), i.e. a discretization of the interior distance field. Next, we place a maximal sphere at the voxel center with the largest radius. Then those voxels whose centers are located inside the new sphere are deleted, and the shortest distances of some voxels are updated, because they are now closer to the new inner sphere (**b**). This procedure continues greedily (**c**)

we can use any *feasible* sphere packing for the construction of our *Inner Sphere Trees*.

The first method that we have developed to compute such *feasible* sphere packings is a simple heuristic that offers a good trade-off between accuracy and speed in practice. This heuristic is currently based on voxelization. Actually, voxel representations of objects are also a representation of the object's volume. However, they are very memory consuming because of the fixed size of the voxels. Hence it seems a good idea to merge the voxels to spheres in order to save some memory. This is exactly the basic idea of our voxel-based sphere packing heuristic.

We start with a flood filling voxelization, but instead of simply storing whether or not a voxel is filled, we additionally store the distance d from the center of each voxel to its closest point on the surface, together with the triangle that realizes this distance (see Fig. 4.1). In our implementation we use a slightly modified version of Dan Morris' *Voxelizer* [35] to compute this initial distance field.

After this initialization we use a greedy algorithm to generate the inner spheres. All voxels are stored in a priority queue, sorted by their distance to the surface. Until the priority queue is empty, we extract the maximum element, i.e. the voxel V^* with the largest distance d^*. We create an inner sphere with radius d^* that is placed on the

Fig. 4.3 An object filled with
the voxel-based sphere
packing method. On the body,
you can see the regular
spheres that were produced
due to the fixed center
positions

center of the voxel V^*. Then, all voxels whose centers are contained in this sphere
are deleted from the priority queue. Additionally, we have to update all voxels V_i
with $d_i < d^*$ and distance $d(V_i, V^*) < 2d^*$. This is because they are now closer to
the sphere around V^* than to a triangle on the hull (see Fig. 4.2). Their d_i must now
be set to the new free radius. This process stops when there is no voxel left.

After this procedure the object is filled densely with a set of non-overlapping
spheres. The restriction to those voxel centers that are located *inside* the object and
the consecutive update of the minimum distances guarantee that the spheres do not
overlap and that they are all located inside the object.

Figure 4.1 summarizes the steps of our voxel-based sphere packing: we start
with a voxelization, compute a distance field, add spheres greedily, and finally get
an object that is filled with spheres.

Basically, the density and thus the accuracy can be somewhat controlled by the
number of initial voxels. However, it is hardly possible to determine the expected
density or the resulting number of spheres in advance. Moreover, due to the fixing
of the sphere centers to the centers of the voxels, this heuristic can produce small
and very regular spheres close to the surface of the object (see Fig. 4.3). This results
in artifacts, in particular temporal aliasing, in the collision response. Therefore, we
have developed another sphere-packing algorithm that provides a better control on
the spheres' density but also avoids these artifacts.

4.3 Protosphere: Prototype-Based Sphere Packings

In this section, we will present a new algorithm, called *Protosphere*, that is able
to efficiently compute a space-filling sphere packing for arbitrary objects. It is independent of the object's representation (polygonal, NURBS, CSG, etc.); the only
pre-condition is that it must be possible to compute the distance from any point to
the surface of the object. Moreover, our algorithm is not restricted to 3D but can be
easily extended to higher dimensions.

Fig. 4.4 The largest sphere
that fits into an object touches
at least three points in 2D,
and four points in 3D,
respectively

The basic idea is very simple and related to *prototype-based approaches* known
from machine learning. This approach directly leads to the *parallel algorithm* that
we have implemented using CUDA. As a byproduct, our algorithm yields an approximation of the object's *medial axis* that has applications ranging from path planning
to surface reconstruction.

4.3.1 Apollonian Sphere Packings for Arbitrary Objects

A simple algorithm to fill an object with a set of non-overlapping spheres is the
following greedy method. For a given object we start with the largest sphere that fits
into the object. Iteratively, we insert new spheres, under the constraints that

(a) they must not intersect the already existing spheres and
(b) that they have to be completely contained inside the object.

The resulting sphere packing is called an "Apollonian sphere packing". One important property of Apollonian packings is that they are known to be space filling.
There exist efficient algorithms to compute Apollonian diagrams for very simple geometrical shapes like cubes or spheres, but they are hardly expandable to arbitrary
objects, let alone their computation time (see Sect. 4.1.2). Hence, in order to transfer
the idea of Apollonian sphere packings to arbitrary objects, we have to make further
considerations.

Let P denote the surface of a closed, simple object in 3D. Consider the largest
sphere s inside P. Obviously, s touches at least four points of P, and there are no
other points of P inside s (see Fig. 4.4). This implies that the center of s is a Voronoi
node (VN) of P. Consequently, it is possible to formulate the greedy space filling
as an iterative computation of a generalized Voronoi diagram (VD) of P plus the set
of all spheres existing so far (see Fig. 4.5).

This basic idea has a major drawback: many algorithms have been devised for
the calculation of the classic VD and for its many generalizations. However, there

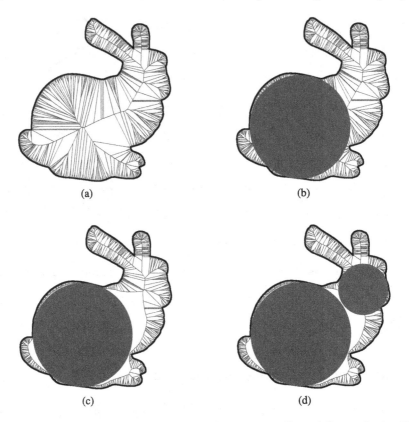

Fig. 4.5 The basic idea of our Protosphere algorithm: compute a Voronoi diagram for the object (**a**), place the largest sphere (**b**), re-compute the Voronoi diagram for the object and the new sphere (**c**), place the largest sphere in the new Voronoi diagram, etc. (**d**)

are relatively few works dedicated to the construction of VDs for spheres in 3D (see Sect. 4.1.4) and, to our knowledge, there is no algorithm available that supports the computation of VDs for a mixed set of triangles and spheres, let alone a fast and stable implementation.

Fortunately, a closer look at the simple algorithm we proposed above shows that we do not need the whole *Voronoi diagram*, but only the *Voronoi nodes*. Hence the core of our novel algorithm is the approximation of the VNs. Again, the basic idea is very simple: we let a single point, the *prototype*, iteratively move towards one of the VNs (see Algorithm 4.1).

The last line guarantees that, after each single step, p is still inside the object, because the entire sphere around p with radius $\|p - q_c\|$ is inside the object.

Moreover, moving p away from the border into the direction $(p - q_c)$ leads potentially to bigger spheres in the next iteration (see Fig. 4.6 for a visualization of our algorithm). Usually, $\varepsilon(t)$ is not a constant, nor chosen randomly, but a cooling

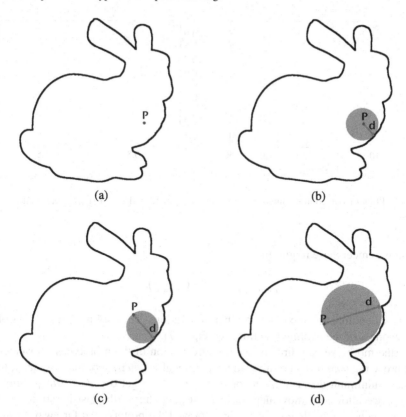

Fig. 4.6 The prototype convergence algorithm: Place prototype P randomly inside the object (**a**). Compute minimum distance d from the prototype P to the surface (**b**). Move prototype P into the opposite direction, away from the surface (**c**). Continue until the prototype converges (**d**)

Algorithm 4.1 convergePrototype(prototype p, object O)

---

place p randomly inside O
while p has not converged **do**
    $q_c = \arg\min\{\|p - q\| : q \in \text{surface of } O\}$
    choose $\varepsilon(t) \in [0, 1]$
    $p = p + \varepsilon(t) \cdot (p - q_c)$

---

function that allows large movements in early iterations and only small changes in the later steps.

The accuracy of the approximated VN depends on the choice of this cooling function and on the number of iterations. Actually, in the first iterations, a large movement of the prototypes should be allowed in order to move very quickly toward the maximum. In the later iterations, when we have almost arrived at the maximum, only fine tuning is required. We choose the following variation of a Gaussian

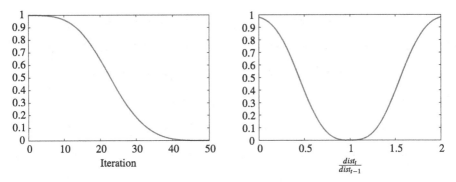

Fig. 4.7 Plots of our cooling functions: $\varepsilon(t)$ with $t_{\max} = 50$ and $c = 4$ (*left*). $\varepsilon(d)$ with $c = 3$ (*right*)

function to meet these requirements:

$$\varepsilon(t) = 1 - e^{-0.5 \cdot \left(\frac{|t - t_{\max}|}{0.5 t_{\max}}\right)^{c}} \tag{4.1}$$

with $t_{\max}$ denoting the maximum number of iterations. The cooling factor c controls the steepness of the cooling function (see Fig. 4.7).

Furthermore, we can directly use the information of the prototypes' movement to improve the *temporal* cooling with an additional *geometric* cooling. Actually, for the new minimum distance d_t in some iteration t we get $0 \le d_t \le 2d_{t-1}$, simply because we allowed a movement of at most d_{t-1} during the last iteration $t - 1$. If d_t is much smaller than d_{t-1}, we have moved the prototype p far away from a probably *better* position that allows a larger sphere. Therefore, we should leave the new position, which is closer to the surface, as fast as possible. Hence, we should allow a large step size in this case.

On the other hand, if d_t is much larger than d_{t-1}, it seems that d_{t-1} was too close to the surface, and probably also d_t is. Therefore, we should quickly escape from this position with a large step size.

Finally, if d_t is almost the same as d_{t-1}, we are probably very close to the optimum. Hence we should reduce the speed of movement and apply only fine tuning.

Summarizing, we need a function $\varepsilon(d)$ that takes these considerations into account, with respect to $\frac{d_t}{d_{t-1}}$, which is known to be in the interval $[0, 2]$. We can use almost the same Gaussian function as for the temporal cooling function in Eq. (4.1). With $x := \frac{d_t}{d_{t-1}}$ we get

$$\varepsilon(d) = 1 - e^{-0.5 \cdot \left(\frac{|x - 1|}{0.5}\right)^{c}} \tag{4.2}$$

Again, c controls the steepness of $\varepsilon(d)$ (see Fig. 4.7).

For the complete cooling function $\varepsilon_{\text{tot}}(d, t)$, we simply combine the two ideas to $\varepsilon_{\text{tot}}(d, t) := \varepsilon(t) \cdot \varepsilon(d)$.

The overall sphere-packing algorithm can be described as shown in Algorithm 4.2.

Algorithm 4.2 spherePacking(object O)

---

while *Number of required spheres is not met* **do**
    Place prototype p randomly inside O
    convergePrototype(p, O)
    s = new sphere at position p
    $O = O \cup s$

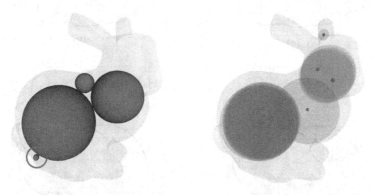

Fig. 4.8 Depending on the prototype's start position, it can run into a local maximum instead of finding the global maximum (*left*). Different prototypes converge to the same end position (*right*)

4.3.2 Parallelization

Using a single prototype does not guarantee to find the global optimum (which is the sought-after VN), because the algorithm presented in the previous section depends on the starting position of the prototype and can end up in a local maximum (see Fig. 4.8). Hence we use a set of independently moving prototypes instead of only a single one. This can be easily parallelized if the prototypes are allowed to move independently. However, a naive implementation has its drawbacks: many prototypes converge to the same end position (see Fig. 4.8). Consequently, we get a lot of similar and thus redundant computations. Obviously, this is not very efficient, even in parallel computing.

Therefore, we use a slightly different approach for our implementation, which is based on a uniform distribution of the prototypes. Actually, we compute a uniform grid and start with a prototype in each cell that is located inside the object. During the movement step of Algorithm 4.1 the prototypes are confined to their cells. This results in a uniform density of the prototypes, and, moreover, the grid can be used to speed up the distance computations. For the latter we additionally compute the discrete distance from each cell to the surface. For further acceleration, we remove those prototypes from the computation, which show the same closest point in two

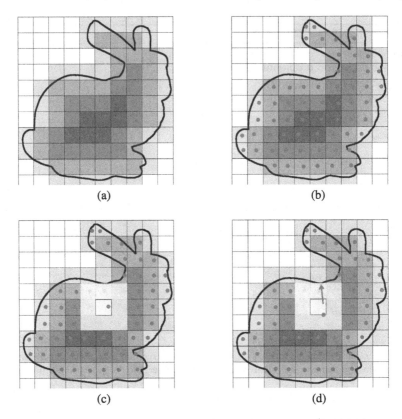

Fig. 4.9 The parallel Protosphere algorithm: We use a discrete distance field. The discrete distance to the surface is color coded (**a**). We place a prototype in each cell of the distance field (**b**). We use the discrete distance only to define a region in which we have to look for closest objects for each prototype (**c**). During the convergence step we clamp the prototypes to their cells (**d**)

Algorithm 4.3 parallelSpherePacking(object O)

In parallel: Initialize discrete distance field
while *Number of required spheres is not met* **do**
    In parallel: Place p_i randomly inside grid cell c_i
    In parallel: convergePrototype(p_i, $O \cup$ inserted spheres)
    In parallel: Find VN $p_m \in \{p_i\}$ with max distance d_m
    Insert sphere at position p_m with radius d_m
    In parallel: Update discrete distance field

---

consecutive iterations and which are therefore clamped twice to the same position. Obviously, those prototypes cannot be Voronoi nodes.

Algorithm 4.3 shows the pseudo-code of the complete parallelized version. Figure 4.9 shows a visualization of the main steps.

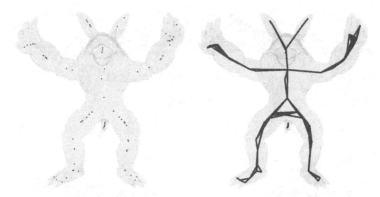

Fig. 4.10 After the convergence of the initial prototypes, our parallel algorithm yields an approximation of the object's Voronoi nodes (*left*). If we connect overlapping spheres, we get an approximation of the *medial axis* (*right*)

Please note that after the convergence of the initial set of prototypes, we get an approximation of the medial axis (see Fig. 4.10). Its accuracy depends on the number of initial prototypes and thus on the size of the grid.

In addition, our algorithm extends Apollonian sphere packings to arbitrary objects. This is the reason for the space-filling property of our algorithm.

4.3.3 Results

We have implemented our algorithm using CUDA. We filled different objects densely with spheres (see Fig. 4.11). The triangle count reaches from 10,000 for the pig until up to 300,000 for the dragon. We are able to fill all objects with 100,000 spheres within a few seconds using a NVIDIA GTX480 graphics card (see Fig. 4.12). The number of iterations of Algorithm 4.1 was set to 50.

In order to track the accuracy, we compared the positions of the prototypes that were computed with our Protosphere algorithm to the exact positions of the Voronoi nodes. Therefore, we used simple objects, like a cube and a sphere, where the VNs positions can be calculated analytically. Actually, the accuracy of the computed Voronoi nodes is >99.99 % compared to the exact Voronoi nodes position.

Surprisingly, the filling rate depends only on the number of spheres but is independent of the objects' shapes, at least with all objects that we have tested (see Fig. 4.13).

4.4 Conclusions and Future Work

Summarizing, we have presented two novel methods for filling arbitrary objects very quickly and stably with sets of non-overlapping spheres. Our prototype-based

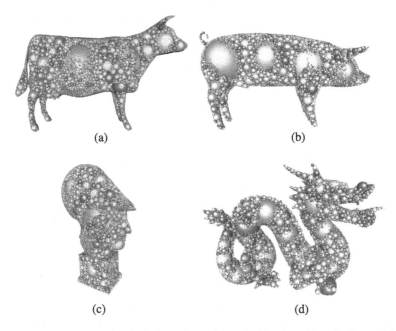

(a)   (b)

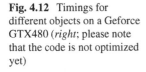

(c)   (d)

Fig. 4.11 The models used for the timings: A cow (**a**), a pig (**b**), a bust (**c**), and a dragon (**d**)

Fig. 4.12 Timings for
different objects on a Geforce
GTX480 (*right*; please note
that the code is not optimized
yet)

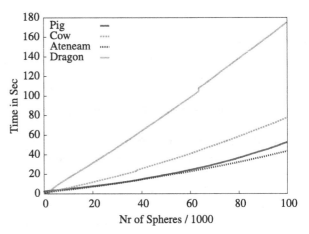

Protosphere algorithm is even optimal in the sense that it produces space filling
sphere packings due to the Apollonian property.

Naturally, sphere packing is an interesting problem per se. But originally, we designed our algorithms as a means to an end; we simply required a method to fill
arbitrary objects with spheres in order to realize our *Inner Sphere Trees* data structure (see Chap. 5). It turns out that the efficient computation of sphere packings for
arbitrary objects, but also the algorithms for their computation, have very interesting properties, which open new ways to solve fundamental problems of computer

Fig. 4.13 The space-filling
rate of our sphere-packing
algorithm

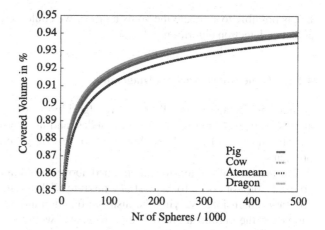

graphics and beyond. For instance, we applied our sphere packings to the real-time
simulation of volume preserving deformable objects (see Sect. 7.2). In the following, we will outline a few other ideas for the future use of such sphere packings.

4.4.1 Future Work

First, we want to improve our Protosphere algorithm in the future. Even if it already
works very fast in its parallel version, there is still room for improvements. Especially the computation of the initial spheres takes some time. We plan to accelerate
this step by using hierarchical grids instead of uniform grids. Probably, this would
allow the real-time approximation of the object's medial axis.

Moreover, we want to extend our algorithm to other object representations than
polygonal meshes, e.g. NURBS, CSG or point clouds. This is basically straightforward: we simply have to adapt the closest point computation.

At the moment, we use a simple greedy choice for the spheres. Replacing this
by a more intelligent optimized choice would probably improve the covered volume
and could further help to solve other optimization problems, e.g. the placement of
beams in radiosurgical treatment planning. Furthermore, we can replace the prototypes by other geometric primitives, like line segments. An appropriate distance
function would allow to compute ellipsoid packings instead of sphere packings.
Also the extension to higher dimensions is straightforward.

The packing of spheres into arbitrary objects also has some interesting theoretical implications. Until now, the density of Apollonian sphere packings has been
investigated only for very simple geometric objects like cubes. There, an exponential distribution of the sphere sizes has been derived. It is unknown if this also holds
for arbitrary objects, even if we already assume this with respect to our results (see
Fig. 4.13). Probably, it is possible to classify objects with respect to their fractal
dimension. Another open problem is the analysis of the voids between the spheres.

If it is possible to estimate the voids a priori, we could derive error bounds for our collision detection algorithm.

4.4.1.1 Generalized Voronoi Diagrams

A major advantage of our Protosphere algorithm is that it initially computes an approximation of the object's Voronoi nodes, and thus on the medial axis. Hence, our algorithm can be used as a blueprint for several generalized Voronoi diagram problems.

For instance, the extensions mentioned above would allow to approximate generalized Voronoi nodes for almost any mixture of different geometric primitives in arbitrary dimensions. Varying the distance function allows further generalizations. Moreover, the optimizations of the performance would probably allow a real-time computation of such generalized VNs. To our knowledge, such a flexible algorithm does not exist yet. Usually, generalized VD algorithms are restricted to either of these extensions, not to mention their performance and their robustness.

Generalized Voronoi diagrams have numerous applications in many scientific disciplines beyond computer graphics and computer science, including chemistry, biology, and material science. However, in order to connect the Voronoi nodes to a complete Voronoi diagram, we will have to add an edge-tracing algorithm.

4.4.1.2 Applications to Computer Graphics

Beyond the computation of generalized VDs, which are widely used in computer graphics, our sphere packings can be applied to other fundamental problems.

For instance, the sphere packing can be used to construct level-of-detail representations of objects by simply sorting the spheres by their size. Furthermore, we can use the sphere sizes and their relative position as a similarity measure to compare different objects or for the search in geometric databases. Obviously, this similarity measure is scale-invariant if we use only the relative sizes of the spheres. Moreover, it can be applied hierarchically.

However, the Protosphere algorithm also has another interesting feature. Actually, it does not only compute a sphere packing, but it also derives automatically the *neighborhood* between the spheres. Connecting adjacent spheres results in a neighborhood graph that we call the *Sphere Graph* (see Fig. 4.14).

This sphere graph can be applied to segmentation problems. Usually, a segmentation of objects into its functional parts is often used for modeling, skeletal extraction or texturing [5, 12, 40]. We assume that our volumetric Sphere-Graph representation has some advantages over the typical surface-based methods. Several heuristics can be used in our Sphere Graph, e.g. a formulation as a min-cut problem, but we can also take into account the sizes of the spheres or their distribution.

Another fundamental problem in computer graphics is the reconstruction of polygonal objects from point clouds that were derived from a 3D scanner. The extension to point clouds mentioned above allows our algorithms to work directly on this

Fig. 4.14 Our Protosphere algorithm does not only compute a sphere packing, but also maintains automatically the adjacency between the spheres, the so called *Sphere Graph*

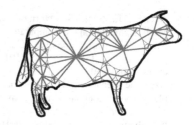

kind of object representation. We can use the direction of the edges in our Sphere Graph with respect to the points in order to determine the interior and exterior of the object. The same technique can be applied to close holes in polygonal meshes. However, we can also formulate this again as a min-cut problem. We assume that such Sphere Graph-based algorithms are very robust to noisy data.

Last but not least, it is also possible to apply our sphere packings to global illumination. Until now, we restricted the sphere packings to fill the interior of single objects. However, we can also use a spherical representation of the *free space* between the objects. This new spherical free-space representation allows us to re-formulate the photon mapping algorithm. Basically, photon mapping is closely related to ray tracing. Instead of tracing rays from the *eye* through the scene, photon mapping traces rays from the *lights* through the scene in order to simulate the distribution of the photons (see [15, 17, 37] for more details). The accuracy of this approach, but also the performance, depends on the number of rays. If we use our Sphere Graph as free-space representation, we can re-formulate this discrete tracing of rays as a continuous network-flow problem. We simply have to define the lights as photon source and the objects as a photon sink, with respect to their material parameters.

Obviously, these are just a few examples of how sphere packings of arbitrary objects and their accompanying space representation, the Sphere Graph, can be applied to very different problems in computer graphics. We are sure that there exist many more interesting applications of our data structures in the future.

References

1. Agarwal, P. K., de Berg, M., Matoušek, J., & Schwarzkopf, O. (1994). Constructing levels in arrangements and higher order Voronoi diagrams. In *Proceedings of the tenth annual symposium on computational geometry, SCG '94* (pp. 67–75). New York: ACM. ISBN 0-89791-648-4. doi:10.1145/177424.177521. URL http://doi.acm.org/10.1145/177424.177521.
2. Anikeenko, A. V., Alinchenko, M. G., Voloshin, V. P., Medvedev, N. N., Gavrilova, M. L., & Jedlovszky, P. (2004). Implementation of the Voronoi-Delaunay method for analysis of intermolecular voids. In A. Laganai, M. L. Gavrilova, V. Kumar, Y. Mun, C. Jeng, K. Tan, & O. Gervasi (Eds.), *Lecture notes in computer science: Vol. 3045. ICCSA (3)* (pp. 217–226). Berlin: Springer. ISBN 3-540-22057-7. URL http://dblp.uni-trier.de/db/conf/iccsa/iccsa2004-3.html.
3. Anishchik, S. V., & Medvedev, N. N. (1995). Three-dimensional Apollonian packing as a model for dense granular systems. *Physical Review Letters, 75*(23), 4314–4317.
4. Aste, T., & Weaire, D. (2000). *The pursuit of perfect packing*. Bristol: Institute of Physics Publishing. ISBN 0-7503-0648-3.

5. Attene, M., Katz, S., Mortara, M., Patane, G., Spagnuolo, M., & Tal, A. (2006). Mesh segmentation—a comparative study. In *Proceedings of the IEEE international conference on shape modeling and applications 2006* (p. 7). Washington: IEEE Computer Society. ISBN 0-7695-2591-1. doi:10.1109/SMI.2006.24. URL http://dl.acm.org/citation.cfm?id=1136647.1136960.

6. Azeddine Benabbou, P. L., Borouchaki, H., & Lu, J. (2008). Sphere packing and applications to granular structure modeling. In R. V. Garimella (Ed.), *Proceedings of the 17th international meshing roundtable*. Berlin: Springer. ISBN 9783540879206. URL http://books.google.com/books?id=11uPPjxBIRsC.

7. Baram, R. M., & Herrmann, H. (2007). Random bearings and their stability. In L. Pietronero, V. Loreto, & S. Zapperi (Eds.), *Abstract book of the XXIII IUPAP international conference on statistical physics*, Genova, Italy, 9–13 July. URL http://st23.statphys23.org/webservices/abstract/preview_pop.php?ID_PAPER=313.

8. Baram, R. M., Herrmann, H. J., & Rivier, N. (2004). Space-filling bearings in three dimensions. *Physical Review Letters, 92*(4), 044301.

9. Birgin, E. G., & Sobral, F. N. C. (2008). Minimizing the object dimensions in circle and sphere packing problems. *Computers & Operations Research, 35*(7), 2357–2375. doi:10.1016/j.cor.2006.11.002.

10. Boada, I., Coll, N., Madern, N., & Sellarès, J. A. (2005). Approximations of 3d generalized Voronoi diagrams. In *EuroCG* (pp. 163–166).

11. Borkovec, M., De Paris, W., & Peikert, R. (1994). The fractal dimension of the Apollonian sphere packing. *Fractals. An Interdisciplinary Journal on the Complex Geometry of Nature, 2*(4), 521–526. URL http://citeseerx.ist.psu.edu/viewdoc/download?doi=10.1.1.127.4067&rep=rep1&type=pdf.

12. Chen, X., Golovinskiy, A., & Funkhouser, T. (2009). A benchmark for 3D mesh segmentation. *ACM Transactions on Graphics, 28*(3) (Proc. SIGGRAPH).

13. Cho, Y., Kim, D., Lee, H.-C., Park, J. Y., & Kim, D.-S. (2006). Reduction of the search space in the edge-tracing algorithm for the Voronoi diagram of 3d balls. In *ICCSA (1)* (pp. 111–120).

14. Conway, J. H., & Sloane, N. J. A. (1992). *Grundlehren der mathematischen Wissenschaften: Vol. 290. Sphere packings, lattices and groups* (2nd ed.). Berlin: Springer.

15. Dutré, P., Bala, K., & Bekaert, P. (2006). *Advanced global illumination* (2nd ed.). Wellesley: A K Peters (http://www.akpeters.com/). URL https://lirias.kuleuven.be/handle/123456789/134118.

16. Fejes Toth, G., Gritzmann, P., & Wills, J. (1989). Finite sphere packing and sphere covering. *Discrete & Computational Geometry, 4*, 19–40. doi:10.1007/BF02187713.

17. Francis, T. (2009). *Realistic image synthesis using photon mapping* (2nd ed.). London: Taylor & Francis. ISBN 9781568811970. URL http://books.google.com/books?id=41c3kgAACAAJ.

18. Hales, T. C. (2005). A proof of the Kepler conjecture. *Annals of Mathematics, 162*(3), 1065–1185.

19. Herrmann, H. J., Mahmoodi-Baram, R., & Wackenhut, M. (2003). Polydisperse packings. *Brazilian Journal of Physics, 33*, 591–594. URL http://www.icp.uni-stuttgart.de/publications/2003/HMW03.

20. Herrmann, H. J., Mahmoodi-Baram, R., & Wackenhut, M. (2006). Dense packings. *Brazilian Journal of Physics, 36*, 610–613. URL http://www.icp.uni-stuttgart.de/publications/2006/HMW06. Proceedings of conference in Ouro Preto.

21. Hifi, M., & M'Hallah, R. (2009). A literature review on circle and sphere packing problems: models and methodologies. *Advances in Operations Research 2009*. URL http://dblp.uni-trier.de/db/journals/advor/advor2009.html.

22. Jerier, J.-F., Imbault, D., Donze, F.-V., & Doremus, P. (2008). A geometric algorithm based on tetrahedral meshes to generate a dense polydisperse sphere packing. *Granular Matter*. doi:10.1007/s10035-008-0116-0.

23. Jerier, J.-F., Richefeu, V., Imbault, D., & Donze, F.-V. (2010). Packing spherical discrete elements for large scale simulations. *Computer Methods in Applied Mechanics and Engineer-*

ing, 199(25–28), 1668–1676. doi:10.1016/j.cma.2010.01.016. URL http://www.sciencedirect. com/science/article/pii/S0045782510000253.

24. Kansal, A. R., Torquato, S., & Stillinger, F. H. (2002). Computer generation of dense poly-disperse sphere packings. *Journal of Chemical Physics, 117*(18), 8212–8218. doi:10.1063/ 1.1511510.

25. Kim, D.-S., Cho, Y., & Kim, D. (2004). Edge-tracing algorithm for Euclidean Voronoi diagram of 3d spheres. In *CCCG* (pp. 176–179).

26. Kim, Y. J., Lin, M. C., & Manocha, D. (2004). Incremental penetration depth estimation be-tween convex polytopes using dual-space expansion. *IEEE Transactions on Visualization and Computer Graphics, 10*(2), 152–163. URL http://visinfo.zib.de/EVlib/Show?EVL-2004-24.

27. Kubach, T. (2009). *Parallel greedy algorithms for packing unequal spheres into a cuboidal strip or a cuboid* (Technical report). Fernuniversität Hagen. URL http://books. google.com/books?id=kZ9scgAACAAJ.

28. Leppmeier, M. (1997). *Kugelpackungen von Kepler bis heute: eine Einführung für Schüler, Studenten und Lehrer*. Wiesbaden: Vieweg. ISBN 9783528067922. URL http://books. google.com/books?id=oXJNGda4MfoC.

29. Li, S. P., & Ng, K.-L. (2003). Monte Carlo study of the sphere packing problem. *Physic-ica. A, Statistical Mechanics and Its Applications, 321*(1–2), 359–363. URL http://www. sciencedirect.com/science/article/B6TVG-47C3PXH-C/1/0cad62b60853861ec908067b2193 69a0.

30. Lubachevsky, B. D., & Stillinger, F. H. (1990). Geometric properties of random disk packings. *Journal of Statistical Physics, 60*(5), 561–583. doi:10.1007/BF01025983.

31. Mahmoodi-Baram, R., & Herrmann, H. J. (2004). Self-similar space-filling packings in three dimensions. *Fractals, 12*, 293–301. URL http://www.icp.uni-stuttgart.de/publications/2004/ MH04a. cond-mat/0312345.

32. Manak, M., & Kolingerova, I. (2010). Fast discovery of Voronoi vertices in the construction of Voronoi diagram of 3d balls. In *2010 international symposium on Voronoi diagrams in science and engineering (ISVD)*, June (pp. 95–104). doi:10.1109/ISVD.2010.22.

33. Medvedev, N. N., Voloshin, V. P., Luchnikov, V. A., & Gavrilova, M. L. (2006). An algorithm for three-dimensional Voronoi s-network. *Journal of Computational Chemistry, 27*(14), 1676–1692.

34. Miller, G. L., Talmor, D., Teng, S.-H., Walkington, N., & Wang, H. (1996). Control volume meshes using sphere packing: generation, refinement and coarsening. In *Fifth international meshing roundtable* (pp. 47–61).

35. Morris, D. (2006). *Algorithms and data structures for haptic rendering: curve constraints, distance maps, and data logging* (Technical Report 2006-06).

36. O'Brien, J. F., & Hodgins, J. K. (1999). Graphical modeling and animation of brittle fracture. In *Proceedings of the 26th annual conference on computer graphics and interactive tech-niques, SIGGRAPH '99* (pp. 137–146). New York: ACM Press/Addison-Wesley Publishing Co. ISBN 0-201-48560-5. doi:10.1145/311535.311550.

37. Pharr, M., & Humphreys, G. (2004). *Physically based rendering: from theory to implementa-tion*. San Francisco: Morgan Kaufmann Publishers Inc. ISBN 012553180X.

38. Schaertl, W., & Sillescu, H. (1994). Brownian dynamics of polydisperse colloidal hard spheres: equilibrium structures and random close packings. *Journal of Statistical Physics, 77*, 1007–1025. doi:10.1007/BF02183148.

39. Schiftner, A., Höbinger, M., Wallner, J., & Pottmann, H. (2009). Packing circles and spheres on surfaces. *ACM Transactions on Graphics, 28*(5). URL http://www.evolute.at/ images/stories/download/packing_preprint.pdf. Proc. SIGGRAPH Asia.

40. Shamir, A. (2008). A survey on mesh segmentation techniques. *Computer Graphics Forum, 27*(6), 1539–1556.

41. Sheehy, D. J., Armstrong, C. G., & Robinson, D. J. (1995). Computing the medial surface of a solid from a domain Delaunay triangulation. In *Proceedings of the third ACM symposium on solid modeling and applications, SMA '95* (pp. 201–212). New York: ACM. ISBN 0-89791-672-7. doi:10.1145/218013.218062. URL http://doi.acm.org/10.1145/218013.218062.

42. Shimada, K., & Gossard, D. C. (1995). Bubble mesh: automated triangular meshing of non-manifold geometry by sphere packing. In *ACM symposium on solid modeling and applications* (pp. 409–419). New York: ACM.
43. Soddy, F. (1936). The kiss precise. *Nature*, 1021. poem.
44. Sutou, A., & Dai, Y. (2002). Global optimization approach to unequal sphere packing problems in 3d. In *Problems in 3D, Journal of Optimization and Applications*. Communicated by P. M. Pardalos.
45. Szpiro, G. (2003). *Kepler's conjecture: how some of the greatest minds in history helped solve one of the oldest math problems in the world*. New York: Wiley. ISBN 0-471-08601-0. URL http://www.loc.gov/catdir/bios/wiley046/2002014422.html; http://www.loc.gov/catdir/description/wiley039/2002014422.html; http://www.loc.gov/catdir/toc/wiley031/2002014422.html.
46. Wang, J. (1999). Packing of unequal spheres and automated radiosurgical treatment planning. *Journal of Combinatorial Optimization*, *3*, 453–463. doi:10.1023/A:1009831621621.
47. Wang, J. (2000). Medial axis and optimal locations for min-max sphere packing. *Journal of Combinatorial Optimization*, *4*, 487–503. doi:10.1023/A:1009889628489.
48. Weller, R., & Zachmann, G. (2009). Inner sphere trees for proximity and penetration queries. In *2009 robotics: science and systems conference (RSS)*, Seattle, WA, USA, June. URL http://cg.in.tu-clausthal.de/research/ist.
49. Weller, R., & Zachmann, G. (2010). Protosphere: a gpu-assisted prototype-guided sphere packing algorithm for arbitrary objects. In *ACM SIGGRAPH ASIA 2010 sketches*, December (pp. 8:1–8:2). New York: ACM. ISBN 978-1-4503-0523-5. doi:10.1145/1899950.1899958. URL http://cg.in.tu-clausthal.de/research/protosphere.
50. Wu, Q. R. (1996). Treatment planning optimization for gamma unit radiosurgery. In *Biophysical science–biomedical imaging—Mayo graduate school*. URL http://books.google.com/books?id=mNt8NwAACAAJ.
51. Zong, C., & Talbot, J. (1999). *Universitext: Vol. 1979. Sphere packings*. Berlin: Springer. ISBN 9780387987941.

Chapter 5
Inner Sphere Trees

In the previous chapter, we have presented new methods to compute sphere packings for arbitrary objects. In this chapter, we will use these sphere packings to define a new data structure for collision detection between rigid objects.

In Chap. 2 we already have seen that BVHs guarantee very fast responses at query time as long as no other information than the set of colliding polygons is required for the collision response. This is because the modern traversal algorithms converge quickly toward a pair of colliding primitives and the algorithm stops immediately when the first intersecting pair is found.

However, most applications require much more information in order to resolve or avoid the collisions. Unfortunately, typical contact information like distances, translational penetration depth or the time of impact suffer from their complex computations and their discontinuous definitions of the resulting force and torque directions. This even aggravates when haptic frequencies of 250–1000 Hz are required or the scene consists of massive models.

This chapter contributes the following novel ideas to the area of collision detection:

- a novel geometric data structure, the *Inner Sphere Trees* (*IST*), which provides hierarchical bounding volumes from the *inside* of an object;
- we propose to utilize a clustering algorithm to construct a sphere hierarchy;
- a unified algorithm that can compute for a pair of objects, based on their ISTs, both an approximate minimal distance and the approximate penetration volume; the application does not need to know in advance which situation currently exists between the pair of objects;
- a *time-critical* variant of the penetration volume traversal, which runs only for a pre-defined time budget, including a new heuristic to derive good error bounds, the *expected overlap volume*;
- a novel collision response scheme to compute *stable* and *continuous* forces and torques, both in direction and value, based on the penetration volume.

Parts of this work have been previously published in [9, 17–20].

R. Weller, *New Geometric Data Structures for Collision Detection and Haptics*, Springer Series on Touch and Haptic Systems, DOI 10.1007/978-3-319-01020-5_5, © Springer International Publishing Switzerland 2013

Our ISTs and consequently, the collision detection algorithm are independent of the geometry complexity; they only depend on the approximation error.

The main idea is that we do not build an (outer) hierarchy based on the polygons on the boundary of an object. Instead, we fill the interior of the model with a set of non-overlapping simple volumes that approximate the object's volume closely. In our implementation, we used spheres for the sake of simplicity, but the idea of using inner BVs for lower bounds instead of outer BVs for upper bounds can be extended analogously to all kinds of volumes. On top of these inner BVs, we build a hierarchy that allows for fast computation of the approximate proximity and *penetration volume*.

The penetration volume corresponds to the water displacement of the overlapping parts of the objects and, thus, leads to a physically motivated and continuous repulsion force and torques. As already mentioned in the introduction, according to Fisher and Lin [4, Sect. 5.1], it is "the most complicated yet accurate method" to define the extent of intersection, which was also reported earlier by O'Brien and Hodgins [11, Sect. 3.3]. However, to our knowledge, there are no algorithms to compute it efficiently as yet.

However, our inner sphere tree not only allows to compute both separation distance and penetration volume, but it also lends itself very well to time-critical variants, which run only for a pre-defined time budget. Moreover, our ISTs can also easily extended to support the time of impact computations that are needed for continuous collision detection. In this, they avoid the time-consuming continuous triangle intersection tests.

Our data structure can support all kinds of object representations, e.g. polygon meshes or NURBS surfaces. The only precondition is that they be watertight. In order to build the hierarchy on the inner spheres, we utilize a recently proposed clustering algorithm that allows us to work in an adaptive manner. Moreover, we present a parallel version of that clustering algorithm that runs completely on modern GPUs.

In order to evaluate the accuracy of our approximative ISTs, we additionally have developed an algorithm that is able to compute an accurate value of the penetration volume. This algorithm is based on tetrahedral decomposition of polygonal objects. Unfortunately, even in combination with acceleration data structures this algorithm cannot operate in real-time. However, this approach can be useful for users that require exact information.

In contrast, the results show that our ISTs can answer both kinds of queries, distance, and penetration volume queries at haptic rates with a negligible loss of accuracy.

5.1 Sphere Packings

Our ISTs rely on dense sphere packings of objects. These sphere packings can be computed by each algorithms that we have presented in Chap. 4. Some optimization

Fig. 5.1 In a wrapped
hierarchy, the parent sphere
covers all its leaf nodes, but
not its direct children

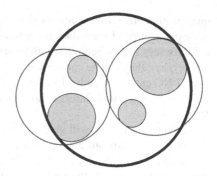

that we will describe in the following section require to store additionally one or
more triangles that are closest to a sphere. However, this information can be derived
easily during the computation of the sphere packing by both algorithms. Basically,
our ISTs are independent of the object's complexity, e.g. the triangle count. Their
running-time depends only on the number of spheres in the sphere packing.

In the following, we will describe how to build an IST from a sphere packing.

5.2 Hierarchy Creation

Based on the sphere packing, we create an *inner* bounding volume hierarchy. To do
so, we use a top-down *wrapped hierarchy* approach according to the notion of Agarwal et al. [1], where inner nodes are tight BVs for all their leaves, but they do not
necessarily bound their direct children (see Fig. 5.1). Compared to layered hierarchies, the big advantage is that the inner BVs are tighter. We use a top-down approach to create our hierarchy, i.e., we start at the root node that covers all inner
spheres and divide these into several subsets.

The partitioning of the inner spheres has significant influence on the performance
during runtime. Previous methods that have been developed for ordinary BVHs, like
the surface area heuristic (see Sect. 2.2) produce optimal hierarchies for surface representations of the objects, but they do not take the objects' volume into account.
Algorithms for building the classical *outer* sphere trees, like the medial-axis approach [2, 7] work well if the spheres constitute a *covering* of the object and have
similar size, but in our scenario we use disjoint inner spheres that exhibit a large
variation in size. Other approaches based on the *k-center problem* work only for
sets of points and do not support spheres.

5.2.1 Batch Neural Gas Hierarchy Clustering

So we decided to use the *batch neural gas* clustering algorithm (BNG) known from
machine learning [3]. BNG is a very robust clustering algorithm which can be formulated as stochastic gradient descent with a cost function closely connected to

quantization error. Like *k-means*, the cost function minimizes the mean squared Euclidean distance of each data point to its nearest center. But unlike k-means, BNG exhibits very robust behavior with respect to the initial cluster center positions (the *prototypes*): they can be chosen arbitrarily without affecting the convergence. Moreover, BNG can be extended to allow the specification of the *importance* of each data point; below, we will describe how this can be used to increase the quality of the ISTs.

In the following we will give a quick recap of the basic batch neural gas and then describe our extensions and application to building the inner sphere tree.

Given points $x_j \in \mathbb{R}^d$, $j = 0, \ldots, m$ and prototypes $w_i \in \mathbb{R}^d$, $i = 0, \ldots, n$ initialized randomly, we set the rank for every prototype w_i with respect to every data point x_j as

$$k_{ij} := \left| \left\{ w_k : d(x_j, w_k) < d(x_j, w_i) \right\} \right| \in \{0, \ldots, n\} \tag{5.1}$$

In other words, we sort the prototypes with respect to every data point. After the computation of the ranks, we compute the new positions for the prototypes:

$$w_i := \frac{\sum_{j=0}^{m} h_\lambda(k_{ij}) x_j}{\sum_{j=0}^{m} h_\lambda(k_{ij})} \tag{5.2}$$

These two steps are repeated until a stop criterion is met. In the original publication by Cottrell et al. [3], a fixed number of iterations is proposed. Indeed, after a certain number of iteration steps, which depends on the number of data points, there is no further improvement. We propose to use an adaptive version and stop the iteration if the movement of the prototypes is smaller than some ε. In our examples, we chose $\varepsilon \approx 10^{-5} \times \text{BoundingBoxSize}$, without any differences in the hierarchy compared to the non-adaptive, exhaustive approach. This improvement speeds up the creation of the hierarchy significantly.

The convergence rate is controlled by a monotonically decreasing function $h_\lambda(k) > 0$ that decreases with the number of iterations t. We use the function proposed in the original publication [3]: $h_\lambda(k) = e^{-\frac{k}{\lambda}}$ with initial value $\lambda_0 = \frac{n}{2}$, and reduction $\lambda(t) = \lambda_0 \left(\frac{0.01}{\lambda_0} \right)^{\frac{t}{t_{\max}}}$, where $t_{\max}$ is the maximum number of iterations. These values have been taken according to Martinetz et al. [10].

Obviously, the number of prototypes defines the arity of the tree. If it is too big, the resulting trees are very inefficient. On the other hand, if it is too small, the trees become very deep and there exist a lot of levels with big spheres that do not approximate the object very well. Experiments with our data structure have shown that a branching factor of 4 produces the best results. Additionally, this has the benefit that we can use the full capacity of SIMD units in modern CPUs during the traversal.

5.2.1.1 Magnification Control

So far, the BNG only utilizes the location of the centers of the spheres. In our experience this already produces much better results than other, simpler heuristics, such as greedily choosing the biggest spheres or the spheres with the largest number of neighbors. However, it does not yet take the extent of the spheres into account. This is, because neural gas uses only the number of data points and not their importance. As a consequence, the prototypes tend to avoid regions that are covered with a very large sphere, i.e., centers of big spheres are treated as outliers and they are thus placed on very deep levels in the hierarchy. However, it is better to place big spheres at higher levels of the hierarchy in order to get early lower bounds during distance traversal (see Sect. 5.3.1 for details).

Therefore, we use an extended version of the classical batch neural gas, which also takes the size of the spheres into account. Our extension is based on an idea of Hammer et al. [6], where *magnification control* is introduced. The idea is to add weighting factors in order to "artificially" increase the density of the space in some areas.

With weighting factors $v(x_j)$, Eq. (5.2) becomes

$$w_i := \frac{\sum_{j=0}^{m} h_\lambda(k_{ij})v(x_j)x_j}{\sum_{j=0}^{m} h_\lambda(k_{ij})v(x_j)} \tag{5.3}$$

where $v(x_j)$ identifies a control parameter to take care of the importance. In Hammer et al. [6], a function of density is used to control the magnification. In our scenario we already know the density, because our spheres are disjoint. Thus, we can directly use the volumes of our spheres to let $v(x_j) = \frac{4}{3}\pi r^3$.

Summing up the hierarchy creation algorithm: we first compute a bounding sphere for all inner spheres (at the leaves), which becomes the root node of the hierarchy. Therefore, we use the fast and stable smallest enclosing sphere algorithm proposed in Gärtner [5]. Then, we divide the set of inner spheres into subsets in order to create the children. To do that, we apply the extended version of batch neural gas with magnification control mentioned above. We repeat this scheme recursively (see Fig. 5.2 for some clustering results).

In the following, we will call the spheres in the hierarchy that are not leaves *hierarchy spheres*. Spheres at the leaves, which were computed by any of the sphere-packing algorithms from the previous chapter, will be called *inner spheres*. Note that hierarchy spheres are not necessarily contained completely within the object.

5.2.1.2 Parallel Hierarchical Batch Neural Gas

The BNG algorithm produces a very good partitioning of the inner spheres, but as a drawback, it is very time-consuming. Actually, we have to execute $O(n)$ BNG calls—one for each hierarchy sphere—where n denotes the number of inner spheres. In case of a balanced tree with height $O(\log n)$ we have an overall running-time of $O(n \log n)$, but with a relatively high hidden constant factor that results from the number of iteration steps.

However, BNG in its pure form, but also the hierarchical BNG calls of our BVH creation, are perfectly suited for parallelization. Assuming that we have $O(n)$ processors we are able to reduce the asymptotic running-time to $O(\log^2 n)$. In the fol-

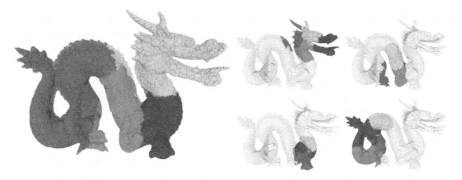

Fig. 5.2 This figure shows the results of our hierarchy building algorithm based on batch neural gas clustering with magnification control. All of those inner spheres that share the same color are assigned to the same bounding sphere. The *left image* shows the clustering result of the root sphere, the *right images* the partitioning of its four children

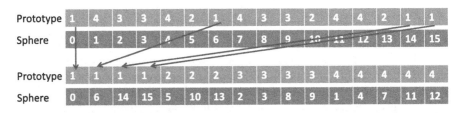

Fig. 5.3 The *top array* stores the indices of the prototype to which the sphere in the array below has been assigned after the initial BNG clustering. In a first step, we sort the spheres with respect to their prototype index (the *two lower arrays*). Note that each sphere is assigned to exactly one prototype

lowing we will sketch the details of this parallel hierarchical BNG implementation using the GPU.

Obviously, on the first level of our hierarchy, the ordering k_{ij} and consequently also $h_\lambda(k_{ij})v(x_j)x_j$ can be computed independently for each sphere x_j. Summing up all those values can be implemented in parallel too, by using a parallel scan algorithm [14]. Also the parallel assignment of spheres to prototypes is straightforward: we simply have to compute the distances of each sphere to the prototypes. Please note that each sphere is assigned to exactly one prototype.

In the next level of the BVH creation, we have to add four new prototypes for each prototype from the previous level (in case of a branching factor of 4). However, triggering an own parallel process for each sub-set of spheres would shoot down the advantages of parallel computing, especially in the deeper hierarchy levels. Therefore, we decided to choose in another way. In the following we will describe its technical details.

First, we sort the spheres with respect to the prototype that the spheres were assigned to (see Fig. 5.3). This can be done in parallel by using a parallel sorting algorithm [12]. This technical detail will allow us later to use fast parallel prefix-sum

	$w_{1,1}...w_{4,4}$			$w_{2,1}...w_{2,4}$			$w_{3,1}...w_{3,3}$				$w_{4,1}...w_{4,1}$				
$h_\lambda(k_{1,j})v(x_j)$	1.3	5.2	8.1	4.2	3.0	9.5	3.6	1.0	1.7	3.4	2.3	2.8	4.8	3.6	2.4	1.3
$h_\lambda(k_{2,j})v(x_j)$	3.1	6.9	1.5	1.4	8.3	6.3	1.2	6.7	4.8	4.3	2.4	7.5	2.2	0.1	3.3	5.1
$h_\lambda(k_{3,j})v(x_j)$	3.1	7.5	3.8	4.9	8.4	3.9	4.4	5.7	9.4	1.3	3.4	4.2	7.3	4.6	4.8	2.2
$h_\lambda(k_{4,j})v(x_j)$	2.1	6.4	9.7	7.4	0.3	8.2	9.2	8.6	7.5	2.9	4.5	0.2	2.3	8.7	6.1	1.7
Prev. Prototype	1	1	1	1	2	2	2	3	3	3	3	4	4	4	4	4
Sphere	0	6	14	15	5	10	13	2	3	8	9	1	4	7	11	12

Fig. 5.4 An example for the second level of the hierarchical BNG. According to Fig. 5.3, each sphere has been assigned to a prototype. We insert 16 new prototypes, $w_{1,1}, \ldots, w_{4,4}$, four for each prototype $w_1, \ldots, w_4$ from the previous level and compute the values that are required by BNG, e.g. $h_\lambda(k_{ij})v(x_j)$. Please note that we do not have to allocate new memory or copy any values from CPU to GPU. We can simply re-use the memory from the previous level because each sphere was assigned to exactly one prototype. Consequently, we get a constant memory consumption for each level

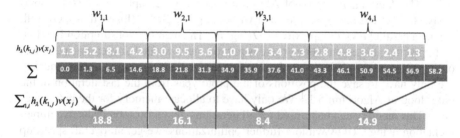

Fig. 5.5 In order to compute the new position of the prototypes for the next iteration, we have to determine $\sum h_\lambda(k_{ij})v(x_j)x_j$. Therefore, we compute the prefix sum (*brown array*) for each of the four prototype arrays from Fig. 5.4. The differences between the values at the boarders directly deliver us the individual sum for each prototype

computations. However, after the sorting we virtually insert four new prototypes for each prototype from the previous hierarchy level. The fact that each sphere has been assigned to exactly one prototype in the previous level allows us to compute the values that are required for BNG (e.g. k_{ij}) in parallel for each sphere. We simply have to ensure that these values are computed for the *right new* prototypes (see Fig. 5.4).

Finally, we have to sum up the individual values to get the new prototype positions; this means we have to compute $\sum_{j=0}^{m} h_\lambda(k_{ij})v(x_j)x_j$ and $\sum_{j=0}^{m} h_\lambda(k_{ij})v(x_j)$. Surprisingly, we can directly re-use the parallel prefix sum from above [14], even if we now need the sums for each new prototype individually: we simply have to subtract the values at the borders of our sorted prototype array (see Fig. 5.5).

Algorithm 5.1 summarized our complete parallel hierarchical BNG implementation.

Algorithm 5.1 Parallel hierarchical BNG

---

while *Not on inner sphere level* **do**
    iteration = 0
    while *iteration<maxNumberIterations* **do**
        iteration++
    In parallel Sort prototype array
    In parallelforall *Spheres* **do**
        compute $h_\lambda(k_{ij})v(x_j)x_j$
        and $h_\lambda(k_{ij})v(x_j)$
    In parallel Compute prefix sum
    In parallelforall *Prototypes in level* **do**
        Compute new position
    read back prototype positions

The prefix sum and the sorting of the prototypes for n inner spheres can be computed in parallel using $O(n)$ processors in $O(\log n)$. Basically, both algorithms are based on an implicit balanced binary tree structure (see [12] and [14] for more details). The "per sphere" steps of Algorithm 5.1 have a complexity of $O(1)$, obviously. If the tree is balanced, the outer while-loop is called $O(\log n)$ times. Overall, we get a parallel time complexity of $O(\log^2 n)$. The memory consumption is $O(n)$.

In practice it is essential that there is not too much traffic between the memories of the CPU and the GPU. In our implementation there is almost no traffic required. We only have to save the positions of the prototypes from the last iteration in the outer loop of Algorithm 5.1.[1] We only have to allocate memory for the prototypes once. This memory can be re-used for all iterations. In our prototypical naive implementation using CUDA without further optimizations, we get an overall speed-up by a factor of 10 compared to the sequential hierarchy computation.

5.3 Traversal Algorithms

Our new data structure supports almost all different kinds of collision queries. Namely *proximity queries*, which report the separation distance between a pair of objects, *penetration volume queries*, which report the common volume covered by both objects and moreover, it also supports *continuous collision detection queries*, which report the time of impact if two objects collide. Obviously, the traversal can easily be modified in order to provide also boolean answers that simply report whether the objects collide or not.

As a by-product, the proximity query can return a witness realizing the distance, the penetration volume algorithm can return a partial list of intersecting polygons

---

[1] However, also this is not really necessary. In the future, we plan to move also the smallest enclosing sphere computation to the GPU. Then we only have to read back the whole hierarchy once.

Algorithm 5.2 checkDistance(A, B, minDist)

---

input : A, B = spheres in the inner sphere tree
in/out: minDist = overall minimum distance seen so far
if A *and* B *are leaves* **then**
    // end of recursion
    minDist = min{distance(A, B), minDist}
else
    // recursion step
    forall *children* a[i] *of* A **do**
        forall *children* b[j] *of* B **do**
            if distance(a[i], b[j]) < minDist **then**
                checkDistance(a[i], b[j], minDist)

---

and the continuous collision detection query can return the first pair of colliding spheres.

We start with a separate discussion of the distance and penetration volume queries in order to point out their specific requirements. In Sect. 5.3.3 we describe how to combine these traversal schemes to a unified algorithm that is able to provide distance and penetration volume information, without the user has to know in advance, whether the objects overlap or not. Furthermore, we will describe a time-critical extension of both algorithms that allows an approximation of the appropriate contact information, distance, and penetration volume, respectively, if a pre-defined time budget should not be exceeded.

Finally, we will describe an algorithm that uses our new data structure to compute the time of impact. Actually, the main focus during the design of our ISTs was the computation of a continuous penetration measure, the penetration volume, at haptic rates. But it turns out that the ISTs also has some nice implications on continuous collision detection.

5.3.1 Distances

Our proximity query algorithm works like most other classical BVH traversal algorithms: we check whether two bounding volumes overlap or not. If this is the case, we recursively step to their children. In order to compute lower bounds for the distance, we simply have to add an appropriate distance test at the right place. This has to be done, when we reach a pair of inner spheres (i.e. the leaves of the ISTs) during traversal (see Algorithm 5.2). According to Chap. 4, these inner spheres are located completely inside the object and, thus, provide a lower bound on the sought-after distance. During traversal there is no need to visit branches of the bounding volume test tree that are farther apart than the current minimum distance because of the bounding property. This guarantees a high culling efficiency.

5.3.1.1 Improvements

In most collision detection scenarios there is a high spatial and temporal coherence, especially when rendering at haptic rates. Thus, in most cases those spheres realizing the minimum distance in a frame are also the closest spheres in the next frames, or they are at least in the neighborhood. Therefore, using the distance from the last frame yields a good initial bound for pruning during traversal. Thus, in our implementation we store pointers to the closest spheres as of the last frame and use their current distance to initialize minDist in Algorithm 5.2.

If the application is only interested in the distance between a pair of objects, then, of course, a further speed-up can be gained by abandoning the traversal once the first pair of intersecting inner spheres is found (in this case the objects must overlap and the distance is zero).

Moreover, our traversal algorithm is very well suited for parallelization. During recursion we compute the distances between four pairs of spheres in one single SIMD implementation, which is greatly facilitated by our hierarchy being a 4-ary tree.

Obviously, Algorithm 5.2 returns only an approximate minimum distance, because it utilizes only the distances of the inner spheres for the proximity query. Thus, the accuracy depends on their density.

Fortunately, it is very easy to alleviate these inaccuracies by simply assigning the closest triangle (or a set of triangles) to each inner sphere. After determining the closest spheres with Algorithm 5.2, we add a subsequent test that calculates the exact distance between the triangles assigned to those spheres. This simple heuristic reduces the error significantly even with relatively sparsely filled objects, and it hardly affects the running time.

5.3.2 Penetration Volume

In addition to proximity queries, our data structure also supports a new kind of penetration query, namely the *penetration volume*. This is the volume of the intersection of the two objects, which can be interpreted directly as the amount of the repulsion force if it is considered as the amount of water being displaced.

The algorithm that computes the penetration volume (see Algorithm 5.3) does not differ very much from the proximity query test: we simply have to replace the distance test by an overlap test and maintain an accumulated overlap volume during the traversal. The overlap volume of a pair of spheres can be easily derived by adding the volumes of the spherical caps.

Due to the non-overlapping constraint of the inner spheres, the accumulated overlap volumes provide a lower bound on the real overlap volume of the objects.

Algorithm 5.3 computeVolume(A, B, totalOverlap)

input : A, B = spheres in the inner sphere tree
in/out: totalOverlap = overall volume of intersection
if A *and* B *are leaves* **then**
    // end of recursion
    totalOverlap + = overlapVolume(A, B)
else
    // recursion step
    forall *children* a[i] *of* A **do**
        forall *children* b[j] *of* B **do**
            if overlap(a[i], b[j]) > 0 **then**
                computeVolume(a[i], b[j], totalOverlap)

Fig. 5.6 Penetration volume of two spheres with radius r_1 and r_2, respectively

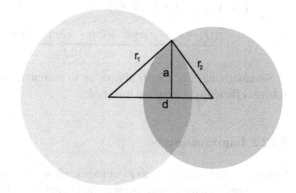

5.3.2.1 Intersection Volume of Spheres

The main challenge during the traversal is the computation of the penetration volume between a pair of spheres. According to Weisstein [15], this can be expressed in a closed formula. Basically, the intersection volume of two intersecting spheres is a lens built of two spherical caps. Without loss of generality we assume that one sphere is centered at the origin and the second sphere is displaced by a distance d on the x-axis (see Fig. 5.6 for the setting). The equations of the spheres can be expressed as

$$x^2 + y^2 + z^2 = r_1^2 \tag{5.4}$$

$$\text{and} \quad (x - d)^2 + y^2 + z^2 = r_2^2, \quad \text{respectively} \tag{5.5}$$

Consequently, the intersection is

$$(x - d)^2 - x^2 = r_2^2 - r_1^2 \tag{5.6}$$

In order to compute the intersection volume, we can simply add the volumes of the two spherical caps with distances $d_1 = x$ for the first sphere and $d_2 = x - d$ for the second sphere. The heights of the spherical caps are

$$h_1 = r_1 - d_1 = \frac{(r_2 - r_1 + d)(r_2 + r_1 - d)}{2d} \tag{5.7}$$

$$\text{and} \quad h_2 = r_2 - d_2 = \frac{(r_1 - r_2 + d)(r_1 + r_2 - d)}{2d} \tag{5.8}$$

In common, the volume of a spherical cap of height h for a sphere with radius r can be expressed by (see e.g. Weisstein [16] for more details):

$$V(R, h) = \frac{1}{3}\pi h^2(3r - h) \tag{5.9}$$

Consequently, we get for the total intersection volume V for two spheres:

$$\begin{aligned}
V &= V(r_1, h_1) + V(r_2, h_2) \\
&= \frac{\pi(r_1 + r_2 - d)^2(d^2 + 2dr_2 - 3r_2^2 + 2dr_1 + 6r_1r_2 - 3r_1^2)}{12d}
\end{aligned} \tag{5.10}$$

Summarizing, Eq. (5.10) allows us to compute the overlap between a pair of spheres efficiently during the traversal.

5.3.2.2 Improvements

Similar to the proximity query implementation, we can utilize SIMD parallelization to speed up both the simple overlap check and the volume accumulation.

Furthermore, we can exploit the observation that a recursion can be terminated if a hierarchy sphere (i.e. an inner node of the sphere hierarchy) is completely contained inside an inner sphere (a leaf) of the other IST. In this case, we can simply add the total volume of all of its leaves to the accumulated penetration volume. In order to do this quickly, we store the total volume

$$\text{Vol}_l(S) = \sum_{S_j \in \text{Leaves}(S)} \text{Vol}(S_j), \tag{5.11}$$

where S_j are all inner spheres below S in the BVH.

This can be done in a preprocessing step during hierarchy creation.

5.3.2.3 Filling the Gaps

The voxel-based sphere packing algorithm described in Sect. 4.2 results in densely filled objects. However, there still remain small voids between the spheres that cannot be completely compensated by increasing the number of voxels. This results in bad lower bounds.

Fig. 5.7 After constructing the sphere packing with the voxel-based method (see Sect. 4.2), each voxel can be intersected by several non-overlapping spheres (*left*). These do not necessarily account for the whole voxel space. In order to account for these voids, too, we simply increase the radius of the sphere that covers the center of the voxel (*right*)

As a remedy, we propose a simple heuristic to compensate this problem: we additionally assign a *secondary radius* to every inner sphere, such that the volume of the secondary sphere is equal to the volume of all voxels whose centers are contained within the radius of the primary sphere (see Fig. 5.7). This guarantees that the total volume of all secondary spheres equals the volume of the object, within the accuracy of the voxelization, because each voxel volume is accounted for exactly once.

Certainly, these secondary spheres may slightly overlap, but this simple heuristic leads to acceptable estimations of the penetration volume. (Note, however, that the secondary spheres are not necessarily larger than the primary spheres.)

For our second sphere packing method, the Protosphere algorithm (see Sect. 4.3), there is, until now, no method known to determine the size of the voids between the spheres.

5.3.3 Unified Algorithm for Distance and Volume Queries

In the previous sections, we introduced the proximity and the penetration volume computation separately. However, it is quite easy to combine both algorithms. This yields a unified algorithm that can compute both the distance and the penetration volume, without the user having to know in advance whether the objects overlap or not.

We start with the distance traversal. If we find the first pair of intersecting inner spheres, then we simply switch to the penetration volume computation.

The correctness is based on the fact that all pairs of inner spheres we visited so far during distance traversal do not overlap and thus do not extend the penetration volume. Thus, we do not have to visit them again and can continue with the traversal of the rest of the hierarchies using the penetration volume algorithm. If we do not meet an intersecting pair of inner spheres, the unified algorithm still reports the minimal separating distance.

5.3.4 Time-Critical Distance and Volume Queries

To yield a time-critical version of the distance query is very easy. We can simply interrupt the traversal at any time and return the minimum distance computed so far. For the initialization we can compute the distance between any pair of inner spheres or simply use the closest pair from the last traversal (see Sect. 5.3.1.1). However, the distance traversal only computes a lower bound of the distance. Using an additional classical *outer* BVH would achieve also an *upper* bound.

Yielding an interruptible version for the penetration volume traversal is more complicated but also more needful. In most cases, a penetration volume query has to visit many more nodes than the average proximity query. Consequently, the running time on average is slower, especially in cases with heavy overlaps.

In the following we will describe a variation of our algorithm for penetration volume queries that guarantees to meet a pre-defined time budget. This is essential for time-critical applications such as haptic rendering.

A suitable strategy to realize time-critical traversals is to guide the traversal by a priority queue Q. Then, given a pair of hierarchy spheres S and R, a simple heuristic is to use $\text{Vol}(S \cap R)$ for the priority in Q. In our experience, this would yield acceptable upper bounds.

Unfortunately, this simple heuristic also may result in very bad lower bounds in cases where only a relatively small number of inner spheres can be visited (unless the time budget permits an almost complete traversal of all overlapping pairs).

A simple heuristic to derive an estimate of the lower bound could be to compute

$$\sum_{\substack{(R,S)\in Q}} \sum_{\substack{R_i\in\text{ch}(R),\\ S_j\in\text{ch}(S)}} \text{Vol}(R_i \cap S_j), \tag{5.12}$$

where $\text{ch}(S)$ is the set of all direct children of node S.

Equation (5.12) amounts to the sum of the intersection of all direct child pairs of all pairs in the priority queue Q. Unfortunately, the direct children of a node are usually not disjoint and, thus, this estimate of the lower bound could actually be larger than the upper bound.

In order to avoid this problem we introduce the notion of *expected overlap volume*. This allows us to estimate the overlap volume more accurately.

The only assumption we make is that, for any point inside S, the distribution of the probability that it is also inside one of its leaves is uniform.

Let (R, S) be a pair of spheres in the priority queue. We define the *density* of a sphere as

$$p(S) = \frac{\text{Vol}_l(S)}{\text{Vol}(S)} \tag{5.13}$$

with $\text{vol}_l(S)$ defined similarly to Eq. (5.11) as the accumulated volume of all inner spheres below S.

Fig. 5.8 We estimate the real penetration volume during our time-critical traversal by the "density" in the hierarchy spheres and the total volume of the leaf spheres

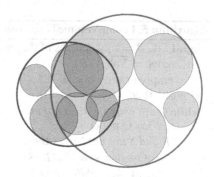

This is the probability that a point inside S is also inside one of its leaves (which are disjoint). Next, we define the *expected overlap volume*, $\overline{\mathrm{Vol}}(R, S)$ as the probability that a point is inside $R \cap S$ and also inside the intersection of one of the possible pairs of leaves, i.e.

$$\overline{\mathrm{Vol}}(R, S) = p(S) \cdot p(R) \cdot \mathrm{Vol}(R \cap S)$$
$$= \frac{\mathrm{Vol}_l(R) \cdot \mathrm{Vol}_l(S) \cdot \mathrm{Vol}(R \cap S)}{\mathrm{Vol}(R) \cdot \mathrm{Vol}(S)} \tag{5.14}$$

(see Fig. 5.8).

In summary, for the whole queue we get the expected overlap volume

$$\sum_{(R,S) \in Q} \overline{\mathrm{Vol}}(R, S) \tag{5.15}$$

Clearly, this volume can be maintained during traversal quite easily.

More importantly, this method provides a much better heuristic for sorting the priority queue: if the difference between the expected overlap $\overline{\mathrm{Vol}}(R, S)$ and the overlap $\mathrm{Vol}(R \cap S)$ is large, then it is most likely that the traversal of this pair will give the most benefit toward improving the bound; consequently, we insert this pair closer to the front of the queue.

Algorithm 5.4 shows the pseudo code of this approach. (Note that $p(S) = 1$ if S is a leaf and therefore $\overline{\mathrm{Vol}}(R, S)$ returns the exact intersection volume at the leaves.)

We initialize the priority queue with the root spheres of the objects. The overlap of the root spheres is trivially an upper bound for the total overlap. Then we pop the element with biggest overlap, subtract the overlap volume from the upper bound computed so far and insert the child pairs instead. A lower bound is simply derived by exclusively summing up the overlap volumes of inner spheres.

Obviously, it is possible to stop the traversal if an user specified accuracy between lower and upper bound is reached, or if the time for this query is exceeded. This maximum running time can be derived in advance, because the computation for a single pair of spheres takes a fixed amount of time.

Overall, we have derived a time-critical algorithm that can traverse a given IST such that the lower bound and the upper bound of the penetration volume approach each other fairly quickly.

Algorithm 5.4 compVolumeTimeCritical(A, B)

---

input : A, B = root spheres of the two ISTs
estOverlap = $\overline{\text{Vol}}(A, B)$
Q = empty priority queue
Q.push(A, B)
while *Q not empty & time not exceeded* **do**
    (R, S) = Q.pop()
    if *R and S are not leaves* **then**
        estOverlap $-$ = $\overline{\text{Vol}}(R, S)$
        forall $R_i \in$ *children of R*, $S_j \in$ *children of S* **do**
            estOverlap $+$ = $\overline{\text{Vol}}(R_i, S_j)$
            Q.push(R_i, S_j)

5.3.5 Continuous Collision Detection

The main focus for the design of the ISTs was the approximation of the penetration volume. However, they can be easily extended for continuous collision detection. There, the ISTs even offer some interesting advantages compared to traditional polygon-based continuous collision detection algorithms.

When BVHs are applied for the acceleration of continuous collision detection queries, often swept volumes are used. Swept volumes are bounding volumes that bound the original object's bounding volumes at the beginning and the end of each query time. The bounding volume property guarantees that there is no intersection of the objects in this time if the BVs do not overlap. We applied this swept-volume method to our ISTs.

We assume a linear motion between the start and the end configuration. Sweeping spheres over time linearly creates a capped cylinder as swept volume (see Fig. 5.9). An intersection test for two capped cylinders is relatively simple. Basically, we have to check if the distance between the line segments (P_t, P_{t+1}) and (Q_t, Q_{t+1}) is smaller than the sum of the radii r_p and r_q (notation according to Fig. 5.9). Therefore, we first compute the minimum distance between the lines that where spanned by the line segments [13]. The line equations are defined as

$$L_p(r) = P_t + r(P_{t+1} - P_t) = P_t + rm_p$$
$$L_q(s) = Q_t + s(Q_{t+1} - Q_t) = Q_t + sm_q \tag{5.16}$$

The squared distance between any two points on the lines is

$$D(r, s) = \left| L_p(r) - L_q(s) \right|^2 \tag{5.17}$$

For the sake of clarity we use the following shortcuts:

$$a := m_p m_p \qquad\qquad b := m_p m_q \qquad\qquad c := m_q m_q$$

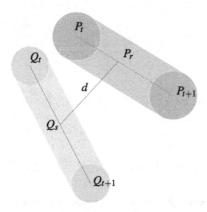

Fig. 5.9 The centers of the spheres move from position P_t to P_{t+1}, and Q_t to Q_{t+1}, respectively, in a time step of the simulation. Spheres in deeper hierarchy levels can only collide if the capped cylinders that are spanned by the moving spheres overlap. The intersection between the capped cylinders can be easily determined by computing the minimum distance d between the line segments (P_t, P_{t+1}) and (Q_t, Q_{t+1}) that is realized by the points P_r and Q_s

$$d := m_p(P_t - Q_t) \qquad d := -m_q(P_t - Q_t) \qquad f := (P_t - Q_t)(P_t - Q_t)$$

and we get

$$D(r, s) = f + ar^2 + 2brs + cs^2 + 2dr + 2es \qquad (5.18)$$

$L_p(r)$ and $L_q(s)$ are continuously differentiable. Consequently, also $D(r, s)$ is continuously differentiable, and we get the minimum by computing the partial derivations and solving for zero. Finally, we get the minimum distance by

$$r_{\min} = \frac{bd - ae}{ac - b^2} \quad \text{and} \quad s_{\min} = \frac{be - cd}{ac - b^2} \qquad (5.19)$$

Additionally, in order to get the minimum distance between the line segments, we have to clamp $r_{\min}$ and $s_{\min}$ to the end of the line segments—this means to the interval $r_{\min}, s_{\min} \in [0, 1]$—and we have to catch the special case of parallel lines, i.e. $ac - b^2 = 0$.

Actually, we are not really interested in an intersection test of two capped cylinders but in the movement of two spheres along the line segments. This allows a further simplification, because we have the additional constraint that $r = s$. Applying this to Eq. (5.18) gives

$$D(r) = f + ar^2 + 2br^2 + cr^2 + 2dr + 2er \qquad (5.20)$$

and we get

$$r_{\min} = \frac{-e - d}{a + 2c + c} \qquad (5.21)$$

for the points that realize the minimum distance.

Fig. 5.10 Determining the
point of impact for a pair of
spheres

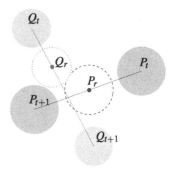

For the *inner spheres* we also have to compute the exact time of impact. There-fore, we have to extend Eq. (5.17). Two spheres collide at a point in time r_{toi} if the distance between the spheres equals the sum of their radii (see Fig. 5.10):

$$(r_p + r_r)^2 = |L_p(r) - L_q(s)|^2 = ((P_t - Q_t) + r_{toi}(m_p - m_q))^2$$
$$r^2 = (\Delta P + r\Delta m)^2$$
(5.22)

Solving for r_{toi} yields

$$r_{toi} = \pm\sqrt{\frac{r^2 - \Delta P^2}{\Delta m^2} + \left(\frac{\Delta P \cdot \Delta m}{\Delta m^2}\right)^2} - \frac{\Delta P \cdot \Delta m}{\Delta m^2}$$
(5.23)

In other words, determining the time of impact for a pair of spheres requires only a quadratic equation to be solved. If you remember the continuous triangle intersection test in Sect. 3.3.4.1: we had to solve 12 costly cubic equations, three vertex/face and nine edge/edge tests. This is the reason for the special suitability of our ISTs for continuous collision detection.

In Algorithm 5.5 we sketch the complete continuous collision traversal for our ISTs. The algorithm is almost the same as for the volume and distance queries, we simply have to replace the distance and volume tests by the continuous sphere tests described above. Obviously, also this algorithm can be optimized using SIMD acceleration.

5.4 Continuous Volumetric Collision Response

In this section, we describe how to use the penetration volume to compute con-tinuous forces and torques in order to enable a sTable 6 DOF haptic rendering or physics-based rigid body simulation. Mainly, there exist three different approaches to resolve collisions: the penalty-based method, the constraint-based method and the impulse-based method. The constraint-based approach computes constraint forces that are designed to cancel any external acceleration that would result in interpene-trations. Unfortunately, this method has at least quadratic complexity in the number

---

Algorithm 5.5 computeTimeOfImpact(A, B, timeOfImpact)

---

input : A, B = spheres in the inner sphere tree
in/out: timeOfImpact = minimum time of impact seen so far
if A *and* B *are leaves* **then**
    // end of recursion
    timeOfImpact = min{timeOfImpact(A, B), timeOfImpact}
else
    // recursion step
    forall *children* a[i] *of* A **do**
        forall *children* b[j] *of* B **do**
            if distance(a[i](t), a[i](t + 1), b[j](t), b[j](t + 1)) < a[i](r) + b[j](r)
            then
                computeTimeOfImpact(a[i], b[j], timeOfImpact)

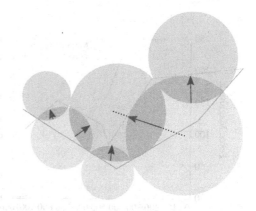

Fig. 5.11 The direction of the penalty force can be derived from the weighted average of all vectors between the centers of colliding pairs of spheres, weighted by their overlap

of contact points. The impulse-based method resolves contacts between objects by a series of impulses in order to prevent interpenetrations. It is applicable to real-time simulations but the forces may not be valid for bodies in resting contact.

So we decided to use the penalty-based method, which computes penalty forces based on the interpenetration of a pair of objects. The main advantages are its computational simplicity, which makes it applicable for haptic rendering and its ability to simulate a variety of surface characteristics. Moreover, the use of the penetration volume eliminates inconsistent states that may occur when only the penetration depth (i.e. the minimum translational vector) is used.

Obviously, the amount of overlap can be directly used to define the *amount* of repelling forces. However, in order to apply such penalty forces in haptic environments or physics-based simulations, also the *direction* of the force is required in addition to its amount.

A simple heuristic would be to consider all overlapping pairs of spheres (R_i, S_j) separately. Let c_i, c_j be their sphere centers and $n_{ij} = c_i - c_j$. Then we compute the overall direction of the penalty force as the weighted sum $n = \sum_{i,j} \text{Vol}(R_i \cap S_j) \cdot n_{ij}$

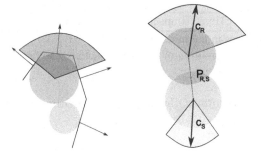

Fig. 5.12 *Left*: we compute a normal cone for each inner sphere. The cone bounds a list of triangles that is associated with the sphere. Note that the spread angle of the normal cone can be 0 if the sphere is closest to a single triangle. *Right*: the axis of the normal cones c_R and c_S are used for the force direction. The center $P_{R,S}$ of the spherical cap defines the contact point

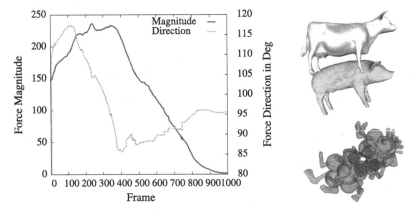

Fig. 5.13 *Left*: force magnitude and direction of the force vector during the cow/pig animation. Right: the test scenes. A cow scraping alongside a pig (*upper*), two instances of a monster with complex extremities tangled up (*lower*)

(see Fig. 5.11). Obviously, this direction is continuous, provided the path of the objects is continuous. However, this simple heuristic also has its drawbacks: in the case of deep penetrations it is possible that some internal intersections point into the false direction. As a result, the objects will be sucked up into each other. Therefore, it can be necessary to flip some of the directions n_{ij}.

In the following, we will present an extension based on normal cones for all spheres throughout the hierarchy that can help to identify these pairs. Moreover, we will show how our ISTs can provide also continuous torques.

Fig. 5.14 Force magnitude and direction in the monster scene (see Fig. 5.13)

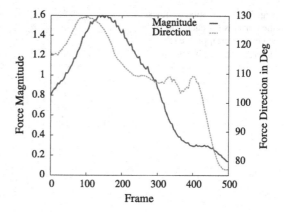

5.4.1 Contact Forces

Algorithm 5.3 and its time-critical derivative return a set of overlapping spheres or potentially overlapping spheres, respectively. We compute a force for each of these pairs of spheres (R_i, S_j) by

$$\mathbf{f}(R_i) = k_c \text{Vol}(R_i \cap S_j)\mathbf{n}_{(R_i)} \qquad (5.24)$$

where k_c is the contact stiffness, $\text{Vol}(R_i \cap S_j)$ is the overlap volume, and $\mathbf{n}_{(R_i)}$ is the contact normal.

Summing up all pairwise forces gives the total penalty force:

$$\mathbf{f}(R) = \sum_{R_i \cap S_j \neq \emptyset} \mathbf{f}(R_i) \qquad (5.25)$$

In order to compute normals for each pair of spheres, we augment the construction process of the ISTs: in addition to storing the distance to the object's surface, we store a pointer to the triangle that realizes this minimum distance. While creating the inner spheres by merging several voxels (see Sect. 4.2), we accumulate a list of triangles for every inner sphere. We use the normals of these triangles to compute normal cones which are defined by an axis and an angle. They tightly bound the normals of the triangles that are stored in the list of each inner sphere.

During force computation, the axes of the normal cones c_R and c_S are used as the directions of the force since they will bring the penetrating spheres outside the other object in the direction of the surface normals (see Fig. 5.12). Note that $\mathbf{f}(R_i) \neq \mathbf{f}(S_j)$.

If the cone angle is too large (i.e. $\alpha \approx \pi$), we simply use the vector between the two centers of the spheres as in the naive approach.

Obviously, this force is continuous in both cases, because the movement of the axes of the normal cones and also the movement of the centers of the spheres are continuous, provided the path of the objects is continuous. See Figs. 5.13 and 5.14 for results from our benchmark. Figure 5.15 shows the individual contact normals for each pair of intersecting spheres.

Fig. 5.15 This image shows
the normals for each pair of
spheres overlapping each
other, computed by our
collision response scheme

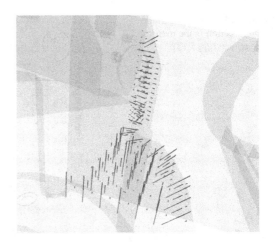

Fig. 5.16 Torque magnitude
and direction in the monster
scene (see Fig. 5.13)

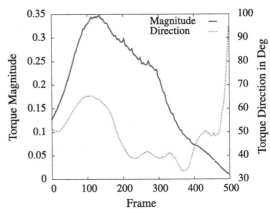

5.4.2 Torques

In rigid body simulation, the torque τ is usually computed as $\tau = (P_c - C_m) \times \mathbf{f}$,
where P_c is the point of collision, C_m is the center of mass of the object and $\mathbf{f}$ is the
force acting at P_c. Like in the section before, we compute the torque separately for
each pair (R_i, S_j) of intersecting inner spheres:

$$\tau(R_i) = (P_{(R_i, S_j)} - C_m) \times \mathbf{f}(R_i) \tag{5.26}$$

Again, we accumulate all pairwise torques to get the total torque:

$$\tau(R) = \sum_{R_i \cap S_j \neq \emptyset} \tau(R_i) \tag{5.27}$$

We define the point of collision $P_{(R_i, S_j)}$ simply as the center of the intersection
volume of the two spheres (see Fig. 5.12). Obviously, this point moves continuously

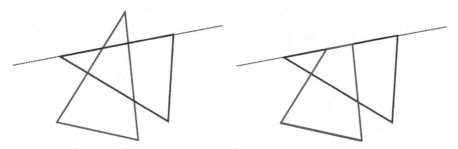

Fig. 5.17 Our tetrahedron intersection method: in the first step, we clip the triangles of one tetrahedron against the planes that span the other one

if the objects move continuously. In combination with the continuous forces $\mathbf{f}(R_i)$ this results in a continuous torque (see Fig. 5.16).

5.5 Excursus: Volumetric Collision Detection with Tetrahedral Packings

To our knowledge, there are no implementations available to compute the exact penetration volume between two polygonal objects. In order to still evaluate the quality of our penetration volume approximation, we had to develop a new algorithm for this task. The algorithm is based on tetrahedralization of polygonal objects. The main principle is very similar to the ISTs.

Initially, instead of computing a sphere packing for the object, we compute a tetrahedralization. Obviously, the non-overlapping tetrahedra fill the objects without any gaps. In order to accelerate the collision queries, we constructed an AABB tree above the tetrahedra. We used AABB instead of spheres, because they fit tetrahedra much tighter.

For the queries we use the same traversal algorithm as for the ISTs (see Algorithm 5.3). We simply replace the computation of the sphere intersection by a method for tetrahedra intersection. Unfortunately, there is no closed formula for the intersection volume of two tetrahedra.

Therefore, we have developed a new method that is based on polygon clipping: we clip the triangles of one tetrahedron with all spanning planes of the other tetrahedron (see Fig. 5.17). In a second step, we tetrahedralize the resulting polyhedron (see Fig. 5.18). The intersection volume can be easily derived from the sum of the volumes of the new tetrahedra.

This simple method allows us to calculate the intersection volume exactly. However, the runtime of this approach is not applicable to real-time collision detection due to bad BV fitting and the costly tetrahedron–tetrahedron overlap volume calculation. In all our example scenes it took more than 2 sec/frame on average.

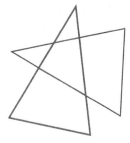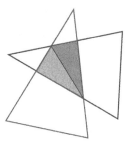

Fig. 5.18 Our tetrahedron intersection method: the second step we tetrahedralize the resulting polyhedron

5.6 Results

We have implemented our new data structure in C++. The testing environment consists of a PC running Windows XP with an Intel Pentium IV 3 GHz dual core CPU and 2 GB of memory.

The benchmark includes hand recorded object paths with distances ranging from about 0–20 % of the objects' BV size for the proximity queries. We concentrated on very close configurations, because they are more interesting in real world scenarios and more challenging regarding the running time. The paths for the penetration volume queries concentrate on light to medium penetrations of about 0–10 % of the objects' total volumes. This scenario resembles the usage in haptic applications best, because the motive for using collision detection algorithms is to avoid heavy penetrations. However, we also included some heavy penetrations of 50 % of the objects' volumes to stress our algorithm. We included those tests in addition to the results of our performance benchmarking suite (see Sect. 6.3) because we used the coherence techniques described above. Our benchmarking suite does not support coherence until now.

We used highly detailed objects with a polygon count ranging up to 370k to test the performance and the quality of our algorithm.[2] The quality of the resulting distances and penetration volumes is closely related to the quality of the underlying sphere packing. Consequently, we filled each object in different resolutions in order to evaluate the trade-off between the number of spheres and the accuracy.

We computed the ground truth data for the proximity queries with the PQP library. We also included the running time of PQP in our plots, even if the comparison seems to be somewhat unfair, because PQP computes exact distances. However, it shows the impressive speed-up that is achievable when using approximative approaches. Moreover, it is possible to extend ISTs to support exact distance calculations, too. In order to compute the ground truth for the penetration volume, we used our tetrahedral approach described in Sect. 5.5. The Figs. 5.19–5.29 show the scenes as well as plots of the results of our measurements.

---

[2]Please visit http://cgvr.informatik.uni-bremen.de/research/ist to watch some videos of our benchmarks.

Fig. 5.19 Test scenes: Oil pump (330k triangles) and Armadillo (700k triangles)

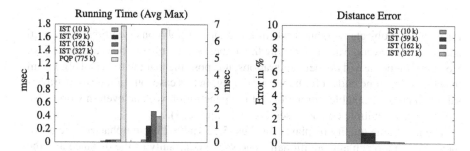

Fig. 5.20 Oil pump scene: average and maximum time/frame (*Left*), relative error compared to accurate distance (*Right*)

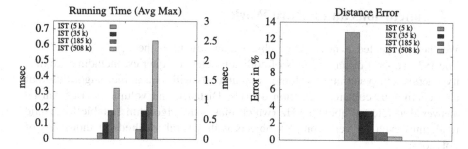

Fig. 5.21 Armadillo scene: average and maximum time/frame (*Left*), relative error compared to accurate distance (*Right*)

The results of our benchmarking show that our ISTs with the highest sphere resolution have an average speed-up of 50 compared to PQP, while the average error is only 1 %. Even in the worst case, they are suitable for haptic rendering with response rates of less than 2 mesc in the highest resolution (see Fig. 5.20). The accuracy can be further improved by the simple extension described in Sect. 5.3.1.1. With the highest sphere count, the error is below floating point accuracy with only a negligibly longer running time (see Fig. 5.21).

Our penetration volume algorithm is able to answer queries at haptic rates between 0.1 msec and 2.5 msec on average, depending on the sphere resolution, even

Fig. 5.22 Distance per frame
in the oil pump scene

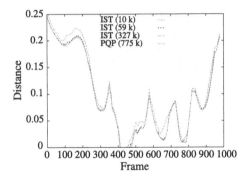

for very large objects with hundreds of thousands of polygons (see Figs. 5.24, 5.26
and 5.27). The average accuracy using the highest sphere resolution is around 0.5 %.
However, in the case of deeper penetrations, it is possible that the traversal algorithm
may exceed its time budget for haptic rendering. In this case, our time-critical traversal guarantees acceptable estimations of the penetration volume even in worst-case
scenarios and multiple contacts (see Fig. 5.28 and 5.29).

The per-frame quality displayed in Figs. 5.22 and 5.25 re-emphasizes the accuracy of our approach and additionally, shows the continuity of the distance and the
volume.

5.7 Conclusions and Future Work

We have presented a novel hierarchical data structure, the *Inner Sphere Trees*.
The ISTs support different kinds of collision detection queries, including proximity queries and penetration volume computations with one unified algorithm, but
also continuous collision detection queries. Distance and volume queries can be
answered at rates of about 1 kHz (which makes the algorithm suitable for haptic
rendering) even for very complex objects with several hundreds of thousands of
polygons.

Fig. 5.23 Test scenes: bolt (171k triangles), pig (10k triangles) and screwdriver (488k triangles)

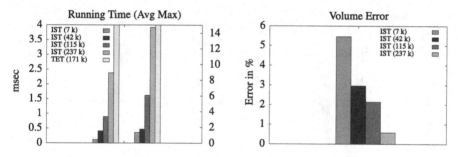

Fig. 5.24 Bolt scene: average and maximum time/frame (*Left*), relative error compared to accurate penetration volume (*Right*)

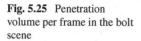**Fig. 5.25** Penetration volume per frame in the bolt scene

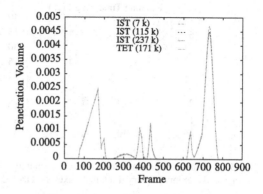

For proximity situations, typical average running times are in the order of 0.05 msec with 500 000 spheres per object and an error of about 0.5 %. In penetration situations, the running times depend, obviously, much more on the intersection volume; here, we are in the order of around 2.5 msec on average with 237 000 spheres and an error of about 0.5 %. The balance between accuracy and speed can be defined by the user. Moreover, the speed is independent of the objects' complexity,

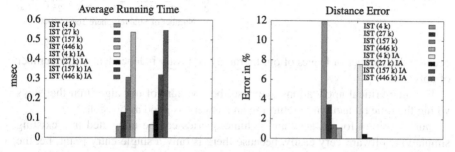

Fig. 5.26 Pig scene: average and maximum time/frame (*Left*), relative error compared to accurate penetration volume (*Right*)

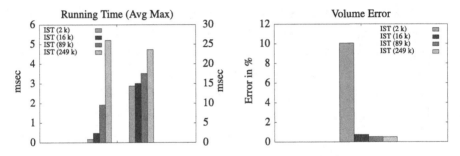

Fig. 5.27 Screwdriver scene: average and maximum time/frame (*Left*), relative error compared to accurate penetration volume (*Right*)

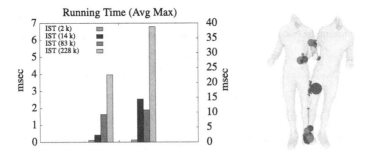

Fig. 5.28 Time-critical penetration volume computations in the torso scene (470k triangles). *Left*: average and maximum query time; the *y* axes are labeled differently

Fig. 5.29 Error relative to the exact penetration volume depending on the number of intersection tests during time-critical penetration volume computations in the torso scene

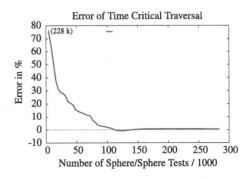

because the number of leaves of our hierarchy is mostly independent of the number of polygons.

For time-critical applications, we describe a variant of our algorithm that stays within the time budget while returning an answer "as good as possible".

Our algorithm for distance and volume queries can be integrated into existing simulation software very easily, because there is only a single entry point, i.e. the application does not need to know in advance whether or not a given pair of objects will be penetrating each other.

The memory consumption of our inner sphere trees is similar to other bounding volume hierarchies, depending on the pre-defined accuracy (in our experiments, it was always in the order of a few MB). This is very modest compared to voxel-based approaches.

Another big advantage of our penetration volume algorithm, when utilized for penalty-based simulations, is that it yields continuous directions and magnitudes of the force and the torque, even in cases of deep penetrations. Moreover, our inner sphere trees are perfectly suited for SIMD acceleration techniques and allow algorithms to make heavy use of temporal and spatial coherence.

Last but not least, we have presented a new method for partitioning geometric primitives into a hierarchical data structure based on the Batch Neural Gas clustering. Our approach considers the object's volume instead of restricting the partitioning to the surface, like most other algorithms do. Moreover, we have implemented a fast and stable parallel version of our hierarchical clustering.

5.7.1 Future Work

However, our novel approach also opens up several avenues for future work, starting with the partitioning of the geometric primitives: it would be interesting to apply our clustering approach also to classical *outer* BVHs. But also for the ISTs there might be some room for improving the hierarchy. For example, it could be better, especially at the borders of an object, to minimize the volume of those parts of hierarchy spheres that are outside of the object, instead of minimizing their volume.

Another option could be the investigation of inner volumes other than spheres. This could improve the quality of the volume covering because spheres do not fit well into some objects, especially if they have many sharp corners or thin ridges.

Moreover, we would like to explore other uses of *inner bounding volume hierarchies*, such as ray tracing or occlusion culling. Note that the type of bounding volume chosen for the "inner hierarchy" probably depends on its use.

An interesting question is the analytical determination of exact error bounds. This could lead to an optimal number of inner spheres with well-defined errors. Therefore we require an analytical or numerical model for the voids between the spheres. In order to minimize the error for distance queries, we could also use a combined *inner* and *outer* hierarchy.

On the whole, ISTs are fast enough for haptic refresh rates. However, there exist configurations, especially in cases of heavy penetrations, where the 1 kHz constraint may not always be met. Therefore, we presented a time-critical version of the volume traversal. Unfortunately, the volumes, and thus the forces and torques, are not guaranteed to be continuous. It would be nice to define a traversal algorithm that is able to compute *continuous* forces for fixed response times. Another issue with respect to the forces is a missing theoretical model that computes frictional forces for a volumetric penetration measure.

Fig. 5.30 ISTs for
non-closed objects: we fill the
space surrounding an object
and break this sphere packing
into several connected
components

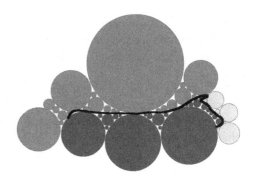

5.7.1.1 Quasi-volumetric Penetration Measure for Thin Sheets

A major drawback of our data structure is their restriction to watertight objects. This
is mainly because we have to compute a sphere packing of the objects' interior. In
real-world applications, e.g. in virtual prototyping tasks in the automotive industry,
thin sheets are widely modeled as a single polygon layer.

In the future we plan to extend our ISTs also to such open geometries by defining
a *quasi-volumetric penetration measure* for thin or non-closed objects. The basic
idea is very simple. Instead of filling the object's interior with spheres, we fill the
free space, or at least a certain region surrounding an object. At the edges we break
these sphere packings into several connected components (see Fig. 5.30). During
the traversal we just have to select the correct connected component to be checked.

This quasi-volumetric penetration measure not only allows to compute volumetric forces and torques for this sheets, but it also avoids the tunneling effect of other
static collision detection approaches.

5.7.1.2 Theoretic Analysis

Another very interesting challenge would be a theoretic analysis of our new data
structure. For polygonal object representations, we get an upper bound of $O(n^2)$ for
the number of colliding polygons and, thus, also for the worst-case running time of
collision detection algorithms.

Until now we could not construct a similar worst-case scenario for sphere packings. Therefore, we assume that the worst-case complexity for the overlap of two
sphere packings is in $O(n)$. However, a proof for that conjecture is still pending.

This proof could have an important impact on the future development of our
ISTs: for instance, it would probably enable us to design new parallel algorithms
with constant running-time even in the worst case, using only $O(n)$ processors.

5.7.1.3 Simulation of Fractures

A long time objective is the extension of our ISTs to deformable objects. Basically,
we could use some kind of parallel Sweep-and-Prune method [8] on the inner sphere

level, but other methods are also possible. However, as a short time objective we plan to apply our ISTs to the simulation of fractures and the material removal in milling simulations.

Here, the volumetric object representation by the sphere packing has several advantages. For instance, during a milling process we can directly remove the spheres and use the resulting sphere packing for a re-triangulation, if spheres are removed completely. In case of a partly removal of large spheres we can use an implicit hierarchy of the large sphere to reconstruct the residual object. The implicit hierarchy has to be computed only once for a single sphere. With an adequate scaling we can re-use this for all other spheres. Consequently, we can avoid a time-consuming re-build of the complete hierarchy.

However, these are just a few ideas for further extensions of our new data structure. We feel certain that there are much more interesting projects in the future.

References

1. Agarwal, P., Guibas, L., Nguyen, A., Russel, D., & Zhang, L. (2004). Collision detection for deforming necklaces. *Computational Geometry, 28*, 137–163.
2. Bradshaw, G., & O'Sullivan, C. (2004). Adaptive medial-axis approximation for sphere-tree construction. *ACM Transactions on Graphics, 23*(1), 1–26. doi:10.1145/966131.966132. URL http://doi.acm.org/10.1145/966131.966132.
3. Cottrell, M., Hammer, B., Hasenfuss, A., & Villmann, T. (2006). Batch and median neural gas. *Neural Networks, 19*, 762–771.
4. Fisher, S., & Lin, M. (2001). Fast penetration depth estimation for elastic bodies using deformed distance fields. In *Proc. international conf. on intelligent robots and systems (IROS)* (pp. 330–336).
5. Gärtner, B. (1999). Fast and robust smallest enclosing balls. In J. Nesetril (Ed.), *Lecture notes in computer science: Vol. 1643. ESA* (pp. 325–338). Berlin: Springer. ISBN 3-540-66251-0. URL http://link.springer.de/link/service/series/0558/bibs/1643/16430325.htm.
6. Hammer, B., Hasenfuss, A., & Villmann, T. (2006). Magnification control for batch neural gas. In *ESANN* (pp. 7–12). URL http://www.dice.ucl.ac.be/Proceedings/esann/esannpdf/es2006-83.pdf.
7. Hubbard, P. M. (1995). Collision detection for interactive graphics applications. *IEEE Transactions on Visualization and Computer Graphics, 1*(3), 218–230.
8. Liu, F., Harada, T., Lee, Y., & Kim, Y. J. (2010). Real-time collision culling of a million bodies on graphics processing units. *ACM Transactions on Graphics, 29*(6), 154:1–154:8. doi:10.1145/1882261.1866180. URL http://doi.acm.org/10.1145/1882261.1866180.
9. Mainzer, D., Weller, R., & Zachmann, G. (2011). Kollisionserkennung und natürliche interaktion in virtuellen umgebungen. In W. Schreiber & P. Zimmermann (Eds.), *Virtuelle Techniken im industriellen Umfeld* (pp. 33–38, 114–116). Berlin: Springer. Chaps. 3.2, 3.4. ISBN 978-3-642-20635-1. URL http://www.springer.com/engineering/signals/book/978-3-642-20635-1.
10. Martinetz, T. M., Berkovich, S. G., & Schulten, K. J. (1993). 'Neural-gas' network for vector quantization and its application to time-series prediction. *IEEE Transactions on Neural Networks, 4*(4), 558–569.
11. O'Brien, J. F., & Hodgins, J. K. (1999). Graphical modeling and animation of brittle fracture. In *Proceedings of the 26th annual conference on computer graphics and interactive techniques, SIGGRAPH '99* (pp. 137–146). New York: ACM Press/Addison-Wesley Publishing Co. ISBN 0-201-48560-5. doi:10.1145/311535.311550.

12. Satish, N., Harris, M., & Garland, M. (2009). Designing efficient sorting algorithms for many-core GPUs. In *Proceedings of the 23rd IEEE international parallel and distributed processing symposium*, May.
13. Schneider, P. J., & Eberly, D. (2002). *Geometric tools for computer graphics*. New York: Elsevier Science Inc. ISBN 1558605940.
14. Sengupta, S., Harris, M., & Garland, M. (2008). *Efficient parallel scan algorithms for GPUs* (Technical Report NVR-2008-003). NVIDIA Corporation. December. URL http://mgarland. org/papers.html#segscan-tr.
15. Weisstein, E. W. (2012). *Sphere-sphere intersection*. URL http://mathworld.wolfram.com/ Sphere-SphereIntersection.html.
16. Weisstein, E. W. (2012). *Spherical cap*. URL http://mathworld.wolfram.com/SphericalCap. html.
17. Weller, R., & Zachmann, G. (2008). *Inner sphere trees* (Technical Report IfI-08-09). Department of Informatics, Clausthal University of Technology, October.
18. Weller, R., & Zachmann, G. (2009). Inner sphere trees for proximity and penetration queries. In *2009 robotics: science and systems conference (RSS)*, Seattle, WA, USA, June. URL http://cg.in.tu-clausthal.de/research/ist.
19. Weller, R., & Zachmann, G. (2009). A unified approach for physically-based simulations and haptic rendering. In *Sandbox 2009: ACM SIGGRAPH video game proceedings*, New Orleans, LA, USA, August. New York: ACM Press. URL http://cg.in.tu-clausthal.de/research/ist.
20. Weller, R., & Zachmann, G. (2011). Inner sphere trees and their application to collision detection. In S. Coquillart, G. Brunnett, & G. Welch (Eds.), *Virtual realities* (pp. 181–202). Berlin: Springer (Dagstuhl). Chap. 10. ISBN 978-3-211-99177-0. doi:10.1007/978-3-211-99178-7.

Part III
Evaluation and Application

Chapter 6
Evaluation and Analysis of Collision Detection Algorithms

The theoretical complexity of almost all hierarchical collision detection approaches is in the worst case quadratic in the number of polygons. This is simply true because it is possible to construct artificial objects like the Chazelle polyhedron (see Fig. 1.1) where each polygon of one object collides with all polygons of another object (see Chap. 1). However, in practice, a quadratic running time of the collision detection for complex objects consisting of millions of polygons is not an option and no one would use quadratic algorithms in real-time scenarios. Actually, situations like this do not occur very often in practical relevant scenarios because most objects behave much better than the artificial ones. This raises the question: What makes an object to behave *good*? And how can we track this *goodness* mathematically?

These are exactly the questions we will answer in the first part of this chapter. In detail, we present a new model to estimate the expected running time of hierarchical collision detection. We show that the *average* running time for the simultaneous traversal of two binary BVHs depends on two characteristic parameters: the overlap of the root BVs and the BV diminishing factor within the hierarchies. With this model we are able to show that the average running time is $O(n)$ or even $O(\log n)$ for realistic cases.

However, theoretically "good behavior" is only one side of the coin. Today a user can choose between a wide variety of different collision detection libraries that are all based on different BVHs (see Chap. 2) and our theoretical observations hold until now only for AABB trees. Moreover, the asymptotic notation hides a constant factor that could make the difference between a smooth 30 frames per second real-time collision detection and unplayable 3 frames per second when choosing the wrong data structure. Actually, it is extremely difficult to evaluate and compare collision detection algorithms in practice because in general they are very sensitive to specific scenarios, i.e. to the relative size of the two objects, their relative position to each other, the distance, etc.

The design of a standardized benchmarking suite for collision detection would make fair comparisons between algorithms much easier. Such a benchmark must be

---

Parts of this work have been previously published in [23, 28, 29].

R. Weller, *New Geometric Data Structures for Collision Detection and Haptics*,
Springer Series on Touch and Haptic Systems, DOI 10.1007/978-3-319-01020-5_6,
© Springer International Publishing Switzerland 2013

designed with care so that it includes a broad spectrum of different and interesting contact scenarios. However, there was no standard benchmark available to compare different algorithms. As a result, it is non-trivial to compare two algorithms and their implementations.

Therefore, we have developed the first benchmarking suite that allows a systematic comparison of pairwise static collision detection algorithms for the rigid objects that we present in the second section of this chapter. Our benchmark generates a number of positions and orientations for a pre-defined distance or penetration depth. We implemented the benchmarking procedure and compared a wide number of freely available collision detection algorithms.

Usually, collision detection is directly coupled with a collision response scheme that resolves collisions between pairs of objects. Hence, the performance of the collision detection is not the only factor that a user has to consider when choosing the right algorithm. Different algorithms provide different kinds of contact information like distances, penetration depth or penetration volume (see Chap. 2) and the quality of the simulation directly relies on the quality of the contact information. This quality of the contact information includes the continuity of the force and torque vectors, but also the amount of noise in the signal. In the third section of this chapter, we present a novel methodology that comprises a number of models for certain collision response scenarios. Our device-independent approach allows objective predictions for physics-based simulations as well as 6 DOF haptic rendering scenarios.

6.1 Related Work

In Chap. 2 we have already seen that there exist a wide variety of different collision detection algorithms that makes it hard for a user to choose the right one for his application. Surprisingly, the literature about methods that allow a fair comparison between collision detection algorithms is very sparse. In most publications a certain scenario that is probably currently available or that makes the freshly published algorithm look good is chosen. However, this may result in a bias and does not guarantee an objective evaluation. In this section we will give a short recap of other methods that were published for the objective comparison and the theoretical analysis of collision detection algorithms.

6.1.1 Theoretical Analysis

In the last few years, some very interesting theoretical results on the collision detection problem have been proposed. One of the first results was presented by Dobkin and Kirkpatrick [4]. They have shown that the distance of two convex polytopes can be determined in time $O(\log^2 n)$, where $n = \max\{|A|, |B|\}$ and $|A|$ and $|B|$ are the number of faces of object A and B, respectively.

For two general polytopes whose motion is restricted to fixed algebraic trajectories, Schömer and Thiel [18] have shown that there is an $O(n^{\frac{5}{3}+\varepsilon})$ algorithm for rotational movements and an $o(n^2)$ algorithm for a more flexible motion that still has to be along fixed known trajectories [19].

Suri et al. [21] proved that for n convex, well-shaped polytopes (with respect to aspect ratio and scale factor), all intersections can be computed in time $O((n + k) \log^2 n)$, where k is the number of intersecting object pairs. They have generalized their approach to the first *average-shape* results in computational geometry [32].

Under mild coherence assumptions, Vemuri et al. [27] showed a linear expected time complexity for the CD between n convex objects. They used well-known data structures, namely octrees and heaps, along with the concept of spatial coherence.

The Lin–Canny algorithm [12] is based on a closest-feature criterion and makes use of Voronoi regions. Let n be the total number of features, the expected run time is between $O(\sqrt{n})$ and $O(n)$ depending on the shape, if no special initialization is done.

In [10], an average-case approach for CD was proposed. However, no analysis of the running time was given.

6.1.2 Performance Benchmarks

There does not exist much work about special benchmarking suites for collision detection algorithms. Most authors simply choose some objects and test them in a way not further described or they restrict their explorations just to some special scenarios. For instance, Otaduy and Lin [14] chose a set of physics-based simulations to test their collision detection algorithms. These scenarios are a torus falling down a spiral peg, a spoon in a cup, and a soup of numbers in a bowl.

Van den Bergen [25] positioned two models by placing the origin of each model randomly inside a cube. The probability of an intersection is tuned by changing the size of the cube. The problem here is that it is stochastic and that a lot of large and irrelevant distances are tested.

A first approach for a comprehensive and objective benchmarking suite was defined by Zachmann [31]. The code for the benchmark is freely available. However, it does not guarantee to produce results with practical relevance because the objects interpenetrate heavily during the benchmark, but collision detection is mostly used to *avoid* interpenetrations. In many simulations objects are allowed to collide only a little bit and then the collision handling resolves the collision by backtracking or a spring-damping approach.

Caselli et al. [3] presented a comparison with the special focus on motion planing. They used different scenes in their probabilistic motion planner for the benchmark. However, this benchmarking suite is restricted to a special scenario and it is not of general utility. Govindaraju et al. [7] created a benchmark for deformable objects. Other researchers have focused on benchmarking of physics engines, of which collision detection is one part. The Physics Abstract Layer (PAL) [1] provides a unified and solid interface to physics engines. Using PAL, a set of benchmarks has been constructed. The collision detection benchmark simulates 64 spheres falling into an inverted square pyramid. The downside of this benchmark is that it is a very special scenario.

6.1.3 Quality Benchmarks

Actually, the literature about the quality of forces and torques in simulated environments is even sparser than that of collision detection benchmarks. Usually, a video or some pictures are presented that should prove the visual quality of the presented algorithms. Most related work is provided by the haptics community. Cao [2] presented a framework for benchmarking haptic systems. This framework emulates a haptic device to which benchmarks can be attached. This benchmark simulates a point-based haptic device with only 3 DOF. Another problem is that it is unsuitable for benchmarking of non-haptic algorithm behavior. Ruffaldi et al. [15] proposed a series of "ground truth" data sets for haptic rendering. These data can be used to assess the accuracy of a particular haptic rendering system, but this benchmark only approximates a single point of contact. Unger et al. [24] presented a user study: they compared the forces during a 3D peg-in-hole task in the real and virtual cases. However, to our knowledge there is no benchmark available that uses an analytical model to compute the ground truth data for a fair comparison of different penetration measures.

6.2 Theoretical Analysis

Bounding volume hierarchies have proven to be a very efficient data structure for collision detection.

The idea of BVHs is to partition the set of object primitives (e.g. polygons or points) recursively until some leaf criterion is met. In most cases each leaf contains a single primitive, but the partitioning can also be stopped when a node contains fewer than a fixed number of primitives. Each node in the hierarchy is associated with a subset of the primitives and a BV that encloses this subset.

Given two BVHs, one for each object, virtually all collision detection approaches traverse the hierarchies simultaneously by an algorithm similar to Algorithm 6.1. It conceptually traverses a bounding volume test tree (see Fig. 2.4 in Chap. 2) until all overlapping pairs of BVs have been visited. It allows to quickly "zoom in" to areas of close proximity and stops if an intersection is found or if the traversal has visited all relevant sub-trees. Most differences between hierarchical CD algorithms lie in the type of BV, the overlap test, and the algorithm for constructing the BVH.

There are two conflicting constraints for choosing an appropriate BV. On the one hand, a BV–BV overlap test during the traversal should be done as fast as possible. On the other hand, BVs should enclose their subset of primitives as tight as possible so as to minimize the number of false positives with the BV–BV overlap tests. As a consequence, a wealth of BV types has been explored in the past (see Chap. 2).

Algorithm 6.1 traverse(A, B)

---

if *A and B do not overlap* **then**
    return
if *A and B are leaves* **then**
    return *intersection of primitives enclosed by A and B*
else
        forall *children A_i and B_j* **do**
            traverse(A_i, B_j)

In order to capture the characteristics of different approaches and to estimate the time required for a collision query, we have to remember the cost function equation (2.1), which we have introduced in Chap. 2:

$$T = N_v C_v + N_p C_p + N_u C_u \quad \text{with}$$

$$T = \text{Total cost of testing a pair of models for intersection}$$

$$N_v = \text{Number of BV Tests}$$

$$C_v = \text{Cost of a BV Test}$$

$$N_p = \text{Number of Primitive Tests} \tag{6.1}$$

$$C_p = \text{Cost of a Primitive Test}$$

$$N_u = \text{Number of BV Updates}$$

$$C_u = \text{Cost of a BV Update}$$

An example of a BV update is the transformation of the BV into a different coordinate system. During a simultaneous traversal of two BVHs, the same BVs might be visited multiple times. However, if the BV updates are not saved, then $N_v = N_u$.

In practice, N_v, the number of overlap tests usually dominates the running time, i.e. $T(n) \sim N_v(n)$, because $N_p = \frac{1}{2}N_v$ in a binary tree and $N_u \leq N_v$. While it is obvious that $N_v = n^2$ in the worst case, it has long been noticed that in most practical cases this number seems to be linear or even sub-linear.

Until now, there is no rigorous average-case analysis for the running-time of simultaneous BVH traversals. Therefore, we present a model with which one can estimate the average number N_v, i.e. the number of overlap tests in the average case. In this work, we restrict ourselves to AABB trees (axis-aligned bounding box trees) which allows us to estimate the probability of an overlap of a pair of bounding boxes by simple geometric reasoning.

Fig. 6.1 General
configuration of the boxes,
assumed throughout our
probability derivations. For
the sake of clarity, boxes are
not placed flush with each
other

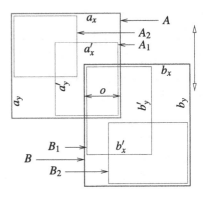

6.2.1 Analyzing Simultaneous Hierarchy Traversals

In this section, we will derive a model that allows to estimate the number N_v, the number of BV overlap tests. This is equivalent to the number of nodes in the BVTT (remember Fig. 2.4 in Chap. 2) that are visited during the traversal. The order and, thus, the exact traversal algorithm are irrelevant.

For the most part of this section, we will deal with 2-dimensional BVHs for the sake of illustration. At the end, we extend these considerations to 3D, which is fairly trivial.

The general approach of our analysis is as follows. For a given level l of the BVTT we estimate the probability of an overlap by recursively resolving it to similar probabilities on higher levels. This yields a product of conditional probabilities. Then we estimate the conditional probabilities by geometric reasoning.

Let $\tilde{N}_v^{(l)}$ be the expected number of nodes in the BVTT that are visited on level l. Clearly,

$$\tilde{N}_v^{(l)} = 4^l \cdot P\big[A^{(l)} \cap B^{(l)} \neq \emptyset\big] \tag{6.2}$$

where $P[A^{(l)} \cap B^{(l)} \neq \emptyset]$ denotes the probability that any pair of boxes on level l overlaps. In order to render the text more readable, we will omit the "$\neq \emptyset$" part and just write $P[A^{(l)} \cap B^{(l)}]$ henceforth.

Let X_l denote the number of nodes we visit on level l in the BVTT.

Overall, the expected total number of nodes we visit in the BVTT is

$$\tilde{N}_v(n) = \sum_{l=1}^{d} \tilde{N}_v^{(l)} = \sum_{l=1}^{d} 4^l P\big[A^{(l)} \cap B^{(l)}\big] \tag{6.3}$$

where $d = \log_4(n^2) = \lg(n)$ is the depth of the BVTT (equaling the depth of the BVHs).

In order to derive a closed-form solution for $P[A^{(l)} \cap B^{(l)}]$ we recall the general equations for conditional probabilities:

$$P[X \wedge Y] = P[Y] \cdot P[X \mid Y] \tag{6.4}$$

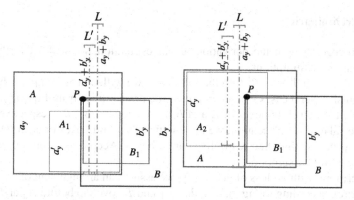

Fig. 6.2 The ratio of the length of segments L and L' equals the probability of A_1 overlapping B_1 (*left*), and A_2 overlapping B_1 (*right*), respectively

and, in particular, if $X \subseteq Y$

$$P[X] = P[Y] \cdot P[X \mid Y] \tag{6.5}$$

where X and Y are arbitrary events (i.e. subsets) in the probability space.

Let $o_x^{(l)}$ denote the overlap of a given pair of bounding boxes when projected on the x-axis, which we call the *x-overlap*. Then,

$$P\big[A^{(l)} \cap B^{(l)}\big] = P\big[A^{(l)} \cap B^{(l)} \mid A^{(l-1)} \cap B^{(l-1)} \wedge o_x^{(l)} > 0\big]$$
$$\cdot P\big[A^{(l-1)} \cap B^{(l-1)} \wedge o_x^{(l)} > 0\big]$$

by Eq. (6.5), and then, by Eq. (6.4),

$$P\big[A^{(l)} \cap B^{(l)}\big] = P\big[A^{(l)} \cap B^{(l)} \mid A^{(l-1)} \cap B^{(l-1)} \wedge o_x^{(l)} > 0\big]$$
$$\cdot P\big[A^{(l-1)} \cap B^{(l-1)}\big]$$
$$\cdot P\big[o_x^{(l)} > 0 \mid A^{(l-1)} \cap B^{(l-1)}\big]$$

Now we can recursively resolve $P[A^{(l-1)} \cap B^{(l-1)}]$, which yields

$$P\big[A^{(l)} \cap B^{(l)}\big] = \prod_{i=1}^{l} P\big[A^{(i)} \cap B^{(i)} \mid A^{(i-1)} \cap B^{(i-1)} \wedge o_x^{(i)} > 0\big]$$
$$\cdot \prod_{i=1}^{l} P\big[o_x^{(i)} > 0 \mid A^{(i-1)} \cap B^{(i-1)}\big] \tag{6.6}$$

6.2.1.1 Preliminaries

Before proceeding with the derivation of our estimation, we will set forth some denotations and assumptions.

Let $A := A^{(l)}$ and $B := B^{(l)}$. In the following, we will, at least temporarily, need to distinguish several cases when computing the probabilities from Eq. (6.6), so we will denote the two child boxes of A and B by A_1, A_2 and B_1, B_2, respectively.

For the sake of simplification, we assume that the child boxes of each BV sit in opposite corners within their respective parent boxes. According to our experience, this is a very mild assumption.

Furthermore, without loss of generality, we assume an arrangement of A, B, and their children according to Fig. 6.1, so that A_1 and B_1 overlap before A_2 and B_1 do (if at all).

Finally, we assume that there is a constant BV *diminishing factor* throughout the hierarchy, i.e.,

$$a'_x = \alpha_x a_x, \qquad a'_y = \alpha_y a_y, \quad \text{etc.}$$

Only for the sake of clarity, we assume that the scale of the boxes is about the same, i.e.,

$$b_x = a_x, \qquad b'_x = a'_x, \quad \text{etc.}$$

This assumption allows us some nice simplifications in Eqs. (6.7) and (6.11), but it is not necessary at all.

6.2.2 Probability of Box Overlap

In this section we will derive the probability that a given pair of child boxes overlaps under the condition that their parent boxes overlap.

Since we need to distinguish, for the moment, between four different cases, we define a shorthand for the four associated probabilities:

$$p_{ij} := P[A_i \cap B_j | A \cap B \wedge o_x > 0]$$

One of the parameters of our probability function is the distance $o_x^{(0)} := \delta$, by which the root box $B^{(0)}$ penetrates $A^{(0)}$ along the x axis from the right. Our analysis considers all arrangements as depicted in Fig. 6.1, where δ is fixed, but B is free to move vertically under the condition that A and B overlap.

First, let us consider p_{11} (see Fig. 6.2). By the precondition, A overlaps B, so the point P (defined as the upper left (common) corner of B and B_1) must be on a certain vertical segment L that has the same x coordinate as the point P. Its length is $a_y + b_y$.

Actually, P can be chosen arbitrarily under the condition that it stays fixed on B as B assumes all possible positions. L would be shifted accordingly, but its length would be the same.

Table 6.1 Effect of the BV diminishing factor α_y on the running time of a simultaneous hierarchy traversal

$\alpha_x \cdot \alpha_y$	$T(n)$
$< 1/4$	$O(1)$
$1/4$	$O(\lg n)$
$\sqrt{1/8} \approx 0.35$	$O(\sqrt{n})$
$3/4$	$O(n^{1.58})$
1	$O(n^2)$

Note that for the sake of illustration, segment L has been shifted slightly to the right from its true position in Fig. 6.2 (left). If in addition A_1 and B_1 overlap, then P must be on segment L'.

Thus,

$$p_{11} = \frac{\text{Length}(L')}{\text{Length}(L)} = \frac{a'_y + b'_y}{a_y + b_y} = \alpha_y. \tag{6.7}$$

Next, let us consider p_{21} (see Fig. 6.2 (right); for the sake of clarity, we re-use some symbols, such as a'_x). For the moment, let us assume $o_{21,x} > 0$; in Sect. 6.2.2.1 we estimate the likelihood of that condition.

Analogously as above, P must be anywhere on segment L', so

$$p_{21} = \alpha_y = p_{11}$$

and, by symmetry, $p_{12} = p_{21}$. Very similarly, we get $p_{22} = \alpha_y$ (see Figs. 6.3 and 6.4).

At this point we have shown that $p_{ij} \equiv \alpha_y$ in our model.

6.2.2.1 Probability of X-Overlap

We can trivially bound

$$P\left[o_x^{(i)} > 0 \,\middle|\, A^{(i-1)} \cap B^{(i-1)}\right] \leq 1$$

Plugging this into Eq. (6.3), and substituting that in Eq. (6.6) yields

$$\tilde{N}_v(n) \leq \sum_{l=1}^{d} 4^l \cdot \alpha_y^l = \frac{(4\alpha_y)^{d+1} - 1}{4\alpha_y - 1} \quad (4\alpha_y \neq 1)$$

$$\in O\left((4\alpha_y)^d\right) = O\left(n^{\lg(4\alpha_y)}\right) \tag{6.8}$$

The corresponding running time for different α_y can be found in Table 6.1. For $\alpha_y > 1/4$, the running time is $O(n^c)$, $0 < c \leq 2$.

In order to derive a better estimate for $P[o_x^{(l)} > 0 \,|\, A^{(l-1)} \cap B^{(l-1)}]$, we observe that the geometric reasoning is exactly the same as in the previous section, except that we now consider all possible loci of point P when A and B are moved only along the x-axis. Therefore, we estimate

$$P\left[o_x^{(l)} > 0 \,|\, A^{(l-1)} \cap B^{(l-1)}\right] \approx \alpha_x. \tag{6.9}$$

Plugging this into Eqs. (6.3) and (6.6) yields an overall estimate

$$\tilde{N}_v(n) \leq \sum_{l=1}^{d} 4^l \cdot \alpha_x^l \cdot \alpha_y^l \in O\left(n^{\lg(4\alpha_x\alpha_y)}\right). \tag{6.10}$$

This results in a table very similar to Table 6.1.

6.2.2.2 The 3D Case

As mentioned above, our considerations can be extended easily to 3D. In 3D, L and L' in Eq. (6.7) are not line segments any longer, but 2D rectangles in 3D lying in the y/z plane. The area of L' can be determined by $(a_y' + b_y')(a_z' + b_z')$ and the area of L by $(a_y + b_y)(a_z + b_z)$. Thus,

$$p_{11} = \frac{\text{area}(L')}{\text{area}(L)} = \frac{(a_y' + b_y')(a_z' + b_z')}{(a_y + b_y)(a_z + b_z)} = \frac{4a_y'a_z'}{4a_ya_z} = \alpha_y\alpha_z. \tag{6.11}$$

The other probabilities p_{ij} can be determined analogously as above so that $p_{11} = p_{12} = p_{21} = p_{22} = \alpha_y\alpha_z$.

Overall, we can estimate the number of BV overlap tests by

$$\tilde{N}_v(n) \leq \sum_{l=1}^{d} 4^l \cdot \alpha_x^l \cdot \alpha_y^l \cdot \alpha_z^l \in O\left(n^{\lg(4\alpha_x\alpha_y\alpha_z)}\right), \tag{6.12}$$

where $d = \log_4(n^2) = \lg(n)$.

Note that Table 6.1 is still valid in the 3D case.

6.2.3 Experimental Support

Intuitively, not only α should be a parameter of the model of the probabilities (see Eqs. (6.7) and (6.9)), but also the amount of penetration of the root boxes. This is not captured by our model, so in this section we present some experiments that provide a better feeling of how these two parameters affect the expected number of BV overlap tests.

We have implemented a version of Algorithm 6.1 using AABBs as BVs (in 3D, of course). As we are only interested in the number of visited nodes in the BVTT, we switched off the intersection tests at the leaf nodes.

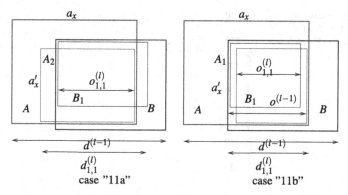

Fig. 6.3 Notations for computing $d_{11}^{(l)}$ for a child pair. If $a_x' > o^{(l-1)}$, the new distance $d_{11}^{(l)}$ is $d_{i,j}^{(l-1)} - 2\omega^{(l)}$ with $\omega^{(l)} = a_x^{(0)}\alpha_x^0(1-\alpha_x) = a_x^{(0)}(1-\alpha_x)$. In the other case, $d_{11}^{(l)}$ equals the overlap $o^{(l-1)}$

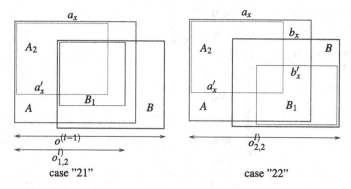

Fig. 6.4 The case "12" is symmetric to "21", and the case "22" is trivial. Here, $\omega^{(l)} = a_x^{(0)}\alpha_x^0(1-\alpha_x) = a_x^{(0)}(1-\alpha_x)$

Fig. 6.5 Some models of our test suite: Infinity Triant (www.3dbarrel.com), lock (courtesy of BMW) and pipes

For the first experiment we used a set of CAD objects, each of them with varying numbers of polygons (see Fig. 6.5).

Fig. 6.6 The number of
visited BVTT nodes for
models shown in Fig. 6.5 at
distance $\delta = 0.4$

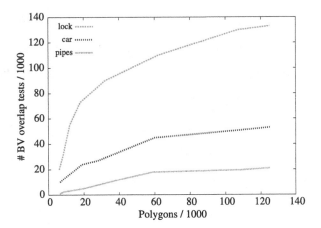

Fig. 6.7 For larger values of
α, our theoretical model
seems to match the
experimental findings fairly
well. In this plot $\alpha = 0.8$

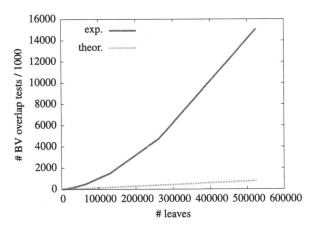

Figure 6.6 shows the number of BV overlap tests for our models depending on
their complexities for a fixed distance $\delta = 0.4$. Clearly, the average number of BV
overlap tests behaves logarithmically for all our models.

For our second experiment we used artificial BVHs where we can adjust the
BV diminishing factors $\alpha_{x,y,z}$. As above, the child BVs of each BV are placed in
opposite corners. In addition, we varied the root BV penetration depth δ.

We plotted the results for different choices of α and n, averaged over the range
0.0–0.9 for δ (see Figs. 6.7 and 6.8). For larger α's, this seems to match our theoretical results. For smaller α our model seems to underestimate the number of
overlapping BVs. However, it seems that the asymptotic running time does not depend very much on the amount of overlap of the root BVs, δ (see Figs. 6.9, 6.10 and
6.11).

Fig. 6.8 Same as Plot 6.7 but with $\alpha = 0.9$

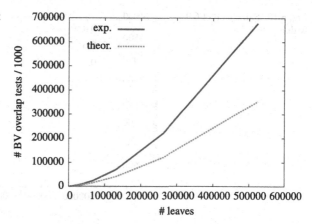

Fig. 6.9 The asymptotic number of overlapping BVs depends mainly on α, the BV diminishing factor, and only to a minor extent on δ, the penetration depth of the root BVs. In this plot $\alpha = 0.6$

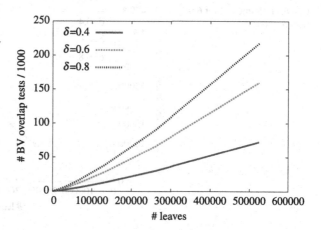

6.2.4 Application to Time-Critical Collision Detection

As observed in [10], almost all CD approaches use some variant of Algorithm 6.1, but often there is no special order defined for the traversal of the hierarchy, which can be exploited to implement time-critical computing.

Our probability model suggests one way how to prioritize the traversal; for a given BVH, we can measure the average BV diminishing factor for each sub-tree and store this with the nodes. Then, during running time, a good heuristic could be to traverse the sub-trees with lower α-values first, because in these sub-trees the expected number of BV pairs we have to check is asymptotically smaller than in the other sub-trees.

In addition, we could tabulate the plots in Figs. 6.12 and 6.13 (or fit a function) and thus compute a better expected number of BV overlaps during running time of time-critical collision detection.

Fig. 6.10 Same as Plot 6.9
with $\alpha = 0.7$

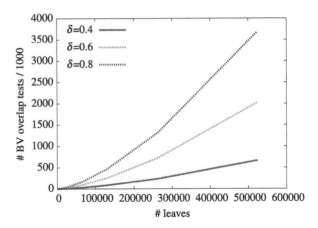

Fig. 6.11 Same as Plot 6.9
with $\alpha = 0.8$

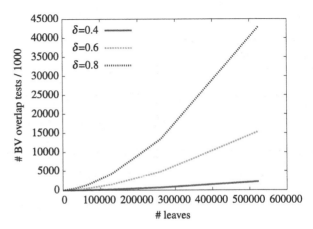

Fig. 6.12 For each number
of leaves in the BVH, the
distribution of overlapping
BVs seems to be nearly the
same. Each BVH has
$n = 65536$ leaves

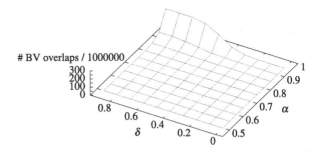

6.3 Performance Benchmark

The theoretic analysis in the previous chapter provides an estimation for the number
of possible bounding volume checks during a simultaneous BVH traversal. However, the analysis is, until now, restricted to AABB hierarchies. Moreover, it delivers
an estimation only for the number of bounding volumes to be tested, and this means:

Fig. 6.13 Same as Plot 6.12
but with $n = 524288$ leaves

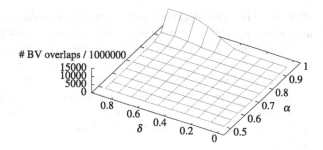

for N_v in the collision detection cost function (see Eq. (6.1)). A complete theoretical analysis of different collision detection approaches should also include the other factors, like the cost for a BV check (C_v), the cost for a BV update (C_u) and, of course, the number and the cost of the primitive tests (N_p and C_p). Especially the latter depends mainly on the distinctive object. For instance, spheres as bounding volumes can be checked very fast for overlap, but they fit flat objects very poorly. In practice this results in a large number of BV tests (a large N_v), but each test is very cheap, i.e. C_v is small. Moreover, due to the bad object fitting, N_p is very large compared to probably better fitting AABBs. Hence, in this example there is a direct connection between the number of BV tests, the number of primitive tests and the shape of the object. A closed formula to solve the cost function (6.1) is not even known for AABBs, not to mention a solution for all available BVHs and all objects.

Consequently, the theoretical analysis is good to guarantee lower bounds on the asymptotic running time of collision detection algorithms and it may help to improve the quality of time-critical traversal algorithms or to create better BVHs, but it is not very helpful when comparing *real implementations* of different collision detection schemes. However, in most applications that require collision detection, this collision detection is the computational bottleneck. And in order to gain a maximum speed of applications, it is essential to select the best suited algorithm.

Unfortunately, it is, not only in theory but also in practice, extremely difficult to compare collision detection algorithms because in general they are very sensitive to specific scenarios, like the shape or the size of the object, the relative position or orientation to each other, etc. Moreover, different collision detection methods provide different kinds of contact information, e.g. the minimum distance or the penetration depth.

Only a standardized benchmarking suite can guarantee a fair comparison between different algorithms. Such a benchmarking suite should include a broad spectrum of different and interesting contact scenarios for different kinds of contact information and a representative set of different objects that do not prefer a special collision detection method in advance.

In this section, we present such a benchmarking suite for static pairwise collision detection between rigid objects. It has been kept very simple so that other researchers can easily reproduce the results and compare their algorithms.

The user only has to specify a small number of parameters. Namely, the objects he wants to test, the number of sample points, and finally, a set of distances or penetration depths. Our algorithm then generates the required number of test positions and orientations by placing the object in the given contact scenario.

Our benchmarking suite is flexible, robust, and it is easy to integrate other collision detection libraries. Moreover, the benchmarking suite is freely available and could be downloaded together with a set of objects in different resolutions that cover a wide range of possible scenarios for collision detection algorithms, and a set of pre-computed test points for these objects.[1] Our benchmarking suite has been already adopted successfully by other researchers (see e.g. Ernst et al. [5] and Ruffaldi et al. [16]).

6.3.1 Benchmarking Scenarios

A main distinction factor of collision detection methods is the kind of contact information that they provide. As already seen in Chap. 2, this information may be the minimum distance between a pair of objects, a penetration depth or a simple boolean answer whether the objects do collide or not. Actually, most freely available collision detection libraries report only the latter information. Usually, these boolean algorithms stop the traversal when they find the first pair of intersecting polygons. However, this is exactly the point of time when the work of algorithms that additionally compute a penetration depth actually starts. Therefore, we introduce two different scenarios in order to guarantee a fair comparison.

- *Scenario I:* Most boolean collision detection methods are based on bounding volume hierarchies. If the bounding volumes of two objects do not intersect, there is no collision and they can be rejected very quickly. If two objects overlap, the recursive traversal during the collision check should quickly converge towards the colliding polygon pairs. The worst case for these algorithms is a configuration where a lot of BVs overlap, possibly down to the leaves, but the polygons do not intersect.

  Consequently, in this scenario we want to construct configurations where the objects are in close proximity, but do not overlap.
- *Scenario II:* was designed to compare also collision detection schemes that additionally compute a measure for the penetration depth. Their running time usually increases with increasing amount of intersection between the objects. In order to compare also this class of algorithms, we compute intersecting object configurations with respect to the amount of overlap.

A *configuration* denotes the relative position and orientation between two objects. For rigid objects, such a configuration can be described by six parameters (see Fig. 6.14): the transformation of object B in the coordinate system of object A, defined by the distance d and the polar coordinates φ_A and θ_A and the orientation of object B, defined by the angles φ_B, θ_B, ψ_B.

---

[1]http://cgvr.informatik.uni-bremen.de/research/colldet_benchmark/.

Fig. 6.14 The relative position and orientation between two rigid objects can be defined by six parameters

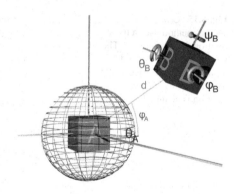

Since we cannot foresee the application of a given collision detection algorithm, the relative positions and orientations are more or less random from a statistical point of view. Therefore, it seems reasonable to factor these parameters out. We achieve this for Scenario I by testing as many configurations as possible for a set of pre-defined distances. For Scenario II, we fix the amount of intersection of the objects. We choose to use the intersection volume as a measure for the penetration depth.

Hence, the main challenge of our benchmark is to compute a large set of configurations for a pair of objects and a pre-defined distance or penetration volume, respectively. In the next section, we will describe two methods to achieve these sets of configurations. The basic ideas of those methods can be used for both scenarios.

Without loss of generality, it is sufficient to rotate only one of the objects in order to get all possible configurations, because we can simply transform one of the objects into the coordinate system of the other. This does not change the relative position of the objects. Therefore, our search space has basically six dimensions.

However, it is impossible to test a continuous 6D search space of configurations; therefore, we have to reduce it by sampling. In order to find a large number of sampling points, we propose two different methods in our benchmarking suite. We call them the *sphere method* and the *grid method*. The sphere method is faster, but it could miss some interesting configurations; conversely, the grid method is more accurate but much slower. Both methods start with a fixed rotation. After a cycle of method-specific translations, the moving object is rotated and the next cycle can start until a user specified number of rotations is reached.

6.3.1.1 The Grid Method

The first method uses a simple axis-aligned grid to find the translations. The center of the moving object is moved to the center of all cells. For each of these, the object is moved towards the fixed object until the required distance or penetration depth is reached. Then, the configuration is stored. Unfortunately, it is not possible to know the number of configurations found by this method in advance.

Fig. 6.15 Our
sphere-method uses a fixed
rotation for every cycle. The
moving object is rotated
around the fixed object. After
a cycle is finished, the
rotation is changed

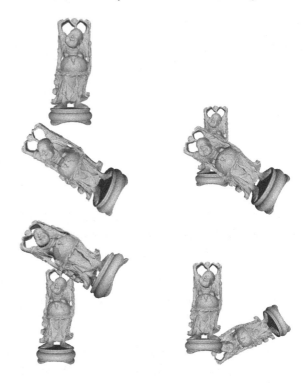

6.3.1.2 The Sphere Method

The main idea of this method is to reduce the time for finding possible configurations. To this end, the 3D search space is reduced to two dimensions by using polar coordinates. Nevertheless, it might happen that some interesting configurations are lacking. Within this method, we place the moving object on a sphere around the fixed object. The sphere should be bigger than the required distance. In the next step, we move the object towards the fixed object on a straight line through the center of the sphere until we reach the required distance or penetration depth, respectively (see Fig. 6.15). Because there could be several points that match the required distance or penetration depth on the straight line, it is possible to miss some configurations (see Fig. 6.16). In addition to the higher speed of this method, it is possible to define the number of located configurations in advance, because every straight line leads to exactly one configuration in the case of the distance.

At the end of this procedure, we have got a large number of configurations for a user specified number of object–object distances or penetration depth. This has to be done only once as preprocessing step, even if we add another collision detection library to the set later, or if we move to other platforms.

However, there is still the question of how to compute the required distances and penetration depth during the search space sampling. In the next two sections, we describe two different methods for each scenario:

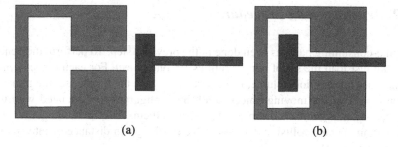

Fig. 6.16 The sphere method will find only configuration (**a**) for the red and the green objects, but it will miss configuration (**b**)

6.3.1.3 Distance Computation

One method to determine the distance between two objects is to use the (boolean) collision detection algorithms themselves. We can build an offset object from the fixed object where the offset equals the specified distance. Then, we can conduct a binary search until we find a point where the moving object is just touching the offset object. However, offset objects can get very complicated for complex objects.

That is why we propose another method: the PQP-library [6, 11] offers the possibility to compute the distance between two objects by using swept spheres. With a given distance, we can also do a binary search until we find a point which matches the specified distance.

However, distance computing is more complicated than collision detection. Thus, this method is more time consuming. On the other hand, it is more accurate and less memory intensive than the offset object method. Therefore, we prefer this method for our benchmark. Another advantage of this method is that we know the exact distance between the objects during the binary search. We can use this information to delete cells in the grid method with a higher distance than the specified one. This accelerates the search for configurations.

Indeed, our benchmarking suite supports both methods for distance computing, because PQP is not Open Source software and, therefore, it is not possible to deliver it directly with our benchmarking suite.

6.3.1.4 Penetration Volume Computation

Computing the penetration volume can be basically performed by using the same methods as for the distance computations. However, constructing an *internal* offset object is more complicated than the computation of an *external* offset object. Therefore, we prefer the binary search method using an algorithm that computes the penetration volume instead of the distance. The tetrahedron-based approach described in Sect. 5.5 can achieve an exact measure for the penetration volume. However, it is relatively slow. Hence, we additionally included the option to approximate the penetration volume by using our Inner Sphere Trees (see Sect. 5).

6.3.2 Benchmarking Procedure

The time-consuming part has been done in the previous step. To perform the benchmark, we just load the set of configurations for one object. For each object–object distance and intersection volume, respectively, we start the timing, set the transformation matrix of the moving object to all the configurations associated with that distance, and perform a collision test for each of them. After that, we get a maximum and an average collision detection time for the given distance or intersection volume, respectively.

6.3.3 Implementation

Besides the distance or the penetration depth between the objects and their configuration, the performance of collision detection libraries mainly depends on the *complexity* and the *shape* of the objects. We used 86 different objects in several resolutions in order to cover a wide range of use cases. All of the objects are in the public domain and can be accessed on our website. In particular, we used models of the Apollo 13 capsule and the Eagle space transporter, because they are almost convex but have a lot of small details on the surface. To test the performance of collision detection libraries on concave objects we chose models of a helicopter, a lustre, a chair, an ATST-walker, and a set of pipes. Moreover, we used a laurel wreath to test intricate geometries. A buddha model, a model of the Deep Space 9 space station, a dragon, and the Stanford Bunny were tested as examples of very large geometries. A model of a castle consists of very small, but also very large triangles. We used it to test the performance at unequal geometries. Accurate models of a Ferrari, a Cobra, and a door lock represent typical complex objects for industrial simulations. Additionally, synthetic models of a sphere, a grid, a sponge, and a torus are included. Figures 6.17, 6.18 and 6.19 show only some of these objects.

We also provide a set of pre-computed configurations. Therefore, we sampled the configuration space for each object and each object's resolution separately. For the sake of simplicity, we tested a model against a copy of itself.

- *Scenario I:* We chose a step size of 15° for the spherical coordinates and a step size of 15° per axis for the rotations of object B. With these values, we generated a set of 1 991 808 sample configurations for each distance.

  We computed sample configurations for distances from 0 up to 30 % of the object size in 1 % steps, because in all example cases, there was no significant time spent on collision detection for larger distances. To compute the configuration of two objects with the exact distance we used PQP.
- *Scenario II:* We used the approximative IST bounding volumes to compute the configurations, because the exact tetrahedral algorithm is some orders of magnitude slower. Although ISTs compute intersection volumes very quickly, we still had to reduce the sampling of the configuration space. Therefore, we changed the

Fig. 6.17   Some of the objects we used to test the collision detection libraries: a model of a castle, a helicopter, and a laurel wreath

step size per axis to 30°. We computed sample configurations for intersection volumes from 0 up to 10 % of the total fixed object volume in 1 % steps. With these values we generated a set of 268 128 sample configurations for each intersection volume. Because most applications of collision detection will try to avoid large intersections, a penetration volume of 10 % should be sufficient as you can see in Fig. 6.20.

One problem that arises with the configuration computation concerns numerical stability. Because we are forced to floating point accuracy, it is not possible to find configurations with an exact distance while doing binary search. On account of this, we use an accuracy of 0.001 % relative to the size of the fixed object in our benchmark. Of course, this accuracy can be changed by the user.

However, computing this large amount of configurations requires a lot of computational power or time. In order to accelerate the configuration computation, we used a PC cluster with 25 cluster nodes, each with 4 Intel Xeon CPUs and 16 GB of RAM. The time needed to calculate configurations for a complete set of distances or intersection volumes varies from object to object between 10 h and 200 h.

Overall, there were required 5 600 CPU days to compute all configurations for each of the 86 objects. All these configurations, as well as the objects and our benchmarking suite can be downloaded from our web site.[2]

Moreover, it is easy to include also other objects: the user simply has to specify the pair of objects he wants to test, the size of the grid, if he wants to use the grid-method or a step size for the spherical coordinates of the sphere method. Moreover, a step size for the rotation of the moving object must be defined and, finally, a distance or a penetration depth. Then, our benchmark automatically generates a set of sample points for these specified parameters.

In a second run, our benchmark contains a script that tests all available algorithms. It measures the times with an accuracy of 1 msec. Moreover, our benchmarking suite also offers scripts for the automatic generation of diagrams to plot the results of the benchmark.

Most collision detection libraries use proprietary internal data structures for data representation. Therefore, it is not possible to pass all kinds of objects directly to the

---

[2]http://cgvr.informatik.uni-bremen.de/research/colldet_benchmark/.

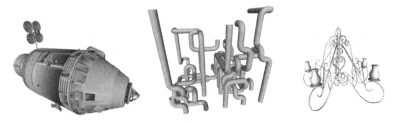

Fig. 6.18 Some more of the test objects: a model of the Apollo 13 capsule, a set of pipes and a lustre

algorithms. We chose OpenSG, a freely available scenegraph system for object management, because it offers support for many file formats, it is portable to many operating systems, and its data structures are well documented and easy to use. We wrote a wrapper for different collision detection libraries in order to convert the OpenSG data to the specific required data structures of the collision detection libraries. During initialization, our benchmark simply checks if the dynamically linked libraries are available and, if so, loads them.

We tested a wide variety of freely available collision detection libraries.

6.3.3.1 Collision Detection Libraries for Scenario I

Most freely available collision detection libraries support only boolean collision queries. Our benchmark provides wrappers for the following libraries.

- *V-Collide:* V-Collide, proposed by Hudson et al. [8], is a wrapper with a simple interface for I-Collide and the RAPID library. In a first step, a sweep-and-prune algorithm is used to detect potentially overlapping pairs of objects. In a second step, the RAPID library is used for the exact pairwise test between a pair of objects. It uses an oriented bounding box test to find possibly colliding pairs of triangles.
- *PQP:* PQP [6, 11] is also based on the RAPID library. As with RAPID, PQP uses oriented bounding boxes. Furthermore, PQP is also able to compute the distance between the closest pair of points. For distance and tolerance queries, a different BV type, the so-called swept spheres, is used.
- *FreeSolid:* FreeSolid, developed by Van den Bergen [26], uses axis-aligned bounding boxes for collision detection. For a fast collision test between the AABB hierarchies, the acceleration scheme described by Van den Bergen [25] is used. FreeSolid can also handle deformations of the geometry.
- *Opcode:* Opcode, introduced by Terdiman [22], is a collision detection library for pairwise collision tests. It uses AABB hierarchies with a special focus on memory optimization. Therefore, it uses the so-called no-leaf case, i.e. BVHs of which the leaf nodes have been removed. For additional acceleration it uses primitive-BV overlap tests during recursive traversal, whereas all other libraries described in

this section only use primitive–primitive-tests and BV–BV tests. Like Freesolid, Opcode also supports deformable meshes.

- *BoxTree:* The BoxTree, described by Zachmann [30], is a memory optimized version of the AABB trees. Instead of storing six values for the extents of the boxes, only two splitting planes are stored. For the acceleration of n-body simulations, the libraries offer support for a grid.
- *Dop-Tree:* The Dop-Tree [31] uses discrete oriented polytopes (where k is the number of orientations) as BVs. k-DOPs are a generalization of axis aligned bounding boxes. The library supports different numbers of orientations. The author mentioned that $k = 24$ guarantees the highest performance. Therefore, we also choose this number for our measurements. The set of orientations is fixed. This library also supports n-body simulation via grids.

6.3.3.2 Collision Detection Libraries for Scenario II

The number of freely available libraries that also support the computation of the penetration depth is sparse. Moreover, we cannot include penetration depth algorithms that are based on conservative advancement (see Sect. 2.3.3), because these algorithms require not only the recent configuration, but also the previous configuration of the objects. Finally, we included only two algorithms that behave very differently for our second scenario:

- *Voxmap–Pointshell Algorithm:* We use an implementation of the Voxmap–Pointshell algorithm (VPS) that was provided by the Deutsches Zentrum für Luft- und Raumfahrt (DLR) [17]. VPS uses different data structures for moving and stationary objects. Fixed objects are represented by a uniform voxel grid where each voxel stores a discrete distance value. Moving objects are represented as pointshells. Pointshells are sets of points uniformly distributed on the surface of the object. Section 2.4.1.2 shows an example of a voxmap and a pointshell. In our quality benchmark (see Sect. 6.4.5.1) we will additionally explain how these data structures can be used to compute an appropriate collision response.
- *Inner Sphere Trees:* The second algorithm is the Inner Sphere Trees that we introduced extensively in Chap. 5. As mentioned before, it computes an approximation of the penetration volume.

6.3.4 Results

We used the pre-computed configurations described in Sect. 6.3.3 to benchmark the aforementioned algorithms. We tested Scenario I and Scenario II separately because a comparison of algorithms providing different kinds contact information cannot be fair.

Fig. 6.19 Even more objects we used in the performance benchmark: a Chinese dragon, a circular box and a gargoyle

Fig. 6.20 The "happy buddha" scene with a total amount of 10 % intersection volume. The objects are in heavy interpenetration; a configuration that usually should not occur in practically relevant scenarios

6.3.4.1 Results for Scenario I

We tested the boolean collision detection libraries on a Pentium D CPU with 3 GHz and 1 GB of DDR2-RAM running Linux. All source code was compiled with gcc 4.0.2 with optimization -O3 except Opcode. This is, because Opcode was originally designed for Windows and uses some non-C++-standard code that produces runtime errors when compiled with optimization -O2 or above. Moreover, the Linux-version of Opcode produces some false-positive messages when the objects are very close together. Therefore, the results of Opcode are not directly comparable to the results of the other libraries. Moreover, we used the boolean version of PQP, which does not compute distances during the test.

The first reasonable finding of our measurements is that those algorithms which use the same kind of BVH behave very similar. Our second finding is that all algorithms have their special strengths and weaknesses in different scenarios. For instance, the AABB-based algorithms like FreeSOLID, Opcode, and the BoxTree are very well suited for regular meshes like the grid or the lustre but also for meshes with very varying triangle sizes, like the castle (see Figs. 6.21 and 6.22). In these cases, they were up to four times faster than the OBB-based libraries or the Dop-Tree.

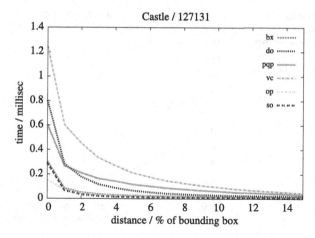

Fig. 6.21 The results of the benchmark for the castle scenario in resolutions with 127 131 vertices. The x-axis denotes the relative distance between the objects, where 1.0 is the size of the object. Distance 0.0 means that the objects are almost touching but do not collide. The abbreviations for the libraries are as follows: bx = BoxTree, do = Dop-Tree, pqp = PQP, vc = V-Collide, op = Opcode, so = FreeSOLID. The AABB-based algorithms perform best in this kind of scenarios

Fig. 6.22 The results of the benchmark for the grid scene with 414 720 vertices. The notation is the same as in Fig. 6.21

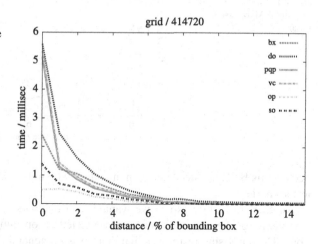

This is because in these test cases, AABBs fit the objects very well and, therefore, the algorithms can benefit from their faster collision check algorithm.

When we used concave and sparse objects, like the lustre or the ATST, or objects with lots of small details, like the Apollo capsule, the situation changed completely and the OBB-based algorithms, namely PQP and V-Collide, performed much better than the AABB-based libraries (see Figs. 6.23 and 6.24). This is because with these kinds of objects, a tight fitting BVH seems to gain more than a fast BV test.

A special role played the DOP-Tree which combines the fast BV tests of the AABB-based algorithms with the tight BVs of the OBB-based libraries. As ex-

Fig. 6.23 The results of the benchmark for the Apollo capsule with 163 198. In these test cases, the OBB-based algorithms are much faster than the AABB-based libraries

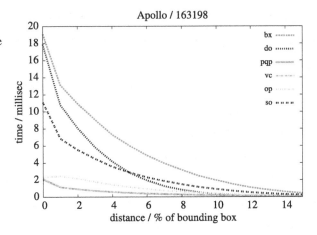

Fig. 6.24 The results of the benchmark for the ATST walker with 20 132 vertices. Like in the Apollo case (Fig. 6.23), the OBB-based algorithms are much faster than the AABB-based libraries

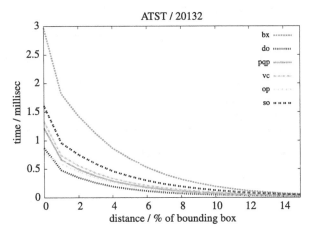

pected, this BVH is placed between the other two kinds of algorithms in most of the test scenarios.

Another interesting aspect we wanted to benchmark is the dependency on the complexity of the objects. Therefore, we tested all our models in different resolutions. The surprising result was that there was no general dependency on the complexity for the algorithms we tested. For instance, in the lustre scene, the times increased nearly linearly with the number of polygons for the AABB-based libraries, whereas it is nearly constant for the OBB-based algorithms. In the grid scenario, the increase was about $O(n \log n)$ for all algorithms (see Fig. 6.26). In the castle scene, the collision detection time seems to be independent from the complexity (see Fig. 6.27) and in the chair scene, the collision detection time decreased for all algorithms with an increasing object complexity (see Fig. 6.28).

Summarizing, there is no all-in-one device suitable for every purpose. Every algorithm has its own strength in special scenarios. Therefore, the users should check their scenario carefully when choosing a special collision detection algorithm.

Fig. 6.25 The results of the benchmark for the lustre scene for a distance of 1 % relative to the object size. The x-axis denotes the number of vertices divided by 1000. The time for collision detection in this scene increases nearly linearly for the AABB-based algorithms

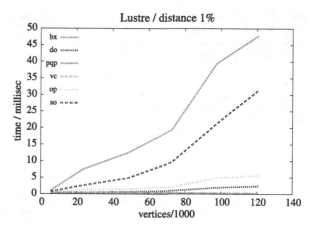

Fig. 6.26 The results of the benchmark for the grid scene for a distance of 1 % relative to the object size. The x-axis denotes the number of vertices divided by 1000. In contrast to the lustre scene (Fig. 6.25) the running time seems to increase in $O(n \log n)$ for all algorithms

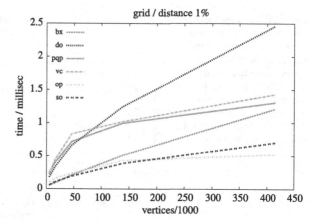

A good compromise seems to be the Dop-Tree, because it combines tight BVs with fast BV tests. Moreover, in some cases, it could be helpful to increase the complexity of the model in order to decrease the time for collision detection, but this does not work in all cases. However, in nearly all test cases, all libraries are fast enough to perform real time collision checks even for very complex objects.

6.3.4.2 Results for Scenario II

In our second scenario, we tested the libraries on an Intel Core2 CPU 6700 @ 2.66 GHz and 2 GB of RAM running Linux. All source code was compiled with gcc 4.3 and optimization setting -O3. Both algorithms that we included in our benchmark, IST as well as VPS (see Sect. 6.3.3.2), work independent of the object's complexity. Therefore, we chose the objects in their highest resolution to compute the required data structures, the sphere packing and the voxmap and pointshell, respectively. The running time of VPS scales linearly with the size of the pointshell. However, the limiting factor of the VPS is actually the high memory consumption of the

Fig. 6.27 The dependency of the collision detection time on the complexity of the models in the castle scene. The distance is fixed to 1 % of the object size. The collision detection time seems to be independent of the complexity

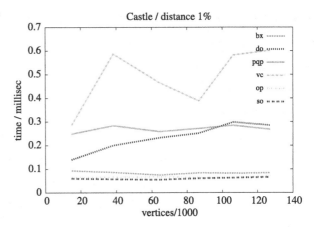

Fig. 6.28 The dependency of the collision detection time from the complexity of the models in the chair scene. Again, the distance is fixed to 1 % of the object size. In contrast to the castle scene (see Fig. 6.27), the collision detection time decreases with an increasing complexity

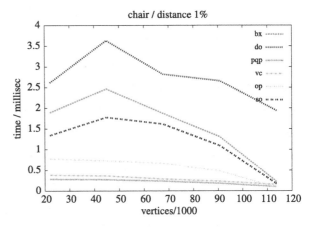

voxmap. For our measurements, we included the highest resolution for the voxmap that just fits into the main memory. The running time of the IST algorithms depends mainly on the number of inner spheres. Therefore, we included different sphere packing resolutions in our measurements.

In case of penetrating objects, we got very similar results for almost all objects in both cases, maximum and average time. Figures 6.29 and 6.30 show the average and maximum running time int the gargoyle scene, Figs. 6.31 and 6.32 show the same plots for the buddha scene. The running time of the ISTs is sub-linear in all cases. Lower and mid-size sphere packings up to 100k spheres outperform the VPS algorithm significantly and they require less than 1 millisecond of computation time in scenarios of small overlaps. Therefore, they are very well suited for haptic rendering. Surprisingly, the running time of the VPS algorithm is not constant as expected. In the worst case, the maximum running time exceeds the average running time by a factor of 2. This is probably due to caching effects. Moreover, the running time seems to increase linearly with a linear increasing penetration volume.

Fig. 6.29 Scenario II, average running time in the happy buddha scene: on the *x*-axis you find the amount of overlap in percent of the object's total volume. The number in parentheses after IST denotes the number of spheres in thousands. The two numbers after VPS denote the number of voxels and points in thousands, respectively

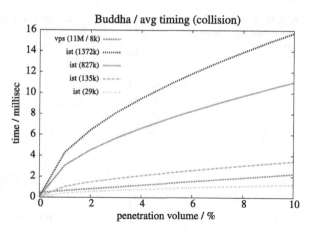

Fig. 6.30 Scenario II, maximum running time in the happy buddha scene

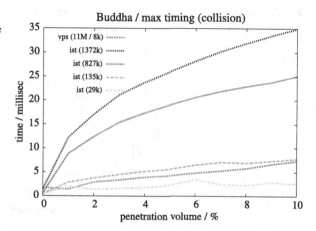

We suppose that this behavior is due to an increasing amount of intersecting points and consequently, an increasing amount of collision response computations.

In order to evaluate this, we also included timings of both algorithms in Scenario I, and this means: with objects in close proximity but without overlap (see Figs. 6.33 and 6.34 for the average and maximum running time, respectively). As expected, the running time of the VPS algorithm is almost linear. However, the ISTs are much faster, even with very detailed sphere packings with up to 800k inner spheres.

Summarizing, the results of our performance benchmark show that it is possible to compare quite different collision detection libraries with respect to their running time. Moreover, our tests can be used to determine objects and a placement of pairs of objects that are not ideal for the special algorithm.

However, the computation time is not enough to fully assess a collision detection algorithm. Often, the quality of the collision responses is another important factor. We will discuss this in more detail in the next section.

Fig. 6.31 Scenario II,
average running time in the
gargoyle scene

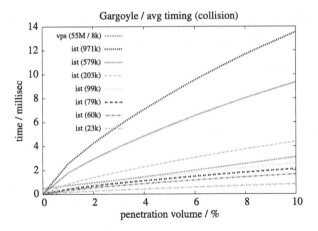

Fig. 6.32 Scenario II,
maximum running time in the
gargoyle scene

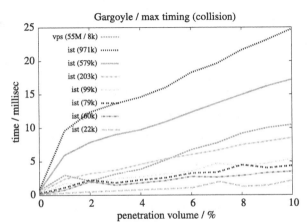

6.4 Quality Benchmark

In order to make games or virtual environments realistic, one of the fundamental
technologies is collision handling. Beside the detection of collisions among virtual objects, it computes a collisions response (such as penetration depth, contact
points, and contact normals) and finally feeds these into a physics-based simulation
or force-feedback algorithm.

Especially with forces, human perception is very sensitive to unexpected discontinuities both in magnitude and direction [9]. This effect is aggravated particularly
when both virtual and haptic feedback are provided to the user: it is known that visual and tactical senses are treated together in a single attentional mechanism and
wrong attention sensing can affect the suspension of disbelief [20]. Consequently, it
is essential that collision detection algorithms provide stable and continuous forces
and torques even in extreme situations, like high impact velocities or large contact
areas. Therefore, a benchmarking suite for collision detection should not only assess
its performance but also the quality of its collision response.

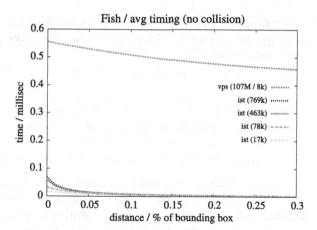

Fig. 6.33 Scenario I with ISTs and VPS, average running time in the fish scene

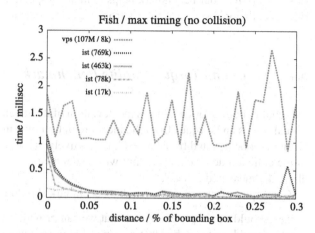

Fig. 6.34 Scenario I with ISTs and VPS, maximum running time in the fish scene

In order to determine the quality of the collision response of an algorithm, we cannot simply re-use the configurations of the performance benchmark and measure the force and torque vectors because computing realistic forces and torques from detailed objects in complex contact scenarios is highly non-trivial.

Because of that, we propose to use fairly simple scenarios and geometries to test the quality of the collision response. We believe that this approach is even more warranted because different collision handling systems use different measures for the force and torque computations. For instance, penalty-based methods usually use a translational penetration depth or the penetration volume; impulse-based collision response schemes often need the first time of impact.

Another advantage of simple scenarios is that we can model them. This allows us to calculate the theoretically expected forces and torques analytically for different collision response schemes. The comparison of this analytically derived ground truth data with the data gathered from the benchmarked algorithms allows us to define several measures, such as deviations and discontinuities of forces and torques, or the measurement of noise.

Our benchmarking suite contains several artificial scenes that support different challenges for collision handling schemes, including scenarios with thin sheets and large contact areas.

Summarizing, our quality benchmarking suite proposed in this section contributes:

- an evaluation method for force and torque quality that analyzes both magnitude and direction values with respect to contact models;
- a validation of our proposed benchmark;
- and a thorough evaluation of two rather different collision detection algorithms.

This empirically proves that our methodology can become a standard evaluation framework. The quality benchmarks allows the identification of the specific strengths and weaknesses and thus, a realistic rating of each benchmarked algorithm. Moreover, our benchmark helps to identify specific scenarios where an algorithm's collision response diverges from the correct results.

6.4.1 Force and Torque Quality Benchmark

Our quality benchmark evaluates the deviation of the magnitude and direction of the virtual forces and torques from the ideal prediction by a model. The ideal force and torque will be denoted by F^i and T^i, respectively, while the ones computed by one of the collision detection algorithm will be denoted by F^m and T^m, which we will also call "measured forces".

Consequently, the scenarios in this benchmark should meet two requirements:

- they should be simple enough so that we can provide an analytical model;
- they should be a suitable abstraction of the most common contact configurations in force feedback or physics-based simulations.

In the following, we will introduce the implemented scenarios (see Sect. 6.4.2) and the methodology that we used to evaluate force and torque quality (see Sects. 6.4.3 and 6.4.4).

6.4.2 Benchmarking Scenarios

Figure 6.35 shows all scenarios and their specific parameters. We will explain the details in the following.

- *Scenario I (a, b): Translation with Constant Penetration*
  A cone is translated while colliding with a block, maintaining a constant penetration. We chose a constant penetration of $\delta = \frac{1}{3}H = \frac{2}{3}r$ and a length of the trajectory of $L + 2a$. Two situations have been differentiated in this scenario:

Fig. 6.35 Scenarios in the force and torque quality benchmark as explained in Sect. 6.4.2. The *upper row* shows 3D snapshots, whereas the *lower* displays parametrized schematics. Trajectories are represented with *dashed curves*. Expected relevant forces and/or torques are shown with *vectors*. Coordinate systems are placed in points where forces and torques are measured—for the cone and the sphere this point is in their AABB center, whereas the position in the z axis for the "Pins" object is in the middle of the pin

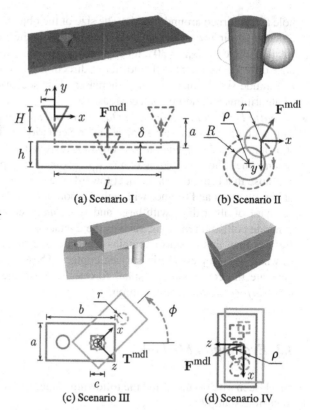

(a) Scenario I   (b) Scenario II

(c) Scenario III   (d) Scenario IV

(a) $h > \delta$ and

(b) $h \to 0$, i.e. the block is a *thin* rectangle.

Ideally, only forces should appear and they should have only a component in the positive y direction. Moreover, these forces should be constant while the cone slides on the block. This scenario evaluates the behavior of algorithms with objects that have flat surfaces or sharp corners. In addition, scenario Ib evaluates how algorithms handle the so-called *tunneling effect* which occurs when thin or non-watertight objects yield too small forces and torques, which allows interpenetration.

- *Scenario II: Revolution with Constant Penetration*
  A sphere is revolved around a cylinder maintaining a constant penetration. The radius of the orbit is $\rho = \frac{5}{3}R = \frac{5}{3}r$. Ideally, only forces should appear (no torque) and they should have uniquely sinusoid components in x and y directions. In addition to that, the measured force magnitude should be constant while the sphere revolves around the cylinder. This is a suitable benchmark for environments with objects that have smooth, rounded surfaces.

- *Scenario III: Rotation of a Square Pin in a Matching Square Hole*
  A so-called *pins* object with a rectangular and a circular pin and a matching *holes* object compose this scenario. The rectangular pin is introduced in the rectangular

hole and is turned around its axis. The size of the objects is $b = 2a$, the side of the rectangular pin is $c = 2r$ and it has a length of a in the z direction. The maximum rotation angle is $\phi_{\max} = 30°$. Ideally, only torques should appear and they should have only a component in the positive z direction. Moreover, the measured torque magnitude should increase as ϕ increases. This scenario evaluates the behavior of algorithms with large contact areas.

- *Scenario IV: Revolution of a Pin Object around the Central Axis of a Hole*
  This scenario uses the same objects as in Scenario III. The start configuration is shown in Fig. 6.35. Then, the pins object is revolved around the central axis of the second one. The orbit radius is $\rho = \frac{1}{10}c = \frac{1}{20}r$. The expected forces and torques are those that bring the *pins* object towards the central axis, i.e. sinusoidal forces on the xy plane and torques with only a z component. This scenario evaluates the behavior of algorithms with large and *superfluous* contact areas that should not generate collision reactions, such as the contact between objects in the xy plane. Besides that, this scenario contains small displacements around a configuration in which two objects are in surface contact. These small displacements should generate the corresponding small forces that push the *pins* object back to the *only-surface-contact* configuration.

6.4.3 Evaluation Method

For each scenario, we measured the following values and recorded them with respect to their time stamp k:

(a) forces F_k^{m},
(b) torques T_k^{m},
(c) penalty values q_k^{m}, and
(d) computation time t_k.

In order to assess these measured values, we have developed ideal analytical models of the expected forces and torques (i). The directions of these force and torque vector models are shown in Fig. 6.35, whereas the magnitudes are considered to be proportional to analytically derivable collision properties, such as

1. $\|F^i\|$ or $\|T^i\| \sim p$, translational penetration depth,
2. $\|F^i\|$ or $\|T^i\| \sim V$, intersection volume.

In each scenario we have determined p and V, respectively, as follows:

- Scenario Ia: $p \sim \delta$ and $V \sim \delta^3$
- Scenario Ib: $p \sim \delta$
- Scenario II: $p = \rho = \mathrm{const}$ and $V = \mathrm{const}$
- Scenario III: $p \sim \sin(\frac{\phi}{2}) - 1$ and $V \sim (\frac{1}{\tan(\phi)} + \frac{1}{\tan(\frac{\pi}{2}-\phi)})(\sqrt{2}\cos(\frac{\pi}{4} - \phi) - 1)^2$
- Scenario IV: $p = \rho = \mathrm{const}$ and $V = c^2 - (c - \rho|\cos\phi|)(c - \rho|\sin\phi|) + \pi r^2 - 4\int_{\frac{\rho}{2}}^{r}(r^2 - \tau^2)\,d\tau$

In order to evaluate the quality of the magnitude, the standard deviation of measured (m) and ideal (i) curves is computed:

$$\sigma_F = \frac{1}{N}\sqrt{\sum_{k=1}^{N}(\|\hat{F}_k^i\| - \|\hat{F}_k^m\|)^2}, \tag{6.13}$$

where $\hat{F} = \frac{F}{\|F\|_{max}}$, and N is the total amount of time stamps. Analogously, the indicator for direction deviation is the angle between ideal and measured values; the average value of this angle is

$$\gamma_F = \frac{1}{N}\sum_{k=1}^{N}\arccos\frac{F_k^i F_k^m}{\|F_k^i\|\|F_k^m\|}. \tag{6.14}$$

Deviation values for the torques (σ_T, γ_T) are computed using T_k^m and T_k^i, instead of force values.

Additionally, we track the amount of noise in the measured signals. A color coded time–frequency diagram using short time Fourier transform can be used to visualize the noise in time domain. In order to define a more manageable value for evaluations, we compute the ratio

$$\nu = \frac{\int S^m}{\int S^i} \tag{6.15}$$

where S^m is the energy spectral density of the measured variable (e.g. $\|F^m\|$) and S^i is the spectrum of the corresponding ideal signal. ν can be evaluated for forces and torques directions and magnitudes separately.

6.4.4 Equivalent Resolutions for Comparing Different Algorithms

The algorithms that we included in our quality benchmark, VPS and IST, are both approximative. This means that they both allow a trade-off between quality and performance. Usually, increasing the resolution of the data structures improves the quality of the contact information, whereas computation time also increases.

However, when comparing such *approximative* collision detection algorithms, it would be nice to compare their quality for a pre-defined *average performance*, or to compare their performance for a given desired quality. In this context, "equivalent" means a resolution such that both algorithms exhibit the same quality of forces and torques. In order to guarantee such a fair comparison, we define the *equivalent resolution*.

Considering two objects in a scenario (A is moving, B is fixed), we define the resolution pair (e_{opt}^A, e_{opt}^B) to be the optimum *equivalent* resolution pair:

$$(e_{opt}^A, e_{opt}^B) = \min\{\eta(e^A, e^B) \mid \bar{i}(e^A, e^B) = \tau\}, \tag{6.16}$$

where τ is the maximum admissible average computation time, $\bar{t}$ and $\eta = \omega_\sigma \sigma + \omega_\gamma \bar{\gamma}$, the equally weighted sum of the standard deviations.

In practice, since time and quality functions of Eq. (6.16) are unknown, we have to derive the equivalence numerically. Therefore, we performed several tests. Actually, we defined three different resolutions within a reasonable[3] domain for each object A and B and for each scenario. Overall, we defined sets of $3 \times 3 = 9$ pairs (e^A, e^B) for the objects. Then, the sets of nine corresponding tests were performed, recording all necessary average computation times ($\bar{t}$) and the global deviations (η) in each of them. Next, we applied a linear regression to values of $\bar{t}$, obtaining the plane which predicts the average computation time for a resolution pair in each scenario. Each of these planes was intersected with $\tau = 0.9$ ms,[4] obtaining the lines formed by all (e^A, e^B) expected to have $\bar{t} = 0.9$ ms for each scenario.

Afterwards, we performed a linear interpolation of η values to selected points on these lines. And finally, these interpolated values were used to get a cubic approximation curve for η in each scenario. The minimum of each of these curves is situated in (e^A_{opt}, e^B_{opt}) for the corresponding scenario.

Being aware of the fact that further refinements would yet be possible, it is considered that the compromise reached is accurate enough to make a fair comparison. The average absolute difference between predicted and measured η values with *equivalent* resolutions was 1.2 % for the VPS algorithm and 2.1 % for the IST algorithm.

6.4.5 Results

In order to test our benchmark, we compared our ISTs (see Chap. 5) with the widely used Voxmap–Pointshell (VPS) approach (see Sect. 2.4.1.2). Both algorithms facilitate and assume a penalty-based haptic rendering method, which allows colliding objects to penetrate each other to some degree. The two algorithms use different definitions of penetration: the one by VPS is closely related to the *(local) translational penetration depth*, while the one by IST is the *intersection volume*.

We will start with a short recap of the VPS algorithm and explain how the algorithm computes the force and torque values. Then, we will discuss the output of our quality benchmark.

6.4.5.1 Force and Torque Computation by VPS

The Voxmap–Pointshell algorithm was initially presented by McNeely et al. [13]. The algorithm computes collision forces and torques of potentially big and complex geometries with 1 kHz update rates. To achieve this goal, two types of data structures

---

[3]Between coarse but acceptable and too fine resolutions.

[4]Collision detection and force computation must lie under 1 ms; hence we chose a reasonable value under this barrier.

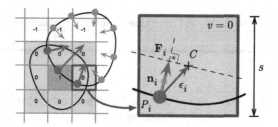

Fig. 6.36 *On the left*, a layered voxmap (*bottom*) is colliding with red pointshell points (*top*), yielding red bold collision forces. *On the right*, the computation of a single collision force related to a colliding point is graphically shown. Single collision forces are computed scaling the normal vector (n_i) of the colliding point (P_i) with the sum of the local ($n_i \varepsilon_i$) and global (vs) penetration of the point in the object

are generated offline for each colliding object-pair: a voxmap and a pointshell (see Fig. 6.36). In this work, we used the fast and accurate voxmap generator presented by Sagardia et al. [17].

Voxmaps are uniform 3D grids in which each voxel stores a discrete distance value $v \in \mathbb{Z}$ to the surface; e.g. for surface voxels $v = 0$ and for first inner layer voxels $v = 1$. Pointshells are sets of points uniformly distributed on the surface of the object; each point has additionally an inwards pointing normal vector.

During collision detection, the normal vectors n_i of colliding points P_i—those which are in voxels with $v \geq 0$—are accumulated, weighted by their penetration in the voxmap to compute the force **F**. Summarizing, this results in the following equation for the local forces:

$$\mathbf{F}_i = \max\{\underbrace{n_i \varepsilon_i}_{(I)} + \underbrace{vs}_{(II)}, 0\} n_i \qquad (6.17)$$

where

(I) denotes a local continuous component, the distance to colliding voxel center in normal vector direction, and

(II) denotes a global discrete component; it is related to the voxmap layer.

The global force acting on the whole object can easily be computed by summing up all local forces:

$$\mathbf{F}_{\text{tot}} = \sum_{\forall i | v(P_i) \geq 0} \mathbf{F}_i. \qquad (6.18)$$

Similarly, we can define local torques $\mathbf{T}_i$: $\mathbf{T}_i$ are the cross products between local forces $\mathbf{F}_i$ and point coordinates P_i, assuming that all magnitudes are expressed in the pointshell frame. We assume that the center of mass is located at the origin:

$$\mathbf{T}_i = P_i \times \mathbf{F}_i. \qquad (6.19)$$

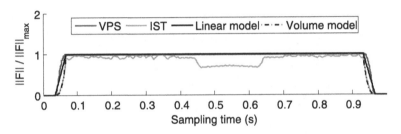

Fig. 6.37 Forces in Scenario I

At the end, all local torques $\mathbf{T}_i$ are summed to compute the total torque $\mathbf{T}_{\text{tot}}$.

$$\mathbf{T}_{\text{tot}} = \sum_{\forall i \mid v(P_i) \geq 0} \mathbf{T}_i. \tag{6.20}$$

The forces and torques of the ISTs were computed according to our new volumetric collision response scheme described in Sect. 5.4.

6.4.5.2 Results

In this section we present the results of our quality benchmark applied to the VPS and the IST data structures. For each scenario, described in Sect. 6.4.2, we store the collision forces $\mathbf{F} \in \mathbb{R}^3$ and collision torques $\mathbf{T} \in \mathbb{R}^3$ that were returned by the algorithms. The magnitudes $\|\mathbf{F}\|$, $\|\mathbf{T}\|$, the orientations $\mathbf{d}$ of these vectors and the direction deviations between the model and the measured values γ are analyzed. As in the case of the performance benchmark, all objects and paths used in the force and torque quality benchmark (see Fig. 6.35) are available on our website.[5] We tested them on an Intel Core2Quad CPU Q9450 @ 2.66 GHz and 3.4 GB of RAM running Linux SLED 11. The libraries were compiled with gcc 4.3.

We have chosen the voxel size u in the voxelized objects such that $H = 60u$, $h = 30u$ (Scenario I), $R = 30u$ (a penetration of $20u$ is maintained) (Scenario II), $c = 20u$ (Scenario III), and $\rho = 20u$ (Scenario IV). The number of voxels was chosen to be $728 \times 24 \times 303$ voxels for the block in Scenario I while the cone has $15\,669$ pointshell points. In Scenario II, for the cylinder, $491 \times 816 \times 491$ voxels we used and $12\,640$ pointshell points for the sphere. In Scenario III the number of voxels was chosen to be $1\,204 \times 604 \times 603$ for the block and $12\,474$ pointshell points for the pin objects. For the last scenario the number of voxel was chosen to be $243 \times 123 \times 123$ voxels for the block and $13\,295$ pointshell points for the pin.

Figures 6.37, 6.38, 6.39, and 6.40 show example plots of the force and torque magnitude analysis in different scenarios. In detail, Fig. 6.37 contains the expected model curves for ideal force magnitudes in Scenario I. Measured curves are superposed to expected curves to give an idea of how reliable they are derived with respect to these proposed collision response models. The standard deviation between

---

[5]http://cgvr.informatik.uni-bremen.de/.

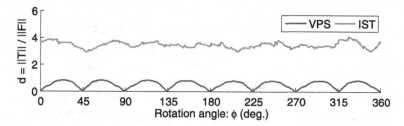

Fig. 6.38 Forces in Scenario II

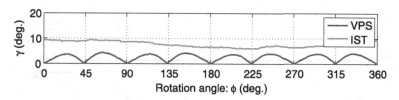

Fig. 6.39 Average angle between analytical model and measured values in Scenario II

measured and ideal curves yields the magnitude deviation $\sigma_F = 0.043$ for VPS and $\sigma_F = 0.176$ for ISTs. In Scenario III, the standard deviation between measured and ideal curves yields the magnitude deviation $\sigma_T = 0.169$ and $\sigma_T = 0.112$ for the torques, respectively. Figure 6.38 shows the curve of $\frac{\|T\|}{\|F\|}$, which should be 0 for Scenario II, since ideally no torques should appear. This quotient gives information about the magnitude of forces or torques that actually should not occur.

In Fig. 6.41 and 6.42, the force and torque components are displayed, giving a visual idea of force and torque direction deviations. Figure 6.39 shows this direction deviation for Scenario II; the associated γ values are $\gamma_F = 2.40$ for VPS and $\gamma_F = 7.64$ for ISTs.

Finally, Fig. 6.43 (VPS) and 6.44 (IST) visualize the results of our noise measurement of the force in the x-direction in Scenario III. The color coded time–frequency diagrams visualize the amount, the time, and the frequency of the signal's noise. The corresponding ν values are $\nu_F = 0.620$ for VPS and $\nu_F = 1.12$ for ISTs, where values closer to 1 denote a minor amount of noise.

All these results show that VPS and IST are very close to their underlying models and that different haptic rendering algorithms can be evaluated. All these results show that our models for penetration are suitable. Furthermore, they prove empirically that our benchmark is valid. Hence, these empirical results show that our benchmark can be helpful in practice. In particular, the benchmark also reveals significant differences between the algorithms: whereas ISTs seem to have a higher standard deviation from the ideal model, VPS tends to deliver a noisier signal quality. The decision between accuracy and noise could be essential for some applications.

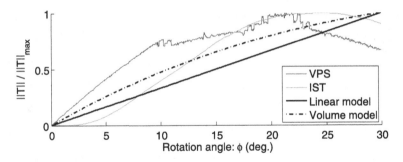

Fig. 6.40 Torques in Scenario III

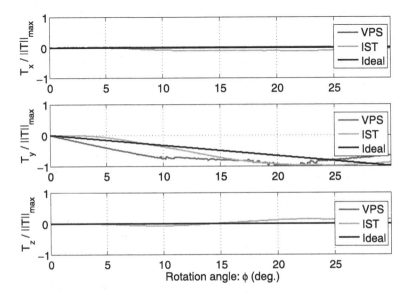

Fig. 6.41 Torques in Scenario III

6.5 Conclusion and Future Work

In summary, we have presented three different methods that allow a theoretical analysis as well as a practical relevant comparison of different collision detection and response methods.

In Sect. 6.2 we have presented an average-case analysis for simultaneous AABB tree traversals, under some assumptions about the AABB tree, which provides a better understanding of the performance of hierarchical collision detections than that which was observed in the past. Our analysis is independent of the order of the traversal. In addition, we have performed several experiments to support the correctness of our model. Moreover, we have shown that the running time behaves logarithmically for real-world models, even for a large overlap between the root BVs.

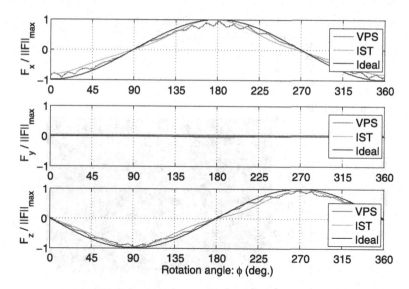

Fig. 6.42 Forces in Scenario IV

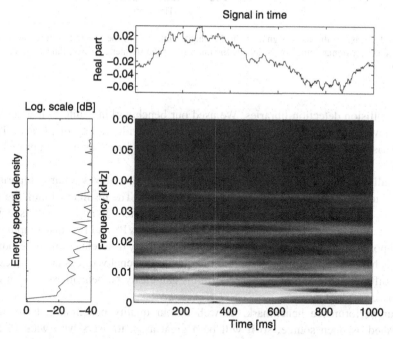

Fig. 6.43 Noise in the force signal of the VPS algorithm. The colored picture shows the time–frequency domain: the colors decode the intensity of the frequency, where dark marks a zero intensity

In Sect. 6.3, we have presented an easy to use benchmarking method and a representative suite for benchmarking objects for static collision detection algorithms for rigid objects. Our benchmark is robust, fast, flexible, and it is easy to integrate

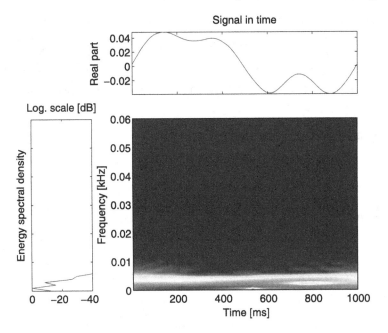

Fig. 6.44 Noise in the force signal of the IST algorithm. Again, the colored picture shows the time–frequency domain: the colors decode the intensity of the frequency, where dark marks a zero intensity

other collision detection libraries. We used our benchmarking suite to test several freely available collision detection libraries with a wide variety of objects. This comparison of several algorithms yields a simple rule for choosing the optimal algorithm.

Finally, in Sect. 6.4, we have introduced a model that allows a fair comparison of the quality of different collision response methods. The results maintain the validity of our analytically derived force and torque models. In addition, the specific differences between the two benchmarked algorithms, VPS and IST, also emphasize the importance of a standardized benchmark for entirely different collision response approaches. Moreover, they show that the quality of penalty forces and torques of quite different collision detection algorithms can easily be benchmarked with our proposed methods.

Our performance benchmark, as well as our quality benchmark, have been published as open source; so it will be a great asset to users who want to figure out the best suited collision handling scheme. Moreover, it will help researchers who want to compare their algorithms to other approaches with a standardized benchmark that delivers verifiable results. Additionally, it helps to identify geometric worst cases for the collision detection method or problematic cases in which the collision response scheme diverges from the correct results.

6.5.1 Future Work

Our work can be used as the basis of different future directions: on the one hand, it would be interesting to provide extensions of our theoretical analysis and practical benchmarks, on the other hand, our results can be directly used to realize new collision detection schemes.

For instance, several existing methods for hierarchical collision detection may benefit directly from our theoretical analysis and model in Sect. 6.2. Especially in time-critical environments or real-time applications it could be very helpful to predict the running time of the collision detection process only with the help of two parameters that can be determined on-the-fly. We will try to speed up probabilistic collision detection by the heuristics mentioned above.

We have already tried to derive a theoretical model of the probabilities that depends on the BV diminishing factor as well as the penetration distance of the two root BVs. This would, hopefully, lead to a probability density function describing the x-overlaps, thus yielding a better estimation of $\tilde{N}_v^{(l)}$ in Sect. 6.2.2. However, this challenge seems to be difficult.

Furthermore, a particular challenge will be a similar average-case analysis for BVHs utilizing other types of BVs, such as DOPs or OBBs. The geometric reasoning would probably have to be quite different from the one presented here. Moreover, it would be very interesting to apply our technique to other areas, such as ray tracing, and we believe one could exploit these ideas to obtain better bounding volume hierarchies.

Also our benchmarking suite offers possibilities for further extensions: for example, the design of a benchmarking suite for more than just two objects and for continuous collision detection algorithms. Another promising future project would be a standardized benchmarking suite for deformable objects; this is still missing but could be very helpful for users. Moreover, a comparison of the *numerical stability* of different implementations could be useful. For instance, during our research we recognized that some algorithms find significantly less intersecting triangles during collision queries than other algorithms (see Fig. 6.45). And the fastest algorithm does not help if it misses interesting contacts.

An application of our results could be the implementation of a performance optimized collision detection library. It could internally implement several different algorithms and choose either of them on a case-to-case basis according to the shape of the objects and their configuration. Moreover, it would be nice to generate a ranking of the different measurements in our quality benchmark, like continuity of forces and torques in magnitude and direction or the noise of the signals, with respect to psychophysical cognition. To achieve that, elaborate user studies need to be done, including testbeds with different haptic devices and investigations of the perception of the different parameters. Moreover, it would be nice to include more complex physics-based collision response phenomena like friction.

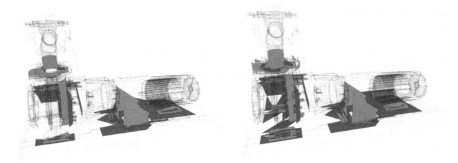

Fig. 6.45 The intersecting triangles that were found by PQP (*left*) and CollDet (*right*) in a typical CAD simulation. You can see that CollDet finds many more intersecting triangles

References

1. Boeing, A., & Bräunl, T. (2007). Evaluation of real-time physics simulation systems. In *Proceedings of the 5th international conference on computer graphics and interactive techniques in Australia and Southeast Asia* (p. 288). New York: ACM.
2. Cao, X. R. (2006). *A framework for benchmarking haptic systems*. Ph.D. thesis, Simon Fraser University.
3. Caselli, S., Reggiani, M., & Mazzoli, M. (2002). Exploiting advanced collision detection libraries in a probabilistic motion planner. In *WSCG* (pp. 103–110).
4. Dobkin, D. P., & Kirkpatrick, D. G. (1985). A linear algorithm for determining the separation of convex polyhedra. *Journal of Algorithms, 6*(3), 381–392.
5. Ernst, M., Schneider, M., & Greiner, G. (2008). Collision detection with early split clipping. In *Proceedings computer graphics international (CGI 2008)*.
6. Gottschalk, S., Lin, M. C., & Manocha, D. (1996). Obbtree: a hierarchical structure for rapid interference detection. In *Proceedings of the 23rd annual conference on computer graphics and interactive techniques, SIGGRAPH '96* (pp. 171–180). New York: ACM. ISBN 0-89791-746-4. doi:10.1145/237170.237244. URL http://doi.acm.org/10.1145/237170.237244.
7. Govindaraju, N. K., Knott, D., Jain, N., Kabul, I., Tamstorf, R., Gayle, R., Lin, M. C., & Manocha, D. (2005). Interactive collision detection between deformable models using chromatic decomposition. *ACM Transactions on Graphics, 24*(3), 991–999.
8. Hudson, T. C., Lin, M. C., Cohen, J., Gottschalk, S., & Manocha, D. (1997). V-COLLIDE: accelerated collision detection for VRML. In R. Carey & P. Strauss (Eds.), *VRML 97: second symposium on the virtual reality modeling language*. New York: ACM Press.
9. Kim, L., Kyrikou, A., Desbrun, M., & Sukhatme, G. S. (2002). An implicit-based haptic rendering technique. In *IEEE/RSJ international conference on intelligent robots and systems*, EPFL, Switzerland, Oct. (pp. 2943–2948). URL http://cres.usc.edu/cgi-bin/print_pub_details.pl?pubid=54.
10. Klein, J., & Zachmann, G. (2003). Time-critical collision detection using an average-case approach. In *Proceedings of the ACM symposium on virtual reality software and technology, VRST '03* (pp. 22–31). New York: ACM. ISBN 1-58113-569-6. doi:10.1145/1008653.1008660. URL http://doi.acm.org/10.1145/1008653.1008660.
11. Larsen, E., Gottschalk, S., Lin, M. C., & Manocha, D. (1999). *Fast proximity queries with swept sphere volumes*, November 14. URL html.http://citeseer.ist.psu.edu/408975.html; ftp://ftp.cs.unc.edu/pub/users/manocha/PAPERS/COLLISION/ssv.ps.
12. Lin, M. C., & Canny, J. F. (1991). A fast algorithm for incremental distance calculation. In *IEEE international conference on robotics and automation* (pp. 1008–1014).

13. McNeely, W. A., Puterbaugh, K. D., & Troy, J. J. (1999). Six degrees-of-freedom haptic rendering using voxel sampling. *ACM Transactions on Graphics, 18*(3), 401–408 (SIGGRAPH 1999).

14. Otaduy, M. A., & Lin, M. C. (2003). CLODs: Dual hierarchies for multiresolution collision detection. In *Symposium on geometry processing* (pp. 94–101).

15. Ruffaldi, E., Morris, D., Edmunds, T., Barbagli, F., & Pai, D. K. (2006). Standardized evaluation of haptic rendering systems. In *Haptic interfaces for virtual environment and teleoperator systems, IEEE VR*.

16. Ruffaldi, E., Morris, D., Barbagli, F., Salisbury, K., & Bergamasco, M. (2008). Voxel-based haptic rendering using implicit sphere trees. In *Proceedings of the 2008 symposium on haptic interfaces for virtual environment and teleoperator systems, HAPTICS '08* (pp. 319–325). Washington: IEEE Computer Society. ISBN 978-1-4244-2005-6. doi:10.1109/HAPTICS.2008.4479964.

17. Sagardia, M., Hulin, T., Preusche, C., & Hirzinger, G. (2008). Improvements of the voxmap-PointShell algorithm-fast generation of haptic data-structures. In *53rd IWK-Internationales Wissenschaftliches Kolloquium*, Ilmenau, Germany.

18. Schömer, E., & Thiel, C. (1995). Efficient collision detection for moving polyhedra. In *11th annual symposium on computational geometry*, June (pp. 51–60).

19. Schömer, E., & Thiel, C. (1996). Subquadratic algorithms for the general collision detection problem. In *12th European workshop on computational geometry*, March (pp. 95–101).

20. Spence, C., Pavani, F., & Driver, J. (2000). Crossmodal links in spatial attention between vision and touch: allocentric coding revealed by crossing the hands. *Journal of Experimental Psychology. Human Perception and Performance*, 1298–1319.

21. Suri, S., Hubbard, P. M., & Hughes, J. F. (1998). Collision detection in aspect and scale bounded polyhedra. In *SODA* (pp. 127–136).

22. Terdiman, P. (2001). *Memory-optimized bounding-volume hierarchies* (Technical report). codercorner.com. URL http://www.codercorner.com/Opcode.htm.

23. Trenkel, S., Weller, R., & Zachmann, G. (2007). A benchmarking suite for static collision detection algorithms. In V. Skala (Ed.), *International conference in Central Europe on computer graphics, visualization and computer vision (WSCG)*, 29 January–1 February 2007. Plzen: Union Agency. URL http://cg.in.tu-clausthal.de/research/colldet_benchmark.

24. Unger, B. J., Nicolaidis, A., Berkelman, P. J., Thompson, A., Klatzky, R. L., & Hollis, R. L. (2001). Comparison of 3-D haptic peg-in-hole tasks in real and virtual environments. *IEEE/RSJ, IROS, 1751–1756*.

25. van den Bergen, G. (1998). Efficient collision detection of complex deformable models using aabb trees. *Journal of Graphics Tools, 2*(4), 1–13. URL http://dl.acm.org/citation.cfm?id=763345.763346.

26. Van den Bergen, G. (1999). A fast and robust gjk implementation for collision detection of convex objects. *Journal of Graphics Tools, 4*(2), 7–25. URL http://dl.acm.org/citation.cfm?id=334709.334711.

27. Vemuri, B. C., Cao, Y., & Chen, L. (1998). Fast collision detection algorithms with applications to particle flow. *Computer Graphics Forum, 17*(2), 121–134.

28. Weller, R., Klein, J., & Zachmann, G. (2006). A model for the expected running time of collision detection using AABB trees. In R. Hubbold & M. Lin (Eds.), *Eurographics symposium on virtual environments (EGVE)*, Lisbon, Portugal, 8–10 May.

29. Weller, R., Mainzer, D., Sagardia, M., Hulin, T., Zachmann, G., & Preusche, C. (2010). A benchmarking suite for 6-dof real time collision response algorithms. In *Proceedings of the 17th ACM symposium on virtual reality software and technology (VRST)* (pp. 63–70). New York: ACM. ISBN 978-1-4503-0441-2. doi:10.1145/1889863.1889874. URL http://cg.in.tu-clausthal.de/publications.shtml#vrst2010.

30. Zachmann, G. (1995). The boxtree: exact and fast collision detection of arbitrary polyhedra. In *SIVE workshop*, July (pp. 104–112).

31. Zachmann, G. (1998). Rapid collision detection by dynamically aligned dop-trees. In *Proceedings of the virtual reality annual international symposium, VRAIS '98* (p. 90). Washington: IEEE Computer Society. ISBN 0-8186-8362-7. URL http://dl.acm.org/citation. cfm?id=522258.836122.
32. Zhou, Y., & Suri, S. (1999). Analysis of a bounding box heuristic for object intersection. *Journal of the ACM, 46*(6), 833–857.

Chapter 7
Applications

In the previous sections, we have presented new data structures and algorithms for collision detection and sphere packings. However, we did not develop these methods just because of their scientific beauty, but because they are really useful in practical relevant scenarios.

Obviously, our data structures for collision detection can be used in almost all situations where collision detection is required. In Chap. 2 we have already mentioned a wide spectrum of possible applications. However, we also used our data structures and algorithms to realize projects that would hardly be possible without them. In this chapter we will present exemplarily three different applications that are based on our research and that are interesting from a scientific or engineering point of view.

We will start with an extension of our sphere-packing algorithm. Based on the dense packing of spheres for arbitrary objects, we will present a new method for the simulation of deformable objects, the *sphere–spring systems*. Sphere–spring systems are an extension of the classical mass–spring systems: we just replace the dimensionless particles by spheres that represents the object's volume. This allows us to define new control parameters; namely, the transfer of volume between the spheres and a novel volume force model. Moreover, maintaining the non-penetration constraint of the spheres during the simulation guarantees volume preservation. Additionally, we present a parallel implementation of this sphere–spring system using the capabilities of modern GPUs. We applied our system to the animation of a complex virtual human hand model.

Our second example presents an application of our ISTs (see Chap. 5) in robotics. In collaboration with KUKA Robotics Corp., we applied our ISTs to interactive obstacle avoidance in highly dynamic environments. The obstacles were maintained via a Kinect camera in real time. Hence, they are represented as a point cloud. Consequently, our applications extends the IST distance computation to fast distance queries for point cloud data.

Parts of this work have been previously published in [61–63].

R. Weller, *New Geometric Data Structures for Collision Detection and Haptics*, Springer Series on Touch and Haptic Systems, DOI 10.1007/978-3-319-01020-5_7, © Springer International Publishing Switzerland 2013

Finally, we present a haptic workspace that allows high fidelity, two-handed multi-user interactions in scenarios containing a large number of dynamically simulated rigid objects and a polygon count that is only limited by the capabilities of the graphics card. Based on this workspace, we present a novel multi-player game that supports qualitative as well as quantitative evaluation of different force-feedback devices in demanding haptic manipulation tasks. The game closely resembles typical tasks arising in tele-operation scenarios or virtual assembly simulations. Using our haptic game, we conducted a comprehensive user study that evaluates the influence of the degrees of freedom on the users' performance in complex bi-manual haptic interaction tasks. The results of our user study show that 6 DOF force-feedback devices outperform 3 DOF devices significantly, both in user perception and in user performance.

7.1 Related Work

In this section, we will present a very short overview on existing methods that are closely related to the applications in this chapter. A complete overview over all previous methods for all three applications would go far beyond the scope of this book. Therefore, we restrict ourselves to a few basic and recent works. The section is subdivided into four parts.

We start with a section about general methods for the simulation of deformable objects. Then, we present the special challenges that arise when simulating a human hand.

The third section outlines recent methods for real-time obstacle avoidance in robotics, with a special focus on approaches that rely on data that is retrieved via depth cameras.

Finally, we discuss user studies that are related to evaluation on the influence of the degrees of freedom in human–computer interactions.

7.1.1 General Deformation Models of Deformable Objects

Actually, there already exist a wide spectrum of methods for the simulation of deformable objects. The survey by Nealen et al. [43] provides a good overview. Basically, we can distinguish two main approaches: geometric and physics-based algorithms. Geometric methods, like meshless deformations [5, 38, 40] or mass–spring systems [8, 11], can be usually computed very fast and most of them are perfectly suited for parallelization. However, physical properties like volume preservation can be modeled only with further, often costly, extensions [17, 55].

Physics-based methods, e.g. the *Finite-Element-Method* (*FEM*) [19] directly support the computation of such physical properties. Unfortunately, they are computationally very expensive and can hardly be used in real-time simulations. Simplifications like the explicit FEM [39] are suited for real-time use, but in the case of large deformations or large time steps they can end up in artifacts.

Another physics-based methods is the *Discrete-Element-Method* (*DEM*). It relies on sphere packings and can be used for the analysis of fractures, but also for the simulation of fluids and granular materials [23]. The DEM is more flexible than the FEM, but it is also computationally even more expensive. Therefore, Munjiza [41] developed a combination of both methods, but it is only applicable to offline simulations.

7.1.2 Hand Animation

Realistic simulation of a virtual hand adds further challenges to the underlying deformable model. Usually, virtual models of the human hand are skeleton-based. The individual limbs of the model are associated with the joints of a virtual skeleton and take over its movements. One of the most simple forms of skeleton-based animations is the so-called *skeleton subspace deformation* (*SSD*) [34]. It is the most widely used technique for real-time character animation. The movements of the limbs of the model are calculated by a simple linear transformation blending technique. However, the SSD also has some drawbacks. For instance, it produces poor results on complicated joints like the thumb.

Some authors presented solutions to overcome these drawbacks by combining the SSD with other techniques. In Magnenant-Thalmann et al. [34], the position of the vertices of the model are corrected by using an exponential function depending on their distance from the joints of the skeleton. Thereby, the deformations look more realistic. Another possibility is the pose-space deformation [32]. They make a correction of the model based on data that is specified for different key poses. The degrees of freedom of motion are interpreted as the spatial dimensions of the pose space. This technique combines the shape interpolation [7] with the skeleton-based animation. The shape interpolation calculates the current target pose of the animation from the given key pose by linear combination. The calculation is very simple, but requires preset poses that have been (possibly expensive) obtained from a reference model. The shape interpolation is often used for facial animation. The *Eigenskin* animation by Kry et al. [29] provides an improvement of the technique that is used by the pose-space deformation. It uses a singular value decomposition to store the data of the preset poses in a compressed form. By this means, the calculation of the correction of the model can also be made by the graphics hardware.

However, all these SSD-based approaches can handle only the visible deformations on the outer skin. There are other algorithms that additionally deal with the simulation of the internal structures and their physical properties. Albrecht et al. [1] developed a model of a human hand that consists of bones, muscles and skin. The movements of this model are triggered by the contractions of the muscles. To represent all aspects of muscle movements, two types of muscles are used: pseudo muscles whose contractions cause the rotations of the limbs and geometric muscles, which emulate the volume of real muscles. The operation of the geometric muscles is described by Kaehler et al. [25]. Each muscle fiber is composed of segments whose volume is simulated by ellipsoids. If the muscles are contracted, these segments are shorter and thicker. The outer skin is connected to the muscles by a mass–spring system and it can take over their deformations. Sueda et al. [52] described a technique that can be used to simulate the deformation of the tendons of the hand. This technique is suitable to expand existing animation systems. The tendons are simulated by cubic B-spline curves. In Chen and Zeltzer [10], the deformation of the muscle is calculated using the FEM. A complex volume is divided into many subspaces (typically tetrahedron). The movements of the nodes of the tetrahedron are represented as a system of equations that is solved by numerical methods. The FEM provides a high degree of physical accuracy, but at the expense of the runtime behavior. Such simulations are typically not suitable for real-time applications. The computational complexity of the FEM is highly dependent on the number of tetrahedra. In order to reduce the computational cost of linear 4-node tetrahedra, also quadratic 10-node tetrahedra can be used to simulate an organically shaped volume [37]. Jaillet et al. [22] presented a technique that uses a system of spheres to simulate deformable volumetric objects like human organs. The movements of the spheres are either calculated using the Lennard–Jones potential or a mass–spring system. However, they did not include volume transfer, therefore, their mass–spring systems are very stiff.

7.1.3 Obstacle Avoidance in Robotics

The movement of autonomous robots in unknown environments offers numerous challenges to both, hard- and software: the robots have to retrieve data to create a map of their environment, they have to localize themselves in this environment and they have to plan paths for their movements while simultaneously avoiding obstacles.

The first challenge is already the retrieval of the data: several different sensor types have been proposed, including monocular cameras [12], stereoscopic cameras [28], laser scanners Weingarten et al. [60] and time-of-flight cameras [44, 47].

In a second step, this sensor data can be combined to create a map of the environment. For instance, May et al. [36] proposed an iterative closest point algorithm for the registration of several depth images. Henry et al. [16] combined depth images and classical color images to construct loop-closed maps of large indoor environments. Obviously, the resulting maps can be used for collision avoidance and path planning using any appropriate collision detection method. However, all these approaches require several seconds for the environment to be reconstructed. Therefore, they can hardly be applied to real-time collision avoidance, and they cannot handle online changes that happen in *dynamic* environments.

Several methods has been proposed for such *online collision avoidance* approaches. Some authors include a high number of additional sensors like infrared or ultrasound to the robots or the environment. These sensors have a limited range of view or produce only coarse data but their combined output can be used to avoid collisions with abruptly popping up objects [18]. Other works use neural networks [6], behavioral Bayesian networks [64] or optical flow algorithms for sequences of images [33] that can be further improved by also including depth images [48]. Kuhn and Henrich [30] introduced the idea to compute distances directly from single images of the environment using computer-vision classification techniques. However, they did not include depth values.

Especially the release of Microsofts inexpensive depth camera Kinect inspired many researchers to new online collision avoidance algorithms that work directly on the depth image, often represented as a point cloud. For example, Biswas and Veloso [9] proposed an error minimization method providing real-time robot pose estimation. However, their approach is restricted to ground robots moving in a 2D space. Also Bascetta et al. [3] represented the robot only by a single point in order to simplify the distance computation. Schiavi et al. [50] compared the obstacle and the robot depth maps by an image plane projection in 3D. The approach that is closest related to our method, was developed simultaneously to ours by Flacco et al. [13]. They also use a KUKA Light-Weight-Robot and a Kinect for the data retrieval. Their primary focus is on the computation of the collision responses based on distances and velocities and less on the acceleration of the distance queries. Actually, the distance computation is derived from a simple spherical approximation of the robot's surface. However, they do not describe any acceleration data structures for the distance queries.

7.1.4 Evaluation of Haptic Interactions

Haptic user interfaces have been actively applied to the domain of human–computer interaction in virtual environments for almost two decades. Many user studies have shown that providing haptic feedback during virtual interaction tasks has positive effects on the perceived realism.

For instance, Basdogan et al. [4] developed a multimodal shared virtual environment. The experiments showed that force feedback during collaboration with a remote partner contributes to the feeling of "sense of togetherness", which is a kind of presence. Moreover, force feedback also helps to improve the user performance. Other authors obtained very similar results with respect to multi-user haptic interactions. Experiments cover a wide spectrum of tasks reaching from training of motor skills in surgery [20], rehabilitation tasks Jung et al. [24], tele-operation [51] to computer games [53]. Moreover, haptic systems can also help to enhance the emotional immersion in real-time messaging. Tsetserukou [54] developed a virtual hug system that supports 3D virtual worlds like Second Life.

Furthermore, some bi-manual haptic workspaces have been developed already: Murayama et al. [42] used two SPIDAR-G devices that provide 6 DOF motion and 6 DOF force feedback. A simple 3D pointing task was used to evaluate the system. The results indicate that bi-manual haptic interactions are more intuitive and efficient with respect to task completion time than single-handed manipulations. Two-handed haptic interaction has also shown to be a promising way for shape model-ing applications: Attar et al. [2] was able to ensure an enhanced precision during interaction; Keefe et al. [26] applied a two-handed tracking system and Phantom devices to help users control their gestures during sketching 3D shapes directly in 3D space.

In addition, there exists a large body of work on two-handed interaction in gen-eral, without a special focus on haptics. For instance, Leganchuk et al. [31] has shown that two-handed interaction combines two types of advantages: first, twice as many degrees of freedom simultaneously available to the user can result in increased motion efficiency; second, single-handed interaction usually requires a higher level of abstraction because of an unnatural, mental composition task. Consequently, bi-manual interaction can reduce the cognitive load. Veit et al. [56] was partly able to validate these assumptions. They conducted a user study to test two-handed freeform deformations using datagloves. The results show an improvement of the user's per-ception, but only if the degree of symmetry was high.

However, the effect of the degrees of freedom on the user's perception is still an active field of research. Jacob et al. [21] proposed a theoretical principle to cap-ture the control structure of an input device: a device that is able to move directly across all dimensions is called an *integral* device, while a device that constrains the user's movement along a single dimension is called a *separable* device. This is an extension to the theoretical framework proposed by Garner [14], called the *perceptual structure*, of objects and tasks by structuring its attributes into integral and separable attributes. They supported this theory by showing that user perfor-mance increases if the perceptual structure of the object being manipulated matches the control structure of the device. However, the matter does not seem to be settled yet, since Veit et al. [57] obtained completely opposite results when conducting a simple manipulation experiment using a dataglove for an integral device versus a touchscreen for a separable device: the results suggest that the simultaneous ma-nipulation of all DOFs does not necessarily lead to better performance. Martinet et al. [35] validated these results when investigating 3D manipulation using a 2D multitouch screen.

However, all of the experiments mentioned in the above two paragraphs were conducted without any force feedback. Consequently, it is impossible to extend the findings directly to haptic environments. For example, Veit et al. [57] explains his results by real-world constraints that reduce the interaction dimensionality in the real world, such as gravity. But with haptic devices it is easy to model these physical constraints as well.

To our knowledge, there is very little work on the comparison of haptic devices with different degrees of freedom. Wang and Srinivasan [59] presented a study about the effect of torque feedback on purely haptic perception of the location of objects in virtual environments. Usually, research concentrated mostly on analyzing devices with an asymmetric number of sensors and actuators. For instance, Verner and Oka-mura [58] found that for tasks like drawing or tracing, devices with 3 DOFs of force and an additional 3 DOFs of positioning can approximate the performance of full force and torque feedback.

7.2 Sphere–Spring Systems and Their Application to Hand Animation

A main goal of virtual reality is a realistic simulation of physical presence in computer-simulated environments. While the level of realism of visual and aural sensations has been improved significantly during the past decades, the simulation of realistic and intuitive interactions is still a challenge. The most important tool for interactions in the real world are our hands. In applications like surgery simulation, virtual prototyping or virtual assembly, a plausible simulation of the human hand is essential to gain the desired grade of realism. On the hardware side, input devices like datagloves already help to transform the motion of the human hand into virtual worlds. But a realistic real-time simulation of a virtual hand model is still an active field of research.

Actually, the human hand is one of the most difficult objects to animate. The reason is its complex structure consisting of bones, muscles, tendons, veins and skin. These parts are made of different materials with different physical properties. Moreover, their interaction provides a variety of complex movement sequences. The hand is divided into separate moveable limbs, their location and mobility is determined by their bones. These bones are rigid bodies, which cannot be deformed. In contrast, the soft tissue parts can be stretched during the movement in some parts and in other parts they are compressed. Thereby, folds and humps become visible on the outer skin. To make a computer model of a human hand look realistic, either the internal structure of the hand with all its parts, or at least the effects that are visible on the skin have to be simulated. Usually, the more detailed the model is, the more complex is the simulation.

In this chapter, we present a virtual hand model that simulates all the essential components of the human hand and their interaction. Therefore, we introduce a new model for the simulation of deformable objects, the *sphere–spring system*. The sphere–spring system is an extension of the well-known mass–spring system. The basic idea is very simple: instead of representing the mass as dimensionless points, we additionally assign a certain volume to each mass point. In detail, the volume of the soft tissue beneath the skin is represented by a system of non-overlapping spheres. The spheres are connected via springs. During simulation, we keep up this non-penetration constraint which directly leads to a volume preserving simulation of the tissue. Like mass–spring systems, our sphere–spring system is perfectly suited for parallelization. Finally, we present a parallel implementation on the GPU using CUDA.

7.2.1 Sphere–Spring System

Our new *sphere–spring system* is an extension of the classical mass–spring system, which is, due to its simplicity, widely used for real-time simulation of deformable objects. In the real world, objects are built of a large number of molecules that are connected via electromagnetic forces. Basically, a mass–spring system is a simplification of this physical model: objects are sampled to a set of discrete particles. In order to simulate the interaction between these particles, they are connected via virtual springs. Usually, the simulation is split into two phases: first, forces between the particles are calculated, and in a second step, the movement of the particles is computed.

In addition to external forces acting on the object, the internal spring forces acting on the particles can be computed following Hooke's spring law:

$$\mathbf{f}_{i \to j} = -\left[k_s \left(|\mathbf{l}| - l_r \right) + k_d \frac{\mathbf{v}\,\mathbf{l}}{|\mathbf{l}|} \right] \frac{\mathbf{l}}{|\mathbf{l}|}$$

$$\mathbf{f}_{j \to i} = -\mathbf{f}_{i \to j}$$

(7.1)

These equations denote the total spring forces acting on two particles p_i and p_j that are connected by a spring, with:

- k_s: the spring constant.
- k_d: the damping constant.
- l_r: the rest length of the spring.
- $\mathbf{l}$: the vector between the positions of the particles: $\mathbf{l} = p_i - p_j$
- $|\mathbf{l}|$: the length of $\mathbf{l}$.
- $\mathbf{v}$: the velocity vector of the spring that can be derived from the velocities v_i and v_j of the particles: $\mathbf{v} = v_j - v_i$.

The new positions of the particles can be computed using Newton's second law of motion:

$$F = ma = m\dot{v} = m\ddot{x}$$

(7.2)

Consequently, computing the movement of particles can be reduced to solving ordinary differential equations.

In our *sphere–spring system*, we do not concentrate the mass in dimensionless points, but we additionally assign a *volume* to each particle. Therefore, we compute a sphere packing to represent the volume of the soft tissue using our *Protosphere* algorithm (see Sect. 4.3). The masses are assigned proportionally to the size of the spheres. Please note that initially the spheres do not overlap. This new representation of the soft tissue offers additional possibilities during the simulation process. The goal is to keep the non-penetration constraint during the simulation and moreover, we want to keep the overall volume of all spheres to be constant. Together, these two constraints result in a volume preserving simulation, which cannot be realized using simple mass–spring systems.

In order to maintain these two constraints during the simulation, we propose two strategies: if two spheres overlap, we add an additional force to resolve the collision. Moreover, we allow the transfer of volume between the spheres. The latter allows us for example to model bulges that appear if the fingers are bent. In the next sections, we will explain both strategies in detail.

Everything else is similar to simple mass–spring systems: we simulate the motion of the spheres following Newton's law and the centers of the spheres are connected via springs. Consequently, our sphere–spring system also inherits all advantages of mass–spring systems: it is easy to implement, and due to the locality of the operations, it is perfectly suited for parallelization.

7.2.1.1 Volume Forces

The first strategy to keep the spheres separated, is to simply add an additional penalty force if two spheres overlap during the simulation. In order to realize this, we present a simple modification of Eq. (7.1).

Obviously, the penalty force should be proportional to the amount of overlap. The penetration volume V_p^{ij} between two spheres can be easily calculated by (see Sect. 5.3.2)

$$V_p^{ij} = \begin{cases} 0 & \text{if } |\mathbf{l}| > r_i + r_j, \\ \frac{4}{3}\pi \left(\min\left(r_i, r_j\right)\right)^3 & \text{if } |\mathbf{l}| + \min\left(r_i, r_j\right) \leq \max(r_i, r_j), \\ \frac{\pi(r_i+r_j-|\mathbf{l}|)(|\mathbf{l}|^2+2|\mathbf{l}|r_i+2|\mathbf{l}|r_j-3r_1^2-3r_2^2+6r_1r_2)}{12\cdot|\mathbf{l}|} & \text{else} \end{cases}$$

$$(7.3)$$

where r_i denotes the radius of the sphere i.

We use this amount of overlap to add an additional penalty force to Eq. (7.1):

$$\mathbf{f}_{i \to j} = -\left[k_s\left(|\mathbf{l}| - l_r\right) + k_d\frac{\mathbf{v}\,\mathbf{l}}{|\mathbf{l}|} + k_v V_p^{ij}\right]\frac{\mathbf{l}}{|\mathbf{l}|}$$

$$\mathbf{f}_{j \to i} = -\mathbf{f}_{i \to j}$$

$$(7.4)$$

With this new volume constant k_v, we can directly control the amount of overlap: the larger we choose k_v, the less overlap is allowed. However, if we choose k_v too large, we recognized some unwanted side-effects. For instance, we need much more iterations to get a stable state of the system. In order to avoid these drawbacks, we additionally propose a method to transfer volume between the spheres.

7.2.1.2 Volume Transfer

Applying volume forces alone is not enough to maintain all our constraints, namely the non-penetration constraint. Therefore, we additionally allow the spheres to transfer parts of their volume to adjacent spheres. In order to guarantee a constant overall volume, the same amount of volume that a sphere emits must be obviously absorbed by another sphere.

Actually, we do not simply transfer the whole penetration volume $V_{\text{penetration}}$ that we have computed using Eq. (7.3), but we introduce an additional transfer factor

k_{trans} to control the amount of transferred volume. Obviously, k_{trans} can be chosen dynamically with respect to the penetration volume to gain another degree of freedom. However, in our prototypical implementation we used a constant factor. Overall, we get for the transfer volume

$$V_{\text{trans}} = k_{\text{trans}} \cdot V_p \tag{7.5}$$

One question is still open: How do we know *where* we should transfer the volume? We will answer this question in the next section.

Direction of Volume Transfer

If an external force acts on a soft object, e.g. if we press a finger into a soft part of our body, we get a dent at the position where the force impacts. This means that the tissue that formerly has filled this dent has been displaced. Actually, the tissue avoids the force. In the volume transfer of our sphere–spring system we emulate this avoiding with a simple heuristic. The tissue seeks regions where no force is acting on it. Therefore, it moves into the opposite direction of the impacting force. Consequently, we also transfer the volume away from the forces.

In detail, the accumulation of all spring forces from Eq. (7.4) and the external forces acting on a sphere s_i deliver the direction and the magnitude of the resulting force f_{s_i}. Because we want to transfer the volume into the direction of f_{s_i}, we simply have to search all adjacent spheres and choose the one sphere s_j that is "mostly" in the transfer direction:

$$s_j \mid s_j \in Adj_{s_i} \wedge$$

$$l_{i \to j} \cdot f_{s_i} > 0 \wedge$$

$$\forall s_k \in Adj_{s_i}, \ s_k \neq s_j \mid l_{i \to k} \cdot f_{s_i} \leq l_{i \to j} \cdot f_{s_i} \tag{7.6}$$

where s_i is the ith sphere in the system, f_{s_i} is the resultant force of the sphere s_i, Adj_{s_i} denotes the set of all adjacent spheres of s_i and $l_{i \to j} = \frac{p_{s_j} - p_{s_i}}{|p_{s_j} - p_{s_i}|}$ is the normalized directional vector from sphere s_i to sphere s_j (see Fig. 7.1).

Obviously the existence of such a sphere is not guaranteed. If all the adjacent spheres k of the current sphere s_i are located in the opposite half space of our force f_{s_i}, we simply do not transfer any volume.

Rest Volume

Unfortunately, the volume transfer alone is not sufficient to guarantee a stable simulation. Just think of a constant external force, like wind, acting on a sphere. The sphere will continuously reduce its volume until it is zero. Consequently, it will never retrieve any volume back from its adjacent spheres, even if the force stops.

Fig. 7.1 Sphere B has two adjacent spheres A and C. The penetration volume will be transferred to A, because A is closest to the direction of the force vector F_b

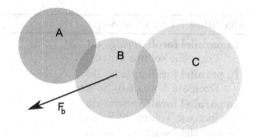

Simply defining a minimum sphere size could avoid this problem. However, a wide variety between the minimum and maximum sphere size leads to numerical problems during simulation. Moreover, the system could never again reach its initial state. Therefore, we propose a different idea to deal with this problem, which is closely related to the rest length of the springs.

Usually, in a mass–spring system, a *rest length* of the springs is defined. If the length of all springs matches their rest length, the system is in an equilibrium state, the so-called *rest pose*. Similarly to the rest length of the springs, we introduce a *rest volume* of the spheres. This rest volume is simply defined as the initial volume of the spheres in the rest pose. During simulation, all spheres try to restore their rest volume, as all springs try to restore their rest length. On the one hand, this additional parameter allows the system to go back to a well defined and stable initial state. On the other hand, it prevents the spheres from transferring all their volume to their neighbors without the chance of ever getting it back.

7.2.2 Parallelization of the Sphere–Spring System

Like classical mass–spring systems, our sphere–spring system is perfectly suited for parallelization, because all basic steps rely on local information only.

In detail we mention the following.

- *Force Volume:* The force volume of Eq. (7.4) can be computed separately for all springs. We simply have to compute the penetration volume and the force for each connected pair of spheres.
- *Volume Transfer:* Actually, parallelizing the volume transfer is not as straightforward as the other steps, because two spheres are involved. Decreasing the volume of one sphere and increasing the volume of another sphere may result in a typical *Write-After-Write* error if different spheres try to increase the volume of the same adjacent sphere.

   However, we can avoid this problem with a simple trick: we divide the decrease and increase of the volume into two separate phases.

   In the first phase, we compute the direction of the volume transfer. Therefore, we have to check all adjacent spheres of each sphere. Obviously, this can be done in parallel. Moreover, we decrease the volume if necessary, and we store the index of that sphere that should receive the volume.

Algorithm 7.1 Iteration-Step

In parallel forall *Springs* **do**
   Compute Volume Force
In parallel forall *Spheres* **do**
   Decrease Volume of Sphere
In parallel forall *Spheres* **do**
   Increase Volume of Sphere
In parallel forall *Spheres* **do**
   Move Sphere

In a second step, we collect the volumes of all adjacent spheres that should be transferred.

- *Sphere Movement:* Just like the particles in mass–spring systems, the movement of the spheres can be computed independently for all spheres. We have to solve the respective ordinary differential equation.

Overall, a single iteration step of our parallel implementation of the sphere–spring system can be summarized as described in Algorithm 7.1.

7.2.3 Application to a Virtual Human Hand Model

In this section, we will briefly describe our virtual hand model to which we applied our sphere–spring system. Usually, simulating a human hand is more complicated than the simulation of a fully elastic body like a pillow. This is mainly because of the additional skeleton inside the hand. Actually, the movement of the skeleton directly affects the deformation of the hand from the inside. Moreover, only parts of the skin may be affected by skeletal transformation, e.g. if we bend only a single finger.

Basically, our hand model is divided into three different layers: the skeleton inside the hand, a layer of spheres that represents the soft tissue, and, finally, the skin on the surface of the hand (see Fig. 7.2). Therefore, we have also different kinds of springs between these layers: some spheres are connected to the skeleton via *skeleton-sphere–springs*, spheres that touch the surface are connected to the skin via *skin-sphere–springs*, and finally, there exist springs between the spheres to realize the sphere–spring system. Additionally, we included springs between the polygons that realize the skin (see Fig. 7.3).

The skeleton of the hand is divided into separate bones. The bones are organized in a typical scenegraph hierarchy. Therefore, transforming the hand, or at least parts of the hand, can be realized by simple matrix multiplications. During the simulation, the bones are treated as rigid bodies.

The connections between the bones and the spheres and the springs between the skin and the spheres, respectively, define which parts of the hand must be moved if a bone transformation is applied.

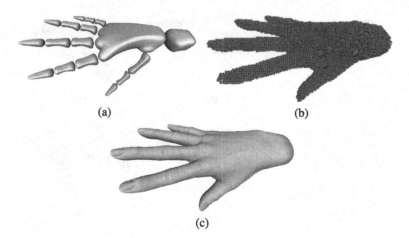

(a)   (b)

(c)

Fig. 7.2 The different layers of our virtual human hand: the skeleton (**a**), the sphere packing (**b**), and the skin (**c**)

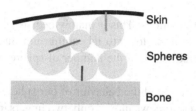

Fig. 7.3 Our model of the virtual hand consists of three different layers: the bones, the spheres, and the skin. Basically, there exist three different types of springs: between the bones and the springs, between adjacent spheres, and between the spheres and the skin

7.2.4 Results

We have implemented our sphere–spring system and the virtual hand model using NVIDIAs CUDA. CUDA offers the possibility to use the same memory for computation and for rendering via OpenGL. Therefore, we are able to use the same data buffers for the simulation and for the rendering. Consequently, we do not have to read or write any data from main memory after the initialization of our sphere–spring system. All our benchmarks were made with a NVIDIA GTX 480 GPU.

We measured the dependency of the running-time from various parameters. In our first scenario, we started with a flat outstretched hand that was then clenched to a fist. This is a worst-case scenario because almost all joints of the hand are involved (see Fig. 7.4). We tested this scenario for different numbers of spheres and different numbers of iterations. Usually, a higher number of iterations results in a higher level of the system's stability. The results are plotted in Fig. 7.5. As expected, a higher number of spheres in the sphere–spring systems requires more computation time. Moreover, the average time per iteration does not remain constant; it decreases with

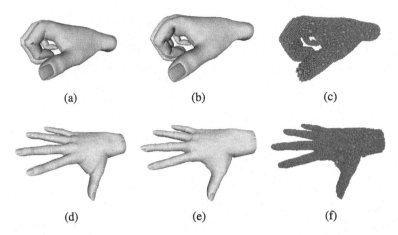

Fig. 7.4 Two different poses of the hand model calculated by a simple skeleton-based algorithm ((**a**), (**d**)) and by our sphere–spring algorithm ((**b**), (**e**)) with the underlying spheres ((**c**), (**f**))

an increasing number of iterations. This is mainly because the running-time of our algorithm decreases when it is closer to its equilibrium. In this case, the amount of volume to be transferred, but also the number of spheres that is involved in the volume transfer, decrease.

In a second scenario we tested the behavior of our sphere–spring system in less complex movements. Therefore, we moved only two fingers instead of including the whole hand as in the first scenario. Again, we tested several numbers of spheres. As expected, we see an increasing running-time with an increasing number of spheres (see Fig. 7.6). Moreover, we also get a higher running-time if more fingers are involved in the movement. However, the additional computational effort is relatively small.

Fig. 7.5 Average running-time of various sphere–spring systems with respect to the number of spheres and to the number of iterations

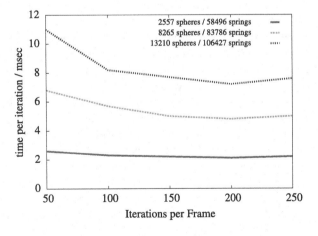

Fig. 7.6 Average
running-time for two different
movements of the virtual
hand. In the first case four
fingers of the hand were
moved simultaneously, while
in the second case only two
fingers were moved

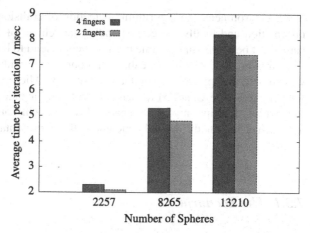

Fig. 7.7 A prototype of the
KUKA Omnirob (©KUKA
Robotics Corp., 2010)

7.3 Real-Time Obstacle Avoidance in Dynamic Environments

During the last years we observed that humans and robots move more and more to
close ranks. Just think about autonomous robotic vacuum cleaners that have already
entered our living rooms. In the future the importance of such tasks that unify human
and robotic workspaces will increase significantly, not only for small service robots,
but also in industrial applications. However, if our foot is hit by a small vacuum
cleaner that lost its way, this does not hurt too much. But a heavy and powerful industrial robot that got astray could injure people seriously. Therefore, the protection
of humans in robotic workspaces has an absolute priority [15].

This means that unexpected collisions between humans and robots have to be
avoided under all circumstances. This challenge can be solved by the design of the
robotic manipulators and on appropriate development of robust collision avoidance
methods. Actually, collision avoidance includes three major parts: the perception

of the environment, the algorithmic detection of collisions based on environment information and finally the corresponding movement of the robot [13]. All those parts must be solved in real time because people tend to behave unpredictably.

In this project, which we realized in cooperation with KUKA Robotics Corp., we explored the applicability of depth sensors like Microsoft's Kinect and our Inner Sphere Trees (see Chap. 5) to real-time collision avoidance. In the following we start with a description of the scenario. Then we will outline our new algorithmic approaches and finally we will conclude with the presentation of some preliminary results.

7.3.1 The Scenario

KUKA has developed the autonomous robotic platform Omnirob (see Fig. 7.7). The Omnirob consists of a 7 DOF KUKA Light-Weight-Robot (LWR) mounted on an autonomously driving car that adds even more degrees of freedom to the platform. The car can localize its position via a laser scanner, if the environment is already known, while the LWR recognizes its position from the rotations of its segments.

In our scenario we added a Kinect depth camera to the end-effector of the LWR in order to scan the environment. In our implementation, the Kinect is controlled via the OpenNI [45] drivers. An open source library for point clouds, the *Point Cloud Library (PCL)* [49], generates 3D point clouds from the depth images delivered by OpenNI.

The main goal of this project was the real-time distance computation between these point clouds and the robot. In contrast to Flacco et al. [13], we neglected the *reaction* of the robot, but concentrated on fast and accurate distance computations. Therefore, we represented the LWR by a detailed polygonal model. We split the geometric model into eight parts and computed Inner Sphere Trees for each of the parts (see Fig. 7.8) in order to accelerate the distance queries.

7.3.2 Accelerating Distance Queries for Point Clouds

Actually, our IST data structure support distance queries between ISTs and point clouds from scratch. We can simply model each point in the point cloud as a single sphere with radius zero and apply the recursive distance traversal from Sect. 5.3.1. However, a single depth image from the Kinect contains approximately 300K points. Performing $300K \times 8$ distance queries by brute force exceeds the desired frame rate even if one IST consists of only a single point, and we use coherence conditions in addition. Our benchmarks showed running-times of about 2 sec/query.

Consequently, we have to reduce the number of point/IST tests significantly in order to guarantee real-time performance. Therefore, we propose two different data structures that allow to filter special regions of interests from the point cloud.

Fig. 7.8 The LWR is
represented by eight parts.
We create an individual IST
for each of these parts

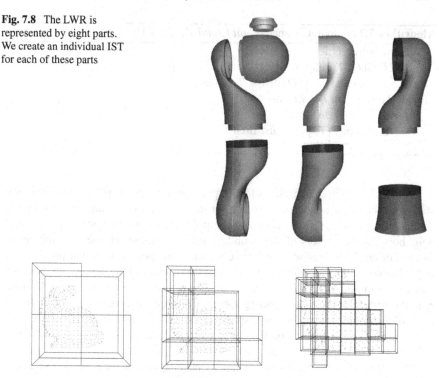

Fig. 7.9 Different octree levels for a point cloud model of a bunny

Namely we used an octree and an uniform grid. Both data structures can compute
regions that are in a predefined neighborhood to an input point. In the following we
will explain the implementation details and we will discuss the particular strengths
and weaknesses of both data structures.

7.3.2.1 Octree

Actually, an octree is a tree data structure for spatial subdivision. Basically, it partitions the 3D space recursively into eight octants. The recursion stops if either there
are no points included in the subregion, or if a certain depth and thus a certain size
of the leaf cells is met.

A main feature of octrees is that they allow fast location of nearest neighbors.
Principally, the nearest neighbor search (NNS) problem takes as input a point q and
returns the point $p_{closest}$ in the point cloud P which is closest to q. When using
octrees for this task, we first have to locate the cell that contains q and then we
explore recursively the cells in the neighborhood until $p_{closest}$ is found. Obviously,
the same technique can be used to define range queries. Range queries deliver all
those points $p_i \in P$ that are located inside a sphere of radius r around some query
point q.

Algorithm 7.2 computeDistance{*Point Cloud P, IST T* }

Compute octree O for P
dist = NNS(O, T.radius)
LeafList = RangeQuery(O, dist + T.radius)
forall *Leaves l_i in LeafList* **do**
   forall p_i *in* l_i **do**
      if *distance*(T, p_i) < *dist* **then**
         dist = distance(T, p_i)

We use these octree operations to compute our regions of interest. In detail, we start with the construction of an octree for the whole point cloud. For a complete distance query between the robot and the point cloud, we first locate the nearest neighbors for the centers of the bounding spheres—these are the root spheres—of each of our ISTs individually. This distance to the nearest neighbor provides an upper bound for the range query: assume that the distance of the nearest neighbor for sphere s_i with radius r_i is d_i. We know that each inner sphere has at most distance r_i to the surface of the root bounding sphere. Consequently, we will find the closest point of the point cloud to any inner sphere in the IST at a distance of at most $d_i + r_i$. Consequently, a range query on the octree with range $d_i + r_i$ delivers all candidates in our region of interest.

Algorithm 7.2 summarizes the distance query algorithm for a single IST and a point cloud.

Please note that if we have already computed a minimum distance for an IST, we can obviously use this value to optimize the minimum distance computations for the other ISTs.

In our implementation we used the octree provided by PCL. In addition to a fast octree construction, this library also supports fast NNS and range queries. Figure 7.9 shows some levels of an octree that was generated with PCL.

7.3.2.2 Uniform Grid

The advantage of octrees is their memory efficiency: we do not waste memory on storing void regions. On the other side, locating points in the tree requires a recursive traversal starting at the root. Moreover, the recursive construction of an octree is relatively expensive. Especially the latter disadvantage is essential because we have to construct a new octree for each frame. Therefore, we evaluated another data structure with a less expensive construction phase: the uniform grid.

Inserting points in a uniform grid is trivial. However, uniform grids usually lack of their high memory consumption. In order to overcome this disadvantage we use spatial hashing that stores only those cells in the grid that are really occupied by points.

The overall algorithm to determine the closest distance from an IST to the point cloud is almost the same as for octrees: we locate the centers of the ISTs in the

Fig. 7.10 A typical point cloud recorded by the Kinect and the polygonal model of the LWR. The *red line* denotes the minimum distance between the LWR and the point cloud (*left*). The complete setup of our application is the KUKA Omnirob with a head mounted Kinect in front of a workspace (*right*)

grid, find the nearest neighbor that defines an upper bound and finally we perform a range query (see Algorithm 7.2). The only difference is in the implementation of the NNS and the range query. Actually, both operations can be implemented by a simple uniform region growing.

7.3.3 Results

We implemented both approaches in a proof-of-concept application. Please note that the code, especially that for the queries, is not optimized yet. All tests were performed on an Intel Core i3-2100 CPU with 3.10 GHz and 4 GB main memory.

Figure 7.10 shows the typical setup: we mounted a Kinect to the end-effector of a KUKA Omnirob. The Omnirob is located in front of a workspace. During the tests we moved the objects on the workspace. The Kinect captures depth images that were used for the minimum distance computations. A single depth image has a resolution of approximately 270K points. Usually, the Kinect captures 30 frames per second.

In our first scenario, we tested the influence of the octree's and the grid's cell size to the performance. Figure 7.11 shows the average time that is required to construct the data structure and Fig. 7.12 shows the average time for a single distance query. On the one hand, the time that is required for the construction decreased with increasing cell size. On the other hand, the query time increased with increasing cell size. We found an optimum for both data structures for a cell size of about 8 cm. Obviously, the grid construction is faster than that of the octree but it requires more time for the queries. For both data structures, the construction time dominates the query time significantly (see Figs. 7.11 and 7.12). However, we were able to provide a close to real-time performance of about 40 msec per frame for both data structures even with our non-optimized implementation (see Fig. 7.13).

In a second scenario, we captured different depth images and merged them to a larger point cloud. This allows a more detailed map of the environment that can be

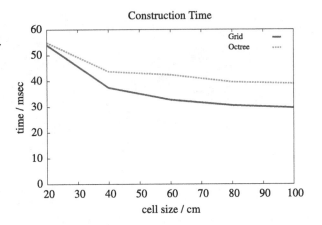

Fig. 7.11 Average construction time for a single point cloud with 270K points. The x-axis denotes different cell sizes of the quadtree and the grid

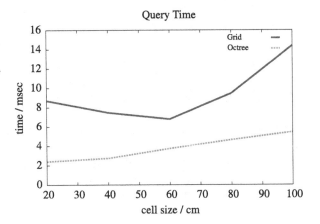

Fig. 7.12 Average query time, this means NNS, range query, and exact IST distance computation, for a single point cloud with 270K points. The x-axis denotes different cell sizes of the quadtree and the grid

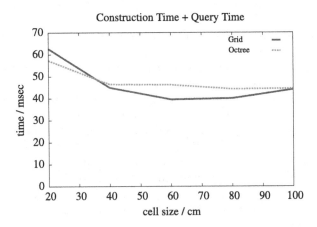

Fig. 7.13 Combined construction and query time from Figs. 7.11 and 7.12

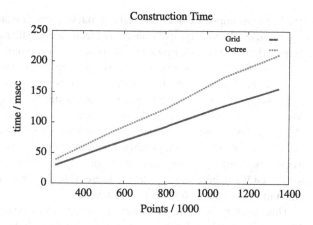

Fig. 7.14 Average construction time for point clouds with respect to the size of the point cloud. The cell size was set to 8 cm

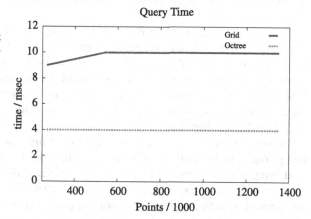

Fig. 7.15 Average query time for point clouds with respect to the size of the point cloud. The cell size was set to 8 cm

applied to path-planning tasks. Please note that we did not require any registration algorithm because the KUKA LWR knows its position and orientation from sensor data. As expected the construction time (see Fig. 7.14) increased linearly with the number of points. However, the query time remained almost constant (see Fig. 7.15).

7.4 3 DOF vs. 6 DOF—Playful Evaluation of Complex Haptic Interactions

Haptics is an emerging technology; it adds the sense of touch to applications in fields like tele-operations, medical simulations, or virtual assembly tasks that are known from the automotive and aircraft industry. In these areas, force feedback already has helped to improve human–computer, as well as human–human interactions in multi-user scenarios for almost two decades.

For a long time, haptic devices were bulky, expensive, and could be installed and handled only by experts. This has changed but in the last few years, when the first low-cost haptic devices entered the market, which were designed especially for desktop use. Besides typical consumer electronic applications like games or online shops, where the sense of touch could be a decision criterion for selecting products, these low-cost devices could also be used to improve the quality of training skills or enhance the desktop of each constructing or design engineer.

However, if a whole engineering office should be equipped with haptic devices cost could be still a limiting factor, even if they are low-cost machines. The cost of haptic devices mainly depends on the number of actuators. Consequently, the low-cost devices for the mass market usually support only 3 DOFs. Obviously, real-world object manipulations comprise not only forces with 3 DOFs but also torques with 3 DOFs. Therefore, rendering these kinds of interactions faithfully requires much more expensive 6 DOF haptic devices.

This raises the question whether or not the enhanced experience is worth the additional cost for the 6 DOF devices, which is precisely the question that this section endeavors to answer.

Intuitively, it seems obvious that users operating with full 6 DOFs should perform much better than users that are provided only 3 DOFs. In fact, the influence of the DOFs in human–computer interaction is still an active field of research, with partly contradictory results, even if they do not include haptics and are restricted to single-hand interactions. However, this section not only presents a qualitative analysis, but also quantitative methodologies to assess the influence of full 6 DOF force and torque rendering objectively.

In order to conduct our user studies, we have implemented a haptic workspace that provides high-fidelity 6 DOF force feedback in object manipulation scenarios containing a large number of dynamically simulated rigid objects. In addition, it supports different kinds of haptic (and non-haptic) devices for bi-manual multi-user interactions. It relies on our new collision detection technique, the Inner Sphere Trees (see Chap. 5) that firstly meets the special requirements, especially the very high simulation frequency and the support to simultaneous simulation of lots of massive objects, of such a haptic workspace.

It is a challenge to define a task that does not favor one of the input methods in advance. In our case, this means we need a task that can be solved with 3 DOF devices as well as with 6 DOF devices with the same level of success. Moreover, we need a task that requires coordinated bi-manual interactions from the users. Therefore, we have developed a simple haptic multi-player game that requires complex, two-handed manipulations of two players within the same environment at the same time.

In order to evaluate the users' performance, we recorded all paths of all objects, including those of the users' hands, for later quantitative and qualitative analysis. Moreover, we utilized a questionnaire to evaluate some of the "softer" factors of such a haptic workspace.

The results support our initial hypothesis that 6 DOF haptic devices outperform 3 DOF haptic devices with respect to user perception and also user performance. This might encourage device manufacturers to make more efforts in the development of cheaper 6 DOF haptic devices for desktop use.

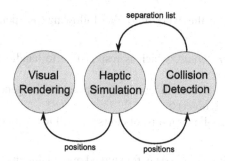

Fig. 7.16 The simulation thread in our haptic workspace computes the collision forces based on the *separation list*, which captures the current collision information. This list is generated in the collision detection thread. Conversely, the haptic thread passes the new positions of the objects to the collision and the (visual) rendering thread

7.4.1 Haptesha—A Multi-user Haptic Workspace

The main challenge when doing haptic rendering is the extremely high frequency that is required: while the temporal resolution of the human eye is limited to approximately 30 Hz, the bandwidth of the human tactile system is about 1000 Hz. In most haptic scenarios, the computational bottleneck remains the collision detection, whereas the force computation can be done relatively fast.

In order to achieve such a high simulation rate, the heart of our haptic workspace is our new geometric data structure, the Inner Sphere Trees (see Chap. 5), which not only allows us to detect collisions between pairs of massive objects at haptic rates, but also enables us to define a novel type of contact information that guarantees *stable* and *continuous* forces and torques, which are based on the penetration volume. This enables us to treat physics-based simulation and haptic rendering in a common way. The only difference between dynamic objects and user-controlled objects is that the forces for the latter are rendered to the haptic device instead of using them for the simulation.

For visual output we use the open source scenegraph OpenSG [46] that supports shading and multi-monitor output.

However, even if the ISTs are very fast, it is not possible to guarantee constant time intervals for the collision detection. Therefore, we extended the algorithm's time-critical approach and included multi-threading support. In the cases of inter-penetrating objects, the computation of the penetration volume can run slower than the required 1000 Hz, because it might have to visit many nodes during traversal, especially in the cases with heavy overlaps. Consequently, an answer of this query type cannot be guaranteed within a predefined time budget as it is needed for haptic applications. Moreover, the force computation requires time, too.

On the other hand, almost all currently available CPUs include multiple cores or, at least, support functions to accelerate multi-threading.

One appropriate strategy to realize time-critical traversals is a decoupling of the force computation and the collision detection by running them asynchronously in different threads. Therefore, we re-use the idea of separation lists once more.

Actually, we divide the work into the following independent threads (see Fig. 7.16):

1. a *haptic simulation thread*, which is responsible to handle the user input and computes the forces;
2. a *collision detection thread*, in which separation lists are generated for each pair of possibly colliding objects;
3. depending on the application it is, of course, possible to add other threads, e.g. a *rendering* thread.

During runtime, the collision detection thread only maintains a separation list and passes it to the haptic thread. In return, the haptic thread passes the current positions of the simulated objects to the collision detection thread for the next query. The haptic thread then uses the current separation list to compute the force, until the next collision detection query is finished.

Usually, especially in haptic simulations running at 1 kHz, the spatial coherence is high and, thus, the separation lists between two synchronizations do not differ very much.

7.4.2 The Design of the Study: A Haptic Game

Usually, when designing haptic user studies, some kind of object docking or path following task is used. Unfortunately, these kinds of tasks are not very well suited when one wants to compare the influence of the degrees of freedom, because, depending on the dock or the path, one of the devices is favored in advance. For example, if a docking task requires a rotation of the object, it is impossible to solve it with a 3 DOF device that does not support changes of the orientation. On the other hand, if the task does not require changes of the object's orientation, there would be no need for a 6 DOF device. Moreover, these tasks usually can be solved with a single-handed device. Consequently, there is no need for coordination between both hands, which is essential in bi-manual interaction tasks.

Consequently, we had to design a new kind of experiment that supports a fair comparison of devices with different degrees of freedom and additionally requires complex bi-manual interactions not only as an option, but as a necessity. Therefore, we use a kind of indirect and imprecise docking task. This means that the objects to place are not directly glued to the haptic tool but must be controlled indirectly following a physics-based simulation. Moreover, the objects do not have to be placed precisely into a predefined docking station, but into a wider goal.

This indirect interaction metaphor that we propose resembles closely typical tasks arising in bi-manual tele-operation scenarios or virtual assembly simulations. Thus, the analysis of the users' performance in this experiment allows for conclusions of practical relevance.

In detail: we have implemented a simple two-player haptic game that is based on our haptic workspace. The players sit face-to-face at a table with two monitors in between (see Fig. 7.17). Each player operates the two identical force-feedback devices

Fig. 7.17 The two-player setup with four haptic devices for our user study

Fig. 7.18 The playing field of our haptic game

on his side, one for each hand. In order to evaluate the differences between 3 and 6 DOF interactions, one of the players uses two 3 DOF devices, namely, two Novint Falcons (see Fig. 7.19, left), whereas his opponent operates two 6 DOF devices that where realized by two Haption Virtuose 6D Desktop devices (see Fig. 7.19, right).

We used these kinds of force-feedback devices, because they have comparable specifications (see Fig. 7.1), they are both designed for desktop use, and there is no other pair of devices that differs in DOFs yet has similar specs.

The playing field is a room with a set of complex objects with different shapes lying on the ground. Each player has a "well" in front of him and controls two rigid virtual hands with his two force-feedback devices. The goal of the game is to pick up the objects and place them in the player's own well in front of him. Figure 7.17

gives an overview of the setup with the four haptic devices; Fig. 7.18 shows a typical view of the playing field.

Even if the task is the same for both players, different strategies can lead to the goal depending on the degrees of freedom of the devices. In tests prior to the final study's design, the 6 DOF operators usually picked up a single object and directly placed it in the well. On the other hand, the 3 DOF users shoveled some of the objects to the front of the well and tried to push them up the well's walls (we dubbed this the "shovel technique"). Consequently, the success of both techniques can be tweaked by the height of the well and the number of objects in the scene. In order to guarantee a fair comparison we adjusted the parameters such that with both techniques the chance to win and the chance to pocket an objects is almost the same for both input devices. Additionally, we chose the objects such that their size and form factor force the users to really use coordinated bi-manual interactions.

For two reasons it is essential that we do not take the winning rate or the number of pocketed objects as distinctive measure: the same probability to win with both kinds of devices proves the fairness and comparability of our results and moreover, the winning rate could also influence the answers of the questionnaire subconsciously.

In order to maintain fairness we also implemented the facility to turn the virtual hands with the 3 DOF devices by mapping rotations to the buttons on the haptic handle (see picture in Fig. 7.19), because it could be complicated for the 3 DOF users to pick up or shovel the objects with the hands remaining in their initial orientation due to the rigidity of the controlled virtual hands. The device has four buttons; we used three of them to change the pitch, yaw, and roll of the virtual hand, while the fourth button changes the direction of the rotation. In addition to the general learning period when operating unknown devices, this relatively complex control paradigm for the three rotational degrees of freedom required some training. Thus each round of the game started with a training phase that ends when both players managed to pocket an object. However, the results of our user study show that almost all participants used the possibility to change the hand's orientation only in the training phase in order to bring the hands into a comfortable orientation. During the game they only made very few attempts to adjust the orientation.

For the evaluation, we recorded the forces and torques acting on the user-controlled hands and additionally, we tracked the covered distances and rotations. This data allows to derive conclusions about the efficiency of the haptic interaction. Furthermore, we recorded the time for the training phase. Moreover, we conducted a user interview after the game using a questionnaire, where we asked the users about the quality of the feedback and their preferences with respect to 3 DOFs vs. 6 DOFs.

The setting of a game was chosen to ensure that, due to the competitiveness, the users are highly concentrated on the challenge and not on the potentially unknown and fascinating devices. After finishing a round, the players swap seats. Thus, each player plays with both kinds of devices. Due to this, we were able to test a large amount of subjects in a relatively small time interval, and moreover, we could keep the learning phase relatively short.

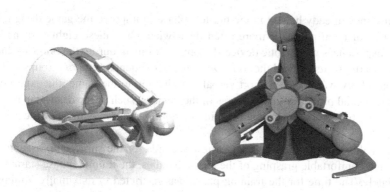

Fig. 7.19 The haptic devices that we used in our evaluation: the 3 DOF Novint Falcon (*left*, courtesy of Novint Technologies Inc., USA) and the 6 DOF Haption Virtuose 6D Desktop (*right*, courtesy of Haption S.A., France)

Table 7.1 The specifications of both force-feedback devices show a comparable workspace and a comparable amount of maximum translational force. The 6 DOF device can additionally render torques

	3 DOF	6 DOF
Manufacturer	Novint	Haption
Model	Falcon	Virtuose 6D Desktop
Translational Workspace	102 mm × 102 mm × 102 mm	Sphere with 120 mm in diameter
Rotational Workspace	–	35° in the 3 directions
Maximum force in translation	10 N	15 N
Maximum torque in rotation	–	0.5 Nm
Price	200$	30,000$

7.4.3 The User Study

In the following, we will give an overview of the user study that we conducted using our haptic game described above.

7.4.3.1 Participants and Protocol

We tested a total number of 47 participants, aged 17 to 34 years. Half of them were high school students visiting our department of computer science, the others were scientific employees with the department. Of the participants, 33 were male and 14 female, three were left-handed and 44 right handed. 27 of them play computer games regularly, and almost all have some experience in gaming, except four who stated they never had played a computer game before. Only five participants use VR devices regularly. Eight subjects did not play our haptic game for the first time, because they already helped in the pre-test phase to improve the game design, but only two of them played it more often than twice. Only these eight persons had made experiences with haptic devices before, six of them during the pre-test-phase.

The participants entered the room with the experimental setup in groups of four persons. They were given a short verbal introduction to the game, the experiment and the special properties and features of the devices, such as the dead-man protection of the 6 DOF device or the mapping of rotations to the buttons of the 3 DOF device.

After this short introduction and a few seconds for the subjects to assume the right and comfortable grasping of the haptic handles, the training phase started immediately. The time for the training phase was restricted to maximally 3 minutes but could end earlier if both players managed to pocket an object. Like the training phase, the game also lasted 3 minutes. During the game, the players received feedback about the score and the time limit by a heads-up display on the screen. After completing the game, the subjects were asked to answer a questionnaire and rate the intuitiveness of control, the quality of the force feedback and so on, on a five-point Likert scale. The Likert scale has suitable symmetry and equidistance for the use of parametric analysis.

7.4.3.2 Results

The groupwise introduction and the attendance of other persons in the room during the test could distract the players. However, the results of our survey show that the concentration during the game was rated very high (3 DOFs: $M = 4.32$, $SD = 0.837$, 6 DOFs: $M = 4.23$, $SD = 1.026$, with the Likert scale ranging from "Heavy distractions" $= 1$ to "No distractions" $= 5$). Also the training time (3 DOFs: $M = 2.51$, $SD = 0.655$, 6 DOFs: $M = 2.81$, $SD = 0.680$, with the Likert scale ranging from "Too short" $= 1$ over "Perfect" $= 3$ to "Too long" $= 5$) and the playing time (3 DOFs: $M = 2.64$, $SD = 0.705$, 6 DOFs: $M = 2.57$, $SD = 0.683$, with the same Likert scale) was rated as sufficient overall.

As mentioned in the introduction, we hypothesized that 6 DOF haptic devices are better suited for complex bi-manual haptic interactions than 3 DOF devices with respect to intuitiveness and the naturalness of the control paradigms, the quality of the force feedback, and other parameters. A paired-samples t-test was conducted to compare the measured values and the results of the survey in 3 DOF and 6 DOF conditions.

Overall, the results support our hypothesis that object manipulation using force feedback with 6 DOFs is more natural and more intuitive: from our survey, we get a highly significant difference in the scores for naturalness of control in the 3 DOF ($M = 2.83$, $SD = 0.816$) and 6 DOF ($M = 3.55$, $SD = 0.717$) case; $t(46) = -6.425$, $p < 0.001$ with the Likert scale reaching from "Not natural" $= 1$ to "Perfect natural" $= 5$. We get a similar highly significant result for the intuitiveness of control (3 DOF ($M = 3.28$, $SD = 0.877$) and 6 DOF ($M = 4.04$, $SD = 0.779$);

Fig. 7.20 The users' perception as voted in the survey. The 6 DOF device was rated significantly better with respect of naturalness and intuitiveness of control

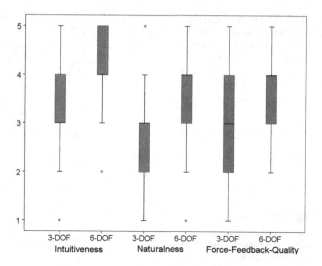

$t(46) = -4.741$, $p < 0.001$ (Likert scale from "Not intuitive" $= 1$ to "Perfectly intuitive" $= 5$)). Also, the quality of the force feedback shows highly significant differences between 3 DOF (M $= 2.98$, SD $= 1.011$) and 6 DOF (M $= 3.66$, SD $= 0.867$) conditions; $t(46) = -4.761$, $p < 0.001$ (Likert scale from "Unsatisfiable" $= 1$ to "Perfect" $= 5$) (see Fig. 7.20). However, the mediocre absolute values show that there is still room for improvements regarding the naturalness and the quality of the forces and torques.

Even though most subjects rated the time given for the training phase as sufficient for both kinds of devices, the paired-samples t-test shows a significant difference between 3 DOF (M $= 2.51$, SD $= 0.655$) and 6 DOF (M $= 2.81$, SD $= 0.680$) conditions; $t(46) = -2.625$, $p = 0.012$. This further supports the results about the intuitiveness of control and the higher naturalness.

In the training phase, the time measured until a player manages to pocket the first object also supports the users' experience we observed through the questionnaire: they needed significantly more time to learn the handling of the 3 DOF devices (M $= 94.66$, SD $= 69.370$) than the 6 DOF devices (M $= 60.74$, SD $= 51.809$); $t(46) = 2.954$, $p = 0.005$ (see Fig. 7.21).

In order to guarantee a fair comparison, we adjusted the task so that the 3 DOF operators and the 6 DOF operators can win with the same chance. The measured results support the validity of our calibration: overall, there were 20 rounds of all games won using a 3 DOF device, and 18 rounds won using a 6 DOF device (9 rounds were a tie).

The number of objects that were pocketed by users using the 6 DOF devices was slightly larger (M $= 5.94$, SD $= 4.532$) than the number of objects pocketed by users using the 3 DOF devices (M $= 5.64$, SD $= 4.321$). However, there is no statistically significant difference between the number of pocketed objects with respect to the DOFs (see Fig. 7.22).

Additionally, a one-way between-subjects ANOVA was conducted to compare the effect of experience on the number of pocketed objects: there was a significant

Fig. 7.21 The time that the
users needed to pocket the
first object during training
with respect to 3 DOF and
6 DOF devices. Clearly, the 3
DOF users needed
significantly more time

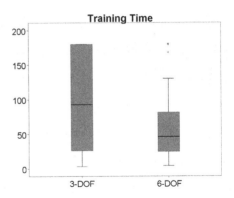

Fig. 7.22 There is no
statistically significant
difference between the
number of pocketed objects
with respect to the DOFs.
Hence, our adjustment of the
game guarantees a fair
comparison between the
different devices

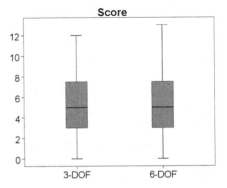

difference between the group that has haptic experience, which is exactly the group
that played the game more than once, and the participants that played the game
only for the first time (Unexperienced 3 DOF: N = 39, M = 4.95, SD = 3.692,
Experienced 3 DOF N = 8, M = 9.00, SD = 5.757, F(1.46) = 6.538, p = 0.014,
Unexperienced 6 DOF: N = 39, M = 5.08, SD = 3.608, Experienced 6 DOF N = 8,
M = 10.13, SD = 6.334, F(1.46) = 9.814, p = 0.003). In both cases, 3 DOF and
6 DOF, the experienced users were able to pocket significantly more objects than
the unexperienced users. However, they were still not able to pocket significantly
more objects with 6 DOF than with 3 DOF or vice versa. Also these results show
that the calibration of our experiment works correctly: the task can be solved with
both kinds of devices with the same succession rate. This implies the fairness of the
game.

Even if the chance to win the game is independent of the degrees of freedom, we
expected differences in the users' performance due to the different techniques: as
already mentioned in the section before, the 3 DOF users usually shoveled the objects on the ground into the direction of the well, whereas the 6 DOF users precisely
picked up the objects. These different strategies directly affects the efficiency of the
haptic interactions. The "shovel"-technique can be successful, but it is inefficient
with respect to the covered distances, because the users need a higher frequency of
forward and backward moving of their hands.

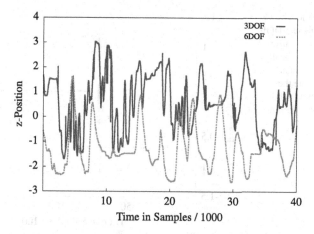

Fig. 7.23 Typical data recorded from the users' interaction during the game. This plot shows the position of the haptic handle in z direction, which is controlled by the users' dominant hand with the 3 DOF and 6 DOF device. Clearly, one can see the typical high frequencies caused by the "shoveling technique," which is often applied by 3 DOF users, whereas the 6 DOF users interact more precisely. Moreover, one can see how the 3 DOF user tries to distract the 6 DOF user at sample time 10k

Fig. 7.24 The distances covered by the users' dominant and non-dominant virtual hands. Clearly, the paths of the 3 DOF users are significantly longer than the paths of the 6 DOF users. Moreover, they prefer to use their dominant hand. Surprisingly, the 6 DOF users cover a slightly longer path with their non-dominant hand

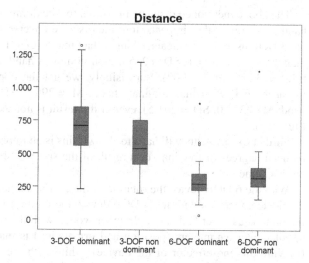

This hypothesis is supported by our measured data: the distances covered by the 6 DOF device that was used with the dominant hand (M = 295.8, SD = 134.0) is significantly (t(46) = −12.034, $p < 0.001$) shorter compared to the paths of the 3 DOF device used with the dominant hand (M = 724.1, SD = 235.0). For the non-dominant hand, we obtain almost the same picture (3 DOF (M = 374.0, SD = 291.5) and 6 DOF (M = 605.0, SD = 251.4); t(46) = −5.991, $p < 0.001$).

Figure 7.23 shows the z-position of the virtual hand in the scene, which is controlled by the user. One can clearly see the typical, high-frequency "shoveling" of

Fig. 7.25 This plot shows the roll-angle of the 3 DOF (*red*) and the 6 DOF users. The 6 DOF users typically rotate their virtual hands continuously, while the 3 DOF users let their hands in almost the same orientation at all times

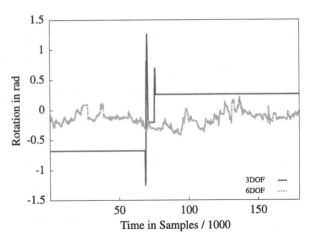

the 3 DOF user and the relatively smooth motion of the 6 DOF user. Moreover, the plots reveal another typical strategy of the 3 DOF users: they tried to distract the 6 DOF users when they had managed to grab an object. You can see this, for instance, at the 5000th sample position: here, the 3 DOF user tried to knock the object out of the 6 DOF user's hand.

The above mentioned distance measures for the dominant and the non-dominant hand have some other impacts, too: the distance covered by the dominant hand of the 3 DOF users is significantly longer than that of their non-dominant hand (dominant hand: M = 724.1, SD = 235.0; non-dominant hand: M = 605.0, SD = 251.4; t(46) = 3.368, p = 0.002). Surprisingly, we get the opposite result when looking at the 6 DOF paths (dominant hand: M = 295.8, SD = 134.0; non-dominant hand: M = 374.0, SD = 291.5), even if the result is not statistically significant (see Fig. 7.24).

Further experiments will have to show if this is an impact of the strain due to the reduced degrees of freedom, or a result of the special "shovel" strategy facilitated by this game.

With the 6 DOF device the rotation of the user's real hands is mapped directly to the device, whereas with the 3 DOF device the rotation virtual hand is mapped to the buttons as described above. In other words, with the 6 DOF device, an integral set of object parameters (position and orientation) is mapped to an integral task (moving the end-effector of the device), while with the 3 DOF device the set of object parameters is treated as a separable set [14, 21].

This has, of course, consequences for the strategies that users employ. Usually, the 3 DOF users first brought their virtual hands in a suitable orientation and changed it only very seldom during the game, whereas the 6 DOF users rotated their real and virtual hands continuously. Figure 7.25 shows a typical situation. Additionally, we computed the Euler angles and accumulated all rotational changes. This shows significant differences, using the paired-samples t-test, for both the dominant and non-dominant hands (6 DOF dominant: M = 90.0, SD = 64.0; and 3 DOF dominant: M = 15.1, SD = 16.0; t(46) = 7.495, p < 0.001; 6 DOF non-

Fig. 7.26 The total amount of rotations applied by the users during the game, which was obtained by accumulating the changes of the Euler angles. Obviously, the 3 DOF users avoid to rotate their virtual hands, probably because the orientation of the virtual hands is mapped to the buttons of the end-effector of the force-feedback device. Usually, they brought it in a comfortable position during the training phase and did not change it during the game

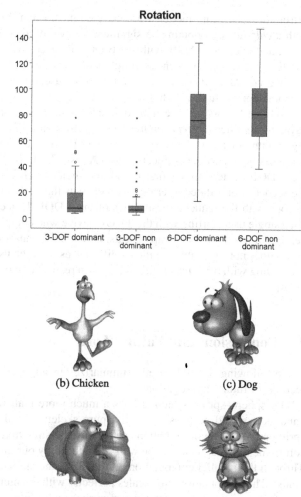

(a) Yellow Cat   (b) Chicken   (c) Dog

(d) Killer Whale   (e) Rhino   (f) Brown Cat

Fig. 7.27 Screenshots of the objects we used in the game. Surprisingly, the rhino (**e**) was pocketed significantly more often than the other objects

dominant: $M = 85.9$, $SD = 27.6$; and 3 DOF non-dominant: $M = 13.6$, $SD = 11.5$; $t(46) = 14.883$, $p < 0.001$) (see Fig. 7.26). This suggests that mapping of rotations to buttons cognitively overwhelmed users in time-critical tasks requiring precision motor control.

We used six different objects in our game, all of them are cartoon animals (see Fig. 7.27). We chose these objects, because their extremities, like the wide-spread arms, oversized feet and ears, or the tails, should simplify the grasping of the objects by clamping them between the fingers of the virtual hands (this facilitated object manipulation considerably). Surprisingly, the only object without strongly protruding extremities, the rhino model, was pocketed most often. We tested the significance with a chi^2-test and obtained a significance level of $p < 0.01$ with the 3 DOF devices, and even $p < 0.001$ with the 6 DOF devices. We believe that this is a hint that the abstraction between the simple handle of the force-feedback device and the detailed virtual hand cognitively overloads the users, but this has to be investigated in more depth in future studies.

All other factors we investigated, like the age, the sex, and the handedness do not have any significant effects on the user's performance. Even the experience in gaming or with other virtual reality devices does not have any effect. We checked this by using one-way between-subjects ANOVA tests. Eight participants that started with the 6 DOF devices in the first round and then switched to the 3 DOF devices in the second round stated after the swap of seats that it was really hard and unnatural to cope with the reduced feasibilities of the 3 DOF devices. Conversely, there was not a single user starting with the 3 DOF device who complained about the extended degrees of freedom after swap of seats. However, the analysis of the users' questionnaires does not show any significant differences between users starting with 3 DOFs and ending with 6 DOFs, or vice versa, with respect to the rating of the different devices.

7.5 Conclusions and Future Work

In the following, we will briefly summarize our applications and outline some directions of future investigation.

Our sphere–spring system allows a much more realistic animation of a human hand as it would be possible with a pure skeletal-based system or a pure mass–spring system. The deformations caused by the stretching and compression of the soft tissue of a real hand can be well reproduced by our model as shown in Fig. 7.4. Through the parallel computation on the GPU, the animation can be greatly accelerated. The computation time scales perfectly with the number of cores of the GPU, therefore we expect an enhanced performance with future hardware.

In the second section of this chapter, we presented an application of our Inner Sphere Trees to real-time collision avoidance for robots in highly dynamic environments. Therefore, we extended our ISTs to distance computations with point cloud data that was captured via a Kinect. The results show a close to real-time performance even with our not yet optimized implementation.

Finally, we presented a new multi-user haptic workspace with support for a large number of haptic devices and a likewise number of dynamic objects with a high polygon count. Its multithreaded architecture guarantees a constant simulation rate of 1 KHz, which is required for stable haptic interactions. Based on our workspace we have implemented a haptic multi-player game with complex bi-manual haptic interactions that we use for a quantitative and qualitative analysis of haptic devices with respect to their number of sensors and actuators.

We conducted a user evaluation with 47 participants. The results show that 6 DOF devices outperform 3 DOF devices significantly, both in user perception and

Fig. 7.28 In the future, we plan to apply our hand animation scheme to natural interaction tasks like virtual prototyping

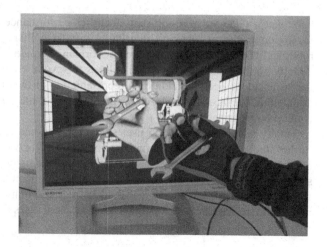

in objective data analysis. For example, the learning phase is much shorter and the users judged the 6 DOF device to be much better with regard to the quality of forces and the intuitiveness of control. However, there is still room left for improvements of the haptic devices: the overall rating of force quality and also naturalness of control is rated only mediocre.

7.5.1 Future Work

Our sphere–spring system can already produce a realistic animation of the human hand, but there is still some room for improvements. In our prototypical implementation of the sphere–spring system, we require approximatively 50 iterations per frame to get a stable state of the system. As for now, we use a simple Euler step during integration. However, the bottleneck of our sphere–spring system is not the integration step, but the calculation of the volume transfer. Therefore, enhanced integration methods like Runge–Kutta, which support larger time steps, could probably increase the speed of our algorithms. Tweaking other parameters, like taking a dynamic version of the volume transfer factor or a dynamic adjustment of the springs after the transfer of volume, is also an option. Another challenge is to provide a theoretical proof of the system's stability.

The long time objective for our real-time hand animation is their application to natural interaction tasks (see Fig. 7.28). Therefore, we have to include collision detection as well as a stable collision response model and the support to frictional forces. Basically, we plan to use a deformable version of the *Inner Sphere Tree* data structure.

The resolution of current depth cameras, like the Kinect, is very limited [27]. Future technologies for real-time depth image acquisition will hopefully provide better resolutions. However, larger point clouds also increase the demands on our collision detection system. All parts of the grid algorithms can be trivially parallelized. We hope that a GPU version will gain a further performance boost. At the moment, we use our collision detection algorithms only for collision avoidance between the robot and the environment. A better performance would also allow path planning directly on the point cloud data. This leads to several challenges for future works: for instance, we need an additional representation of the objects' volumes, instead of only their surface. Probably, a real-time version of the sphere-packing algorithms could produce relief.

Finally, also our pioneering user study leaves some challenges for the future: further studies are necessary to find the best trade-off between cost and performance regarding bi-manual complex haptic interactions. This could include asymmetric setups of the haptic devices, e.g. 6 DOF for the dominant hand and cheaper 3 DOF for the other hand. Obviously, it would be nice to compare other haptic but also non-haptic devices and to investigate other kinds of tasks like object recognition.

References

1. Albrecht, I., Haber, J., & Seidel, H. P. (2003). Construction and animation of anatomically based human hand models. In *Proc. of the 2003 ACM SIGGRAPH/Eurographics symposium on computer animation* (pp. 98–109).
2. Attar, F. T., Patel, R. V., & Moallem, M. (2005). Hived: a passive system for haptic interaction and visualization of elastic deformations. In *World haptics conference* (pp. 529–530). doi:10.1109/WHC.2005.75.
3. Bascetta, L., Magnani, G., Rocco, P., Migliorini, R., & Pelagatti, M. (2010). Anti-collision systems for robotic applications based on laser time-of-flight sensors. In *2010 IEEE/ASME international conference on advanced intelligent mechatronics (AIM)*, July (pp. 278–284). doi:10.1109/AIM.2010.5695851.
4. Basdogan, C., Ho, C.-H., Srinivasan, M. A., & Slater, M. (2000). An experimental study on the role of touch in shared virtual environments. *ACM Transactions on Computer-Human Interaction*, 7, 443–460. doi:10.1145/365058.365082. URL http://doi.acm.org/10.1145/365058.365082.
5. Becker, M., Ihmsen, M., & Teschner, M. (2009). Corotated sph for deformable solids. In E. Galin & J. Schneider (Eds.), *NPH* (pp. 27–34). Aire-la-Ville: Eurographics Association. URL http://dblp.uni-trier.de/db/conf/nph/nph2009.html.
6. Benavidez, P., & Jamshidi, M. (2011). Mobile robot navigation and target tracking system. In *IEEE international conference on system of systems engineering*. doi:10.1109/SYSOSE.2011.5966614.
7. Bergeron, P., & Lachapelle, P. (1985). Controlling facial expression and body movements in the computer generated short " 'tony de peltrie' ". In *SIGGRAPH 85 tutorial notes*.
8. Bielser, D., Maiwald, V. A., & Gross, M. H. (1999). Interactive cuts through 3-dimensional soft tissue. *Computer Graphics Forum*, *18*(3), 31–38.
9. Biswas, J., & Veloso, M. M. (2012). Depth camera based indoor mobile robot localization and navigation. In *ICRA* (pp. 1697–1702).
10. Chen, D. T., & Zeltzer, D. (1992). Pump it up: computer animation based model of muscle using the finite element method. In *Computer graphics (SIGGRAPH 92 conference proceedings)* (Vol. 26, pp. 89–98). Reading: Addison Wesley.
11. Chen, Y., Zhu, Q. h., Kaufman, A. E., & Muraki, S. (1998). Physically-based animation of volumetric objects. In *CA* (pp. 154–160).
12. Clemente, L. A., Davison, A. J., Reid, I. D., Neira, J., & Tardos, J. D. (2007). Mapping large loops with a single hand-held camera. In W. Burgard, O. Brock, & C. Stachniss (Eds.), *Robotics: science and systems*. Cambridge: MIT Press. ISBN 978-0-262-52484-1.

13. Flacco, F., Kroger, T., De Luca, A., & Khatib, O. (2012). Depth space approach to human-robot collision avoidance. In *ICRA* (pp. 338–345). New York: IEEE. ISBN 978-1-4673-1403-9. URL http://dblp.uni-trier.de/db/conf/icra/icra2012.html.

14. Garner, W. R. (1974). *The processing of information and structure*. Potomac: Lawrence Erlbaum Associates.

15. Haddadin, S., Albu-Schäffer, A., De Luca, A., & Hirzinger, G. (2008). Collision detection and reaction: a contribution to safe physical human-robot interaction. In *IROS* (pp. 3356–3363). New York: IEEE.

16. Henry, P., Krainin, M., Herbst, E., Ren, X., & Fox, D. (2012). RGB-D mapping: using kinect-style depth cameras for dense 3D modeling of indoor environments. *International Journal of Robotics Research, 31*(5), 647–663.

17. Hong, M., Jung, S., Choi, M.-H., & Welch, S. W. J. (2006). Fast volume preservation for a mass–spring system. *IEEE Computer Graphics and Applications, 26*, 83–91. doi:10.1109/MCG.2006.104. URL http://dl.acm.org/citation.cfm?id=1158812.1158873.

18. Hu, H., & Gan, J. Q. (2005). Sensors and data fusion algorithms in mobile robotics.

19. Hunter, P. (2005). *Fem/bem notes* (Technical report). University of Oaklans, New Zealand.

20. Hutchins, M., Stevenson, D., Adcock, M., & Youngblood, P. (2005). Using collaborative haptics in remote surgical training. In *Proc. first joint eurohaptics conference and symposium on haptic interfaces for virtual environment and teleoperator systems (WHC 05)* (pp. 481–482). Washington: IEEE Computer Society.

21. Jacob, R. J. K., Sibert, L. E., McFarlane, D. C., & Preston Mullen, M. Jr. (1994). Integrality and separability of input devices. *ACM Transactions on Computer-Human Interaction, 1*, 3–26. doi:10.1145/174630.174631. URL http://doi.acm.org/10.1145/174630.174631.

22. Jaillet, F., Shariat, B., & Vandrope, D. (1998). Volume object modeling and animation with particle based system. In *Proc. 8th ICECGDG* (Vol. 1, pp. 215–219).

23. Jing, L., & Stephansson, O. (2007). *Fundamentals of discrete element methods for rock engineering: theory and applications. Developments in geotechnical engineering*. Amsterdam: Elsevier. ISBN 9780444829375. URL http://books.google.com/books?id=WS9bjQ0ORSEC.

24. Jung, Y., Yeh, S.-C., & Stewart, J. (2006). Tailoring virtual reality technology for stroke rehabilitation: a human factors design. In *CHI '06 extended abstracts on human factors in computing systems, CHI '06* (pp. 929–934). New York: ACM. ISBN 1-59593-298-4. doi:10.1145/1125451.1125631. URL http://doi.acm.org/10.1145/1125451.1125631.

25. Kaehler, K., Haber, J., & Seidel, H. P. (2001). Geometry-based muscle modeling for facial animation. In *Proc. of graphics interface 2001* (pp. 37–46).

26. Keefe, D. F., Zeleznik, R. C., & Laidlaw, D. H. (2007). Drawing on air: input techniques for controlled 3D line illustration. *IEEE Transactions on Visualization and Computer Graphics, 13*(5), 1067–1081.

27. Khoshelham, K., & Elberink, S. O. (2012). Accuracy and resolution of kinect depth data for indoor mapping applications. *Sensors, 12*(2), 1437–1454. doi:10.3390/s120201437. URL http://www.mdpi.com/1424-8220/12/2/1437.

28. Konolige, K., & Agrawal, M. (2008). Frameslam: from bundle adjustment to real-time visual mapping. *IEEE Transactions on Robotics, 24*(5), 1066–1077.

29. Kry, P. G., James, D. L., & Pai, D. K. (2002). Eigenskin: real time large deformation character skinning in hardware. In *Proc. ACM SIGGRAPH symposium on computer animation* (pp. 153–159).

30. Kuhn, S., & Henrich, D. (2007). Fast vision-based minimum distance determination between known and unknown objects. In *IEEE international conference on intelligent robots and systems*, San Diego/USA.

31. Leganchuk, A., Zhai, S., & Buxton, W. (1998). Manual and cognitive benefits of two-handed input: an experimental study. *ACM Transactions on Computer-Human Interaction, 5*, 326–359. doi:10.1145/300520.300522. URL http://doi.acm.org/10.1145/300520.300522.

32. Lewis, J. P., Cordner, M., & Fong, N. (2000). Pose space deformations: a unified approach to shape interpolation and skeleton-driven deformation. In *SIGGRAPH 00 conference proceedings*. Reading: Addison Wesley.

33. Low, T., & Wyeth, G. (2005). Obstacle detection using optical flow. In *Proceedings of the 2005 Australasian conf. on robotics & automation*.

34. Magnenant-Thalmann, N., Laperriere, R., & Thalmann, D. (1988). Jointdependent local deformations for hand animation and object grasping. In *Proc. of graphics interface 88* (pp. 26–33).

35. Martinet, A., Casiez, G., & Grisoni, L. (2010). The effect of dof separation in 3d manipulation tasks with multi-touch displays. In *Proceedings of the 17th ACM symposium on virtual reality software and technology, VRST '10* (pp. 111–118). New York: ACM. ISBN 978-1-4503-0441-2. doi:10.1145/1889863.1889888. URL http://doi.acm.org/10.1145/1889863.1889888.

36. May, S., Fuchs, S., Droeschel, D., Holz, D., & Nüchter, A. (2009). Robust 3d-mapping with time-of-flight cameras. In *Proceedings of the 2009 IEEE/RSJ international conference on intelligent robots and systems, IROS'09* (pp. 1673–1678). Piscataway: IEEE Press. ISBN 978-1-4244-3803-7. URL http://dl.acm.org/citation.cfm?id=1733343.1733640.

37. Mezger, J., & Strasser, W. (2006). Interactive soft object simulation with quadratic finite elements. In *Proc. AMDO conference*.

38. Müller, M., & Chentanez, N. (2011). Solid simulation with oriented particles. In *ACM SIGGRAPH 2011 papers, SIGGRAPH '11* (pp. 92:1–92:10). New York: ACM. ISBN 978-1-4503-0943-1. doi:10.1145/1964921.1964987. URL http://doi.acm.org/10.1145/1964921.1964987.

39. Müller, M., Dorsey, J., McMillan, L., Jagnow, R., & Cutler, B. (2002). Stable real-time deformations. In *Proceedings of the 2002 ACM SIGGRAPH/Eurographics symposium on computer animation, SCA '02* (pp. 49–54). New York: ACM. ISBN 1-58113-573-4. doi:10.1145/545261.545269. URL http://doi.acm.org/10.1145/545261.545269.

40. Müller, M., Heidelberger, B., Teschner, M., & Gross, M. (2005). Meshless deformations based on shape matching. In *ACM SIGGRAPH 2005 papers, SIGGRAPH '05* (pp. 471–478). New York: ACM. doi:10.1145/1186822.1073216. URL http://doi.acm.org/10.1145/1186822.1073216.

41. Munjiza, A. (2004). *The combined finite-discrete element method*. New York: Wiley. ISBN 9780470841990. URL http://books.google.co.in/books?id=lbznrSzqcRkC.

42. Murayama, J., Bougrila, L., Akahane, Y. K., Hasegawa, S., Hirsbrunner, B., & Sato, M. (2004). Spidar g&g: a two-handed haptic interface for bimanual vr interaction. In *Proceedings of EuroHaptics 2004* (pp. 138–146).

43. Nealen, A., Mueller, M., Keiser, R., Boxerman, E., & Carlson, M. (2006). Physically based deformable models in computer graphics. *Computer Graphics Forum, 25*(4), 809–836. doi:10.1111/j.1467-8659.2006.01000.x.

44. Ohno, K., Nomura, T., & Tadokoro, S. (2006). Real-time robot trajectory estimation and 3d map construction using 3d camera. In *IROS* (pp. 5279–5285). New York: IEEE.

45. OpenNI (2010). *OpenNI user guide*. OpenNI organization, November. URL http://www.openni.org/documentation.

46. OpenSG (2012). *Opensg—a portable scenegraph system to create realtime graphics programs*. URL http://www.opensg.org/.

47. Prusak, A., Melnychuk, O., Roth, H., Schiller, I., & Koch, R. (2008). Pose estimation and map building with a time- of- flight- camera for robot navigation. *International Journal of Intelligent Systems Technologies and Applications, 5*(3/4), 355–364. doi:10.1504/IJISTA.2008.021298.

48. Ravari, A. R. N., Taghirad, H. D., & Tamjidi, A. H. (2009). Vision-based fuzzy navigation of mobile robots in grassland environments. In *IEEE/ASME international conference on advanced intelligent mechatronics, 2009. AIM 2009*, July (pp. 1441–1446). doi:10.1109/AIM.2009.5229858.

49. Rusu, R. B., & Cousins, S. (2011). 3d is here: point cloud library (pcl). In *International conference on robotics and automation*, Shanghai, China.

50. Schiavi, R., Bicchi, A., & Flacco, F. (2009). Integration of active and passive compliance control for safe human-robot coexistence. In *Proceedings of the 2009 IEEE international confer-*

ence on robotics and automation, ICRA'09 (pp. 2471–2475). Piscataway: IEEE Press. ISBN 978-1-4244-2788-8. URL http://dl.acm.org/citation.cfm?id=1703775.1703850.

51. Stylopoulos, N., & Rattner, D. (2003). Robotics and ergonomics. *Surgical Clinics of North America, 83*(6), 1321–1337. URL http://view.ncbi.nlm.nih.gov/pubmed/14712869.

52. Sueda, S., Kaufman, A., & Pai, D. K. (2008). Musculotendon simulation for hand animation. *ACM Transactions on Graphics, 27*(3). URL http://doi.acm.org/10.1145/1360612.1360682.

53. Swapp, D., Pawar, V., & Loscos, C. (2006). Interaction with co-located haptic feedback in virtual reality. *Virtual Reality, 10*, 24–30. doi:10.1007/s10055-006-0027-5.

54. Tsetserukou, D. (2010). Haptihug: a novel haptic display for communication of hug over a distance. In *EuroHaptics (1)* (pp. 340–347).

55. Vassilev, T., & Spanlang, B. (2002). A mass–spring model for real time deformable solids. In *East-west vision.*

56. Veit, M., Capobianco, A., & Bechmann, D. (2008). Consequence of two-handed manipulation on speed, precision and perception on spatial input task in 3d modelling applications. *Journal of Universal Computer Science, 14*(19), 3174–3187. Special issue on human–computer interaction.

57. Veit, M., Capobianco, A., & Bechmann, D. (2009). Influence of degrees of freedom's manipulation on performances during orientation tasks in virtual reality environments. In *VRST 2009: the 16th ACM symposium on virtual reality and software technology,* Kyoto (Japan), November.

58. Verner, L. N., & Okamura, A. M. (2009). Force & torque feedback vs force only feedback. In *WHC '09: proceedings of the world haptics 2009—third joint EuroHaptics conference and symposium on haptic interfaces for virtual environment and teleoperator systems* (pp. 406–410). Washington: IEEE Computer Society. ISBN 978-1-4244-3858-7. doi:10.1109/WHC.2009.4810880.

59. Wang, S., & Srinivasan, M. A. (2003). The role of torque in haptic perception of object location in virtual environments. In *HAPTICS '03: proceedings of the 11th symposium on haptic interfaces for virtual environment and teleoperator systems (HAPTICS'03)* (p. 302). Washington: IEEE Computer Society. ISBN 0-7695-1890-7.

60. Weingarten, J. W., Gruener, G., & Siegwari, R. (2004). A state-of-the-art 3d sensor for robot navigation. In *IEEE/RSJ int. conf. on intelligent robots and systems* (pp. 2155–2160).

61. Weller, R., & Zachmann, G. (2009). Stable 6-DOF haptic rendering with inner sphere trees. In *International design engineering technical conferences & computers and information in engineering conference (IDETC/CIE),* August. San Diego: ASME. URL http://cg.in.tu-clausthal.de/research/ist. CIE/VES Best Paper Award.

62. Weller, R., & Zachmann, G. (2011). 3-dof vs. 6-dof—playful evaluation of complex haptic interactions. In *IEEE international conference on consumer electronics (ICCE), 2011 digest of technical papers,* January. Washington: IEEE Computer Society. URL http://cg.in.tu-clausthal.de/research/haptesha.

63. Weller, R., & Zachmann, G. (2012). User performance in complex bi-manual haptic manipulation with 3 dofs vs. 6 dofs. In *Haptics symposium,* Vancouver, Canada, March 4–7. URL http://cg.in.tu-clausthal.de/research/haptesha/index.shtml.

64. Yinka-Banjo, C., Osunmakinde, I., & Bagula, A. (2011). Collision avoidance in unstructured environments for autonomous robots: a behavioural modelling approach. In *Proceedings of the IEEE 2011 international conference on control, robotics and cybernetics (ICCRC 2011),* New Delhi, India, 20 March.

Part IV
Every End Is Just a New Beginning

Chapter 8
Epilogue

In this chapter we will summarize the main contributions presented in this book and we will venture to describe avenues for future work in the field of collision detection and related areas. We will restrict the summary in this chapter to very basic concepts and results. In the individual sections of the respective chapters you will find much more detailed presentations (see Sects. 3.6, 4.4, 5.7, 6.5, and 7.5). The same applies for the future work section. You will find the more technical improvements and extension of our new data structures, evaluations methods, and applications in the individual chapters. In this chapter, we try to draw a wider picture of future challenges related to collision detection in particular and to geometric acceleration structures in general.

8.1 Summary

Collision detection is one of the "technologies" for enabling all kinds of applications that deal with objects in motion. Often collision detection is the computational bottleneck. An increasing graphical scene complexity, enabled by the explosive development on GPUs, also makes increasing demands on the collision detection process. Simply relying on the further increase of the computational power just postpones rather than eliminates this problem.

A major challenge is still the collision detection for complex deformable objects. Pre-computed bounding volume hierarchies become invalid and must be recomputed or updated. This is often done on a per-frame basis. In Chap. 3 we presented two new data structures, the *kinetic AABB-Tree* and the *kinetic BoxTree*, that need significantly less update operations than previous methods. We even showed that they are optimal in the number of bounding volume updates by proving a lower bound on the number of update operations. Also in practice they outperform existing algorithms by an order of magnitude. Our new data structures gain their efficiency from an *event-based* approach that is formalized in the kinetic data structure framework. Moreover, we also extended this method to the collision detection process

R. Weller, *New Geometric Data Structures for Collision Detection and Haptics*,
Springer Series on Touch and Haptic Systems, DOI 10.1007/978-3-319-01020-5_8,
© Springer International Publishing Switzerland 2013

itself. The resulting *kinetic Separation-List* enables real-time continuous detection of collisions in complex scenes. Compared to classical swept volume algorithms we measured a performance gain of a factor of 50.

Another challenge in the collision handling process is to determine "good" contact information for a plausible collision response. Actually, the *penetration volume* is known to be the best penetration measure because it corresponds to the water displacement of the overlapping parts of the objects and thus leads to physically motivated and continuous repulsion forces and torques. However, no one could compute this penetration measure efficiently as yet. In Chap. 5 we presented the first data structure, called *Inner Sphere Trees*, that yields an approximation of the penetration volume even for very complex objects consisting of several hundreds of thousands of polygons. Moreover, these volume queries can be answered at rates of about 1 kHz (which makes the algorithm suitable for haptic rendering) and an error of about 1 % compared to the exact penetration volume. The basic idea of our *Inner Sphere Trees* is very simple: In contrast to previous methods that create bounding volume hierarchies from the *surfaces* of the objects, we fill the objects' interior with sets of *non-overlapping volumetric primitives*—in our implementation we used spheres—and create an *inner* bounding volume hierarchy. In order to partition our inner primitives into a hierarchical data structure, we could not simply adopt the classical surface-optimized methods; so we have developed a *volume-based* heuristic that relies on an optimization scheme known from machine learning.

However, the main challenge was less the hierarchy creation, but the computation of an appropriate sphere packing. Actually, there were no algorithms available that could compute sphere packings for arbitrary objects efficiently as yet. Therefore, we have developed a new method that we presented in Chap. 4. Basically, it extends the idea of space-filling Apollonian sphere packings to arbitrary objects by successive approximating Voronoi nodes. Originally designed as a means to an end, we are pretty confident that we just hit the tip of an iceberg with this new spherical volume representation. Section 4.4.1 outlines some ideas on how sphere packings can be applied to many other fundamental problems in computer graphics, including global illumination and the segmentation of 3D objects.

Another example is the definition of a new deformation model for the volume preserving simulation of deformable objects based on our sphere packings that we presented in Sect. 7.2. Basically, these so-called *Sphere–Spring Systems* are an extension of classical mass–spring systems with an additional volume assigned to the masses. We applied our model to the real-time animation of a virtual hand model. Also our *Inner Sphere Trees* enabled us to realize interesting applications that are summarized in Chap. 7 too: In Sect. 7.3 we explored new methods for real-time obstacle avoidance in robotics using the minimum distance between point clouds that was derived by a Kinect and our *Inner Sphere Trees*. In Sect. 7.4 we first described a new multi-user haptic workspace that we then used to evaluate the influence of the degrees of freedom in demanding bi-manual haptic interaction tasks. The results of our extensive user study shows that 6 DOF devices outperform 3 DOF devices significantly, both in user perception and performance. This is partly contradictory to previous user studies that did not include haptic feedback.

Fig. 8.1 The Holodeck as a
symbol for the long term
objective in VR

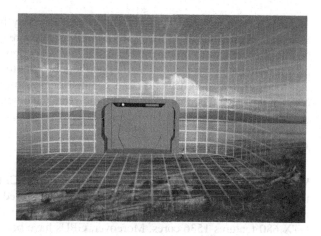

However, there already exist a wide variety of different collision detection approaches and, obviously, not all of them will have been replaced by our new data structures on short term. Actually, also our new data structures have their drawbacks, like the restriction to watertight models of our *Inner Sphere Trees*, or the requirement of flightplans for our kinetic data structures. Furthermore, different applications need different types of contact information; e.g. for path-planning in robotics it is sufficient to detect whether two objects collide or not. It does not need any further contact information. Additionally, most collision detection algorithms are very sensitive to specific scenarios, i.e. to the relative size of the objects, the relative position to each other, the distance, etc. This makes it very difficult to select the collision detection best suited for a special task. In order to simplify this selection process, but also in order to give other researchers the possibility to compare their new algorithms to previous approaches, we have developed two representative and easy to use benchmarks that delivers verifiable results—namely, a performance benchmark for static collision detection libraries for rigid objects (see Sect. 6.3) and a quality benchmark that evaluates the quality of forces and torques computed by different collision response schemes (see Sect. 6.3). The results of our benchmarks show that they are able to crave out the strengths and weaknesses of very different collision handling systems.

However, simply stressing collision detection algorithms with worst case objects like Chazelle's polyhedron is easy but not very conducive. The results of our benchmarks shows that such worst cases do not occur very often in practical cases. Usually, we observed an almost logarithmic performance for most objects. In Sect. 6.2 we presented a theoretical average-case analysis for simultaneous AABB-Tree traversals to confirm this observation.

8.2 Future Directions

Figure 8.1 shows the Holodeck known from Star Trek™ to symbolize the long term objective: A fully immersive and interactive virtual environment that cannot be distinguished from reality. Obviously, we are still far away from its implementation. However, improvements in hardware as well as software development offer today possibilities that were unimaginable just a few years ago. In this section, we will present some medium-term objectives on the long way to the Holodeck, with special focus on collision detection and geometric data structures that will probably concern the research community during the years to come.

8.2.1 Parallelization

While we can identify a stagnancy in the frequency of CPUs in the last few years, the further performance gain today is primarily achieved by packing more cores into a single die. We get the same picture for GPUs; for instance, a recent NVIDIA GTX 680 features 1536 cores. Moreover, GPUs have become fully programmable in the last years. While parts of the collision detection pipeline lend themselves well for parallelization, this is more complicated for other parts. For example, it is straightforward to assign pairs of objects in the narrow phase to different cores for a simultaneous check on the CPU.

GPU cores actually are not suitable to recursive hierarchy traversal, because of their lack of an instruction stack. Hence, collision detection for GPUs requires completely different algorithms and data structures. First approaches have been published on non-hierarchical collision detection on the GPU, but we think that there is still room for improvements. For instance, we are pretty sure that our kinetic data structures as well as our Inner Sphere Trees would greatly benefit from parallelization.

8.2.2 Point Clouds

Most work has been done on collision detection for polygonal objects. However, hardware that generates 3D content in the form of point clouds has become extremely popular. For instance, due to the success of Microsoft's Kinect an advanced real-time tracking system is located in each child's room today. The output of Kinect is basically a depth image and thus some kind of point cloud. Real-time interactions relying directly on such depth images will benefit from fast collision detection that does not require a conversion to polygonal objects as intermediate step.

Moreover, 3D photography becomes more and more popular. Advanced effects in 3D photo editing would benefit from fast point cloud-based collision detection methods too.

8.2.3 Natural Interaction

Until now, the Kinect's accuracy is restricted to track only coarse movements of the body. We are quite sure that future developments will allow a precise tracking of the human hands and fingers. This would enable us to use our primary interaction tools—our hands—to naturally manipulate objects in virtual environments. Obviously, there already exist hardware devices for finger tracking, like data gloves, but they always cause a tethering of the user.

However, there are also challenges on the software side. Until now, there is no physically plausible simulation model available that allows complex grasps and precise operations like turning a screw with the index finger and the thumb. In today's virtual prototyping tasks objects are most often simply glued to the virtual hand. However, such precise operations require a detailed physics-based deformable hand model and an appropriate simulation of the fingers' frictional forces.

8.2.4 Haptics

While the improvements in visual and aural sensations are impressive, one sense is widely neglected in the simulation of virtual environments: the sense of touch. However, force feedback defines a natural and expected cue on how to resolve collisions with the environment and hence it adds a significant degree of immersion and usability. For instance, in natural interaction scenarios as described above, it would prevent a deviation of our real hands from the virtual ones.

Until now, haptic devices are bulky, expensive and require technical expertise for installation and handling. The first cheap devices that were designed for the consumer market are very limited in their degrees of freedom and in their amount of force.

Also on the software side there are unsolved challenges with respect to haptics. Our *Inner Sphere Trees* are able to meet the high frequency demands of 1000 Hz for haptic simulations, but it is hardly possible to provide appropriate forces for thin sheets that often appear in virtual assembly tasks. Moreover, the determination of surface details that are visually represented by textures but have no corresponding representation in the object's geometry is still a challenge.

8.2.5 Global Illumination

Even if the quality of real-time graphics has improved significantly in the last years, almost everybody is able to detect large differences between real-time renderings via OpenGL or DirectX on the one hand and CGI animated films that are produced in a time consuming offline rendering on the other hand. This gain of quality mainly relies on global illumination techniques, like ray tracing, that allow a realistic simulation of advanced lightning effects, like refractions or subsurface scattering. Such global illumination models are still not applicable to real-time rendering, especially if deformable or at least moving objects are included.

The problems that arise with global illumination are very similar to collision detection. Actually, most of these techniques require recursive intersection computations between the scene and a ray as a basic operation (see Sect. 2.6.1). Geometric data structures like BVHs are used to accelerate these intersection tests. Similarly to collision detection, these data structures become invalid if the scene changes.

8.2.6 Sound Rendering

Sound rendering draws two major challenges: first, if a sound occurs at some place in a virtual environment, it has to be distributed through the scene. This means that we have to compute echoes and reflections in order to make it sound realistic. This problem is very similar to global illumination problems and can be approximated by tracing rays through the scene. However, we also think that our *Sphere Graph* would be suited well to compute sound propagations.

The second challenge is the production of the sounds itself. Today, usually prerecorded samples are used. If an event happens, e.g. if we knock over a virtual vase that falls down and breaks into pieces, we hear the respective pre-recorded sound of braking vases. However, it is hardly possible to provide a sound database that covers every possible sound in highly interactive scenes. For instance, a vase falling on a wooden floor sounds different from a hit on a stone floor. Consequently, *synthesis* of sounds from material properties and contact information will improve the sound quality as well as save the cost and time for the pre-recording of samples.

Printed in the United States
By Bookmasters